INTRODUCTION
TO QUALITATIVE
RESEARCH METHODS

INTRODUCTION TO QUALITATIVE RESEARCH METHODS

A PHENOMENOLOGICAL APPROACH TO THE SOCIAL SCIENCES

ROBERT BOGDAN
AND
STEVEN J. TAYLOR

A WILEY-INTERSCIENCE PUBLICATION

JOHN WILEY & SONS, New York • London • Sydney • Toronto

Library of Congress Cataloging in Publication Data
Bogdan, Robert.
    Introduction to qualitative research methods.

    "A Wiley-Interscience publication."
    Bibliography: p.
    Includes index.
    1. Sociology—Methodology. 2. Sociological research.
3. Phenomenology. I. Taylor, Steven J., 1949-   Joint
author. II. Title.

HM24.B612   301'.01'8   75-19407
ISBN 0-471-08571-5

Printed in the United States of America

10 9 8 7 6 5 4 3 2

Foreword

Robert Bogdan and Steven Taylor have produced a pioneering work. It is a textbook on a crucial social science enterprise where none has existed before. It is not too many years since Barney Glaser and Anselm Strauss provided for the first time a coherent theoretical rationale and a conceptual framework for legitimizing participant observation. Their gift was a line of reasoning and a rhetoric that permitted us to organize our talk about fieldwork in a respectable manner. But to talk about fieldwork and to do it are very different things. Glaser and Strauss invited us to go into the field and "discover categories" that would inevitably "emerge." They provided us with a bible that explained and justified and evoked faith in fieldwork. Bogdan and Taylor show us how to do it!

With the publication of their 1973 volume focusing on "strategies for a natural sociology," Schatzman and Strauss continued the important line of contributions initiated by Glaser and Strauss. Bogdan and Taylor breathe new life into this cumulative process of developing qualitative research methods, theories, and techniques. Not only do they move issues from a strategic to a tactical level, but they attempt something that Schatzman and Strauss deliberately avoided—the presentation of a "how-to" handbook. Unlike the Schatzman and Strauss book, which the authors recommend be read in sequence and in its entirety, Bogdan and Taylor provide a coherent volume that is also a reference work, the index of which will be heavily used. A final difference between these two complementary volumes lies in the greater catholicity of Bogdan and Taylor. These authors extend their treatment of qualitative research to include not only participant observation and interviewing but also the use of personal documents: an art that has received little attention since the days of *The Polish Peasant in Europe and America.*

Introduction to Qualitative Research Methods will be welcomed by students, teachers, and researchers at all levels. It seems strange that one book can address so many diverse audiences. But this one does it and does it well. For the undergraduate student and teacher it provides an easily understandable guidebook, free from jargon, clearly written, and systematically organized. It takes them step by step through the maze. And for those undergraduates encountering sociology for the first time in this manner, it will surely be an exciting adventure. For the graduate student and teacher it is a clear exposition of the intricate relations between theory and method and, for those engaged in research, it is an encyclopedia of fieldwork: a reference book that will become dirty, torn, thumbprinted, underscored, and scribbled in from constant use. No matter how much experience researchers have at this kind of work, it is likely that they will find themselves taking notes as they read. I did. Among other things, the volume serves as a checklist of the many details one must remember every time a new field study is initiated. Regardless of how much experience they have had, competent aircraft pilots always run through such a checklist before taking off.

The most empirically valid and dependable evidence obtainable consists in the anecdotal materials elicited during the course of fieldwork. But as some sage once put it, you get what you pay for. The price of doing fieldwork is extremely high, not in dollars (fieldwork is less expensive than most other kinds of research) but in physical and mental effort. It is very hard work. It is exhausting to lead two lives simultaneously. A double life is frequently required of the fieldworker who is involved as a participant in whatever little world is under study while at the same time attempting to record and make sense out of that world as an observer. Particularly energetic fieldworkers may risk added fatigue by trying to live a "private life" in addition to those other lives.

The intellectual effort must be high and continuous in this type of research. It is scary because the research outcomes are unpredictable. The nightmare of every qualitative researcher, novice or experienced, is "What if I don't find anything?" The fact that one is always able to find something because there is always something there is not reassuring. The emphasis in qualitative research is on discovery as well as verification. As important as it is, the process of replication and verification is a routine, precisely specified procedure. Hypothesis testing has known and predictable outcomes. Little intellectual effort is required in such research in contrast to the imagination, sensitivity, and creativity that permit the investigator to get the most out of qualitative research.

Bogdan and Taylor cannot provide those qualities, but they can and do provide the opportunity for the adventuresome scholar to maximize his or her effectiveness. It must become clear to most students very early in the educational process that the "classics" and the prizewinners, the works of enduring quality in sociology, are almost inevitably based on adventures in the field. A great deal of literature has been published between William F. Whyte's classic study of white corner boys in Boston and Elliot Liebow's more recent award winner on black corner boys in Washington, D. C. There have been several generations of high-quality fieldworkers producing useful, credible, and enduring research. They range from E. C. Hughes, Alfred Lindesmith, and David Riessman through Howard Becker, Blanche Geer, and Ned Polsky to Laud Humphries and Jacqueline Wiseman. Readers who would transcend this bit of name-dropping are referred to their library card catalogue and the excellent set of references provided in this volume. Can there be any student of the social sciences who needs a reference to Thomas and Znaniecki's classic analysis of personal documents?

It is appalling that there should be so little literature on so much of sociology's methods and techniques. Our methodological literature has tended to focus on that small fragment of procedural logic that is easiest to handle. But what of the student or scholar who would follow the path of W. I. Thomas or Erving Goffman? Where are the procedural guidelines? It seems primitive to suggest that only those students privileged to work with experienced qualitative researchers can hope to learn those methods. Talented teachers such as Blanche Geer who have been able to systematically educate even a handful of students for fieldwork are rare. There are a few volumes such as those by Oscar Lewis or Rosalie Wax that instill in the reader a sense of awe and respect for the fieldwork skills of the authors, but they don't really tell us how to do it. Bogdan and Taylor not only tell us how to do it, but show us how to do it. Furthermore, in the second part of the book they provide examples from their own research of what the "product" can look like.

Participant observation is no panacea. It will not cure the ills of the discipline or of the world. There are, in fact, kinds of problems for which such methods seem clearly inappropriate. But there is a very important place for qualitative research in the understanding of human behavior and social processes. I hope that *Introduction to Qualitative Research Methods* will help it take this proper place.

IRWIN DEUTSCHER

Professor of Sociology
Case Western Reserve University

Cleveland, Ohio
February 1975

Preface

A glance at book exhibits at social science conventions or at book reviews and advertisements in professional journals reveals a new vocabulary: "the human perspective," "the social construction of reality," "phenomenology," and "ethnomethodology." Over the past decade, there has been growing interest in the subjective, in meaning, and in commonsense understandings. This interest has been accompanied by changes in the way we conduct research. The questionnaire, the formal interview, and the laboratory experiment, though still important, are no longer as dominant as they once were. The questions that the new approaches raise require methods that are descriptive and holistic. We call these qualitative methods.

In recent years, a number of books have appeared that deal with qualitative methods. Most of these, however, have been confined to a single approach: participant observation. Moreover, many discuss issues that are of interest only to those with professional experience in data collection. They do not provide those unfamiliar with qualitative methods with an adequate introduction, a discussion of the range of possible approaches, or guidance on how to conduct a study. The purpose of this book is to provide these things.

We have intended to avoid writing a cultist book: one that appeals only to those who are single-minded in their research approach or theoretical interest. While we discuss qualitative methods as they relate to the phenomenological perspective, we believe that they have much to offer, as proven in the past, to other theoretical perspectives. Our interest in this newer theoretical thrust reflects our own preferences and concerns. But we want to resist orthodoxy in broad theoretical and methodological issues and in specific techniques and strategies used to carry out a study. Thus, we take care throughout the text to remind the reader that we merely present the ways in which we have conducted qualitative research.

This book includes an introduction and two major parts. The Introduction deals with qualitative methodology in general and with the theoretical issues at stake. Part One contains a "how to do it" approach to qualitative methods. Chapters 2 to 4 deal with participant observation. In Chapter 5 we discuss personal documents and open-ended interviewing. Chapter 6 includes a number of vignettes on particularly creative qualitative studies.

In Part Two we move to a discussion of how to present findings. After a short introduction, we present a number of articles based on research of the kind conducted in Part One. Many of the examples we use in our discussion in Part One come from the studies found in Part Two. All of these articles have been written by us. Some have appeared in other publications; others have been presented at professional meetings; still others appear here for the first time. We present these not because they epitomize professional scholarship, but rather because they exemplify a variety of ways in which to write up findings. We also chose them because they are of such a nature as might catch the interest and imagination of people new to the field.

A few words of thanks to those who helped. While we were writing this book, we worked at the Center on Human Policy at Syracuse University. The people at the Center have created the kind of atmosphere that makes creativity a joy and a must. The many people at the Center who have engaged in qualitative research have provided us with many of the insights and experiences shared in this book. But most importantly, they have helped to show us that the products of research can be directed toward social action and social change. While some have been called students, they have been our teachers. We thank them. A special thanks to Burton Blatt of the Center and the Division of Special Education and Rehabilitation at Syracuse and to Blanche Geer of the Department of Sociology and Anthropology at Northeastern University. It was Burton Blatt who first encouraged the writing of the chapters on participant observation.* He, along with Bill Beneville, Doug Biklen, Janet Bogdan, Irwin Deutscher, and Jack Douglas, read earlier drafts of this book and

---

*That chapter was first published, in much modified form, by Robert Bogdan (*Participant Observation in Organizational Settings*, Syracuse, N.Y.: Syracuse University Division of Special Education and Rehabilitation, 1972). Selected sentences and paragraphs, as well as rewritten sections of the entire book, are used in Part One by permission of the publisher.

made many suggestions that we have incorporated into the text. While we have cited in the footnotes many authors and researchers we have found helpful, Blanche Geer's contribution to this book deserves special mention. While we accept responsibility for specific contents, many of our perspectives on theory and method were learned from her.

ROBERT BOGDAN
STEVEN J. TAYLOR

The Center on Human Policy
Syracuse University
Syracuse, New York
April 1975

Contents

INTRODUCTION
TO QUALITATIVE
RESEARCH METHODS

Introduction

GO TO THE PEOPLE

Method

The term *methodology* in a broad sense refers to the process, principles, and procedures by which we approach problems and seek answers. In the social sciences the term applies to how one conducts research. As in everything we do, our assumptions, interests, and goals greatly influence which methodological procedures we choose. When stripped to their essentials, *most debates over methods are debates over assumptions and goals, over theory and perspective.*

Two major theoretical perspectives have dominated the social science scene.[1] One, *positivism,* traces its origins to the great social theorists of the nineteenth and early twentieth centuries and especially to Auguste Comte and Emile Durkheim.[2] The positivist seeks the *facts* or *causes* of social phenomena with little regard for the subjective states of individuals. Durkheim advised the social scientist to consider "social facts," or social phenomena, as "things" that exercise an external and coercive influence on human behavior.[3]

The second theoretical perspective, which, following the lead of Irwin Deutscher,[4] we will describe as *phenomenological,* stems most prominently from Max Weber.[5] The phenomenologist is concerned with *understanding* human behavior from the actor's own frame of reference. As Jack Douglas writes:

> The "forces" that move human beings, as human beings rather than simply as human bodies . . . are "meaningful stuff." They are internal ideas, feelings, and motives.[6]

The phenomenologist examines how the world is experienced. For him or her the important reality is what people imagine it to be.

Since the positivists and the phenomenologists approach different problems and seek different answers, their research will typically demand different methodologies. The positivist searches for "facts" and "causes" through methods such as survey questionnaires, inventories, and demographic analysis, which produce quantitative data and which allow him or her to statistically prove relationships between operationally defined variables.[7] The phenomenologist, on the other hand, seeks understanding through such qualitative methods as participant observation, open-ended interviewing, and personal documents. These methods yield descriptive data which enable the phenomenologist to see the world as subjects see it.

This book is first and foremost about qualitative methodologies: how to collect data in the form of people's own words, utterances, gestures, and behavior. It is a book on how to approach problems phenomenologically.

We are not saying that positivists *cannot* use qualitative methods to address their own interests. Descriptive data can be viewed as indicators of group norms or values and other social forces which cause, or determine, human behavior.[8] We *are* saying that the search for causes is neither the main subject of this particular book nor where our interests lie.

We return to the phenomenological perspective later in this chapter, for it is at the heart of this work. It is this perspective that guides our research and embodies our assumptions. We now move to a discussion of the history of qualitative methods, their various forms, and other issues related to qualitative research.

1975

A HISTORY OF QUALITATIVE METHODS

Most writers on the subject trace the origins of qualitative methodology to Frederick LePlay's observational study of European families and communities in the nineteenth century.[9] Some authors, in fact, argue that LePlay's research represents the first "scientific" sociological research. For example, Robert Nisbet writes:

> But *The European Working Classes* is a work squarely in the field of sociology, the first genuinely scientific sociological work in the century. . . . Durkheim's *Suicide* is commonly regarded as the first "scientific" work in sociology, but it takes nothing away from Durkheim's achievement to observe that it was in LePlay's studies of kinship and community types in Europe that a much earlier effort is to be found in European sociology to combine empirical observation with the drawing of crucial inference—and to do this acknowledgedly within the criteria of science.[10]

It was later in the nineteenth century and in the beginning of the twentieth, however, that qualitative methodology, and specifically field research, came into its own in European and American anthropological research. One can only speculate on the reasons why it was so readily accepted by anthropologists and so easily ignored by sociologists. Presumably, anthropologists, unlike sociologists, were unable to use most other methods, such as demographic analysis and survey questionnaires, to study so-called primitive societies. Moreover, while anthropologists were unfamiliar and consequently deeply concerned with the everyday lives of the people they studied, sociologists probably took it for granted that they already knew everything there was to know about the everyday lives of the people in their society.

In any case, the use of qualitative methods first became popular in American sociology in the studies of the "Chicago School" sometime after the turn of the century.[11] W. I. Thomas and Florian Znaniecki, two of the most influential sociologists of their time, wrote in 1927:

> We are safe in saying that personal life-records [personal documents] constitute the perfect type of sociological material, and that if social science has

to use other materials at all it is only because of the practical difficulty of
obtaining at the moment sufficient number of such records to cover the
totality of sociological problems. . . .[12]

In the period from 1920 to 1940 people who called themselves students
of society were familiar with personal documents and participant
observation.

As important as these early studies were, interest in qualitative methodology waned throughout the 1940s and into the fifties with the growth
in prominence of positivist theories and quantitative methods. Even today it is common for students to complete advanced degrees in sociology
without ever even hearing the phrase "personal documents." One of the
authors recently received a letter from the chairperson of the faculty-
recruiting team of the department of sociology at a large state university.
In reference to the author's interest in qualitative methodology, the
letter stated: "I am writing to let you know that our department recently
decided to look for someone in the area of 'nonstandard' methodology."

The 1960s and 1970s have, nevertheless, seen a reemergence in the
use of qualitative methods. The number of published studies based on
these methodologies has steadily increased[13] and there are now volumes
of collected essays[14] and monographs[15] on how to gather and interpret
qualitative data. The prospects for the future? Uncertain, of course. Yet
if the experience of recent years is any indication, if the interest in
phenomenological perspectives continues to grow, we should expect
qualitative methodologies to be around for quite a while.

QUALITATIVE METHODS

As mentioned earlier, _qualitative methodologies refer to research procedures
which produce descriptive data: people's own written or spoken words and observable behavior._ This approach, as we see it, directs itself at settings and the
individuals within those settings holistically; that is, the subject of the
study, be it an organization or an individual, is not reduced to an isolated
variable or to an hypothesis, but is viewed instead as part of a whole.

The methods by which we study people of necessity affects how we
view them. When we reduce people to statistical aggregates, we lose sight
of the subjective nature of human behavior. Qualitative methods allow
us to know people personally and to see them as they are developing
their own definitions of the world. We experience what they experience

in their daily struggles with their society. We learn about groups and experiences about which we may know nothing. Finally, qualitative methods enable us to explore concepts whose essence is lost in other research approaches. Such concepts as beauty, pain, faith, suffering, frustration, hope, and love can be studied as they are defined and experienced by real people in their everyday lives. As E. W. Burgess has suggested:

> In the life history is revealed as in no other way the inner life of the person, his moral struggles, his successes and failures in securing his destiny in a world too often at variance with his hopes and ideals.[16]

On the next several pages we will describe the two approaches which have served as the mainstays of qualitative methods and on which we will concentrate in this book: participant observation and personal documents, including unstructured interviewing. As we will later note, these are not the only methods by which one can gain phenomenological understanding.

Participant Observation

The phrase *participant observation* has not enjoyed a clear definition in the social sciences. *It is used here to refer to research characterized by a period of intense social interaction between the researcher and the subjects, in the milieu of the latter.*[17] *During this period, data are unobtrusively and systematically collected.*

Observers immerse themselves in the lives of the people and the situations they wish to understand. They speak with them, joke with them, empathize with them, and share their concerns and experiences. Prolonged contact in the setting allows them to view the dynamics of conflict and change and thus see organizations, relationships, and group and individual definitions in process. They therefore enjoy a unique vantage point in relation to the practitioners of other methodologies.[18]

Those who are new to the methodology often wonder how participant observers differ from observant people in their natural settings. While the difference will become clearer as we discuss the techniques of the method, a few comments should be directed toward this issue now. First, participant observers usually carry out their activities in settings in which they have no direct personal stake. That is, their career, status, friendships, past, future, and self-definition are not directly intertwined with the settings being studied. Participants, on the other hand, are intimately tied to the setting and are consequently less able to understand situations from all people's perspectives. Moreover, participants are inclined to share with others certain taken-for-granted assumptions that researchers question. Second, researchers can devote all of their time to observing in the setting, whereas participants have many constraints on their time. In most situations in which participants are involved they must perform tasks with a certain degree of competence and are, therefore, expending time and energy. For example, an occupational therapist must serve a number of clients; a teacher must teach and confront problems that arise in a classroom; and a police must process criminals. In short, participants lack the time and concentration necessary for intensive observation. Third, researchers are much more systematic in making observations than the people in daily life. Researchers record detailed field notes soon after leaving the field. Therefore, they must concentrate on words and actions in order to later recall them. Finally, researchers are trained in the craft of observation and analysis, are familiar with the problems of observation, and bring to the field a unique perspective for understanding.

What we have just said does not mean that the techniques outlined later in this book cannot be used by people in order to develop a greater understanding of settings in which they work and live. As a matter of fact, several successful participant observation studies have been conducted by researchers who were intimate participants of the settings they studied.[19] However, participant observation is a demanding work. The observer must devote an enormous amount of time and energy in order to observe in the field and record notes after leaving the setting.

Personal Documents, Including Unstructured Interviewing

By *"personal documents"* we mean those materials in which people reveal in their own words their view of their entire life, or a part of it, or some other aspect about themselves.[20] Personal documents include such diverse materials as diaries, letters, autobiographies, and transcripts of long, open-ended interviews. Whether used as autonomous sources of understanding or as resources from which hypotheses can be generated, personal documents permit us to study facets of people, events, and settings which are not directly observable.

We gain an intimate view of organizations, relationships, and events from the perspective of one who has experienced them him- or herself and who may have different premises about the world than we have. As such, personal documents offer a cutting edge by which we can examine our most basic commonsense assumptions about the nature of reality. Howard Becker makes this point well in his introduction to Shaw's study of Stanley, a "juvenile delinquent":

> By putting ourselves in Stanley's [the author's] skin we can feel and become aware of the deep biases about such people that ordinarily permeate our thinking and shape the kinds of problems we investigate. By truly entering into Stanley's life, we can begin to see what we take for granted (and ought not to) in designing our research—what kinds of assumptions about delin-quents, slums, and Poles are embedded in the way we set the questions we study. Stanley's story allows us, if we want to take advantage of it, to begin to ask questions about delinquency from the point of view of the delinquent.[21]

Life stories or autobiographies allow us to see people in the context of their entire lives, from birth to the present. Subjects become people who have experienced successes as well as failures and who look to the future with hope as well as fear. These types of documents help us develop a fuller understanding of the stages and critical periods in the process of development.

Finally, personal documents enable us to view a person in relation to the history of his or her time and to examine how he or she is influenced by various social, religious, political, and economic currents. We see the intersection between the lives of people and the history of their societies. As C. Wright Mills has written, viewing these relationships is one of the most important dimensions of social science:

> The over-all questions of the social sciences . . . come readily to the mind that has firm hold of the orienting conception of social science as the study of biography, history, and of the problems of their intersection within the social structure. To study these problems, to realize the human variety, requires that our work be continuously and closely related to the level of historical reality—and to the meanings of this reality for individual men and women.[22]

We say more about the different kinds of personal documents in Chapter 5; however, we are concerned primarily with documents which represent either intimate conversations and correspondence or personal stories and experiences as told to a researcher.

THE STANCE OF THE QUALITATIVE RESEARCHER

In qualitative methods, the researcher is necessarily involved in the lives of the subjects. He or she is involved to a certain degree simply by virtue of his or her relationship with the subjects. As Cottle points out:

> For a method as fundamental as visiting with people, listening, speaking, and allowing conversations to proceed as they will, means that one's own life is implicated in the life of another person, and one's own feelings are evoked by the language, history and accounts of this other person.[23]

And even more than this involvement, the researcher must identify and empathize with his or her subjects in order to understand them from their own frames of reference. Herbert Blumer writes:

> To try to catch the interpretive process by remaining aloof as a so-called "objective" observer and refusing to take the role of the acting unit is to risk the worst kind of subjectivism—the objective observer is likely to fill in the process of interpretation with his own surmises in place of catching the process as it occurs in the experience of the acting unit which uses it.[24]

There has been a tendency in the social sciences to view certain groups of people in distinct categories and to consequently devalue their perspectives. "Deviants," for example, have been viewed as somehow different from all other people; their behavior have been explained by special theories. Many have been reluctant to become involved with those who are different or to listen to what they have to say. An incident related to us by Burton Blatt is relevant here. It occurred while he and Fred Kaplan were collecting material for their photographic essay, *Christmas in Purgatory,*[25] which depicts the atrocious conditions in state institutions for the "mentally retarded" with pictures secretly taken by Blatt and Kaplan. On one particular occasion, a resident at one of the institutions discovered Kaplan's camera which was secured to his belt and hidden from view by his sports jacket. The resident immediately reported what he had seen to an administrator whose attention Blatt had monopolized until that point. The administrator laughed and casually dismissed the report with the remark: "Boy, these retardates can really have an imagination." A word to the wise is sufficient—resist the temptation to be smug in your own perspective. Understand others, all others, for what they are and for how they see the world.

There is, however, *a real sense in which the qualitative researcher remains detached from his or her subjects and their perspectives.*[26] She or he must be able to stand back from subjects' perspectives. They are viewed as neither true nor false, good nor bad. *The researcher seeks not truth and morality, but rather, understanding.*   bracketing.

While in the situation, the researcher suspends his or her own beliefs and predispositions, as well as those of his or her subjects. As Bruyn notes, he or she views things as though they were happening for the first time.[27] Nothing is taken for granted. Everything is a subject of inquiry.

For some this idea of semiemotional detachment in the field may sound condescending and inhumane. In point of fact, qualitative methods are extremely humanistic. *Every subject in a setting is viewed as an equal to every other.* The researcher considers a juvenile delinquent's perspective to be as important a source of understanding as that of a judge or a detention home director. What the "paranoid" has to say is as important as what a psychiatrist has to say. Moreover, those whom society often ignores—the poor and the "deviant"—receive a forum in the research reports and monographs.[28] Oscar Lewis, famous for his studies among the poor in Latin America, writes, "I have tried to give a voice to a people who are rarely heard."[29] In another work, Lewis remarks:

> This book has grown out of my conviction that anthropologists have a new function in the modern world: to serve as students and reporters of the great mass of peasants and urban dwellers of the underdeveloped countries. . . . We know little about the psychology of the people, particularly the lower classes, their problems, how they think and feel, what they worry about, argue over, anticipate, or enjoy.[30]

Through qualitative methods we learn about people we would not otherwise know. We hear them speak about themselves and their experiences and, though we do not accept their perspectives as truth, develop an empathy which allows us to see the world from their points of view.

TRUTH VERSUS PERSPECTIVES

As noted in the preceding section, *truth is an evasive concept.* One person may describe an experience in one way and another person may describe that same experience in quite another way. Yet both may be "telling the truth" according to their own perspectives: their own interpretations, rationalizations, fabrications, prejudices, and exaggerations.[31]

In our own research at state institutions for the "mentally retarded" (see Chapters 8 and 12), we have found that people who work and live in such settings present contradictory pictures of what institutions are like.[32] Perspectives and understandings differ from person to person, from staff to resident, from administrator to ward attendant, from volunteer to official visitor, from maintenance staff to nurse, and from physician to therapist. These people differ not only in their understandings of institutional goals and practices but in their views of each other.

We have seen vivid scenes and behavior such as rocking and head-banging by residents interpreted in markedly disparate fashion. One attendant explained self-mutilation and head-banging as a direct result of severe mental retardation, while another claimed that a resident may bang his head against the wall as a response to sheer boredom and lack of programming. Similarly, one staff person remarked sadly, "These patients could really be helped if there were a program for them," while another praised the institution for its program: "I know I have the best recreation program in the country. We do everything for these kids." The staff's views of residents further exemplify the gross differences in perceptions. One attendant remarked, "You can't train these kids. They're too low-grade." Another staff member revealed a much more positive view of institutionalized residents: "With the right training, he can walk. A lot of people think these kind of kids are dumb, but they're just as sharp as you and I."

When such contradictory statements emerge during research, who should be believed? Is there actually one perspective, perhaps that of the administrators or that of the residents, that more accurately than all others reflects the reality of institutional life? Could we average out the comments of various people in the setting to arrive at a fair picture of truth? Is there a truthful view?

In searching for some true or objective perspective, one cannot help but ask why people say different things. Might we assume, for example, that some people lie about their experiences in institutions? Do attendants lie? Or is it the administrators who wish to deceive? And what of the residents, do they tell the truth? The fact of the matter is that every person who works and lives in an institution, or in any setting, sees things differently from every other person there. The now trite phrase "beauty is in the eye of the beholder" perhaps most easily conveys the idea that people view the same things in different ways. *Not only do people interpret things differently, they focus their attention on different things.* Hence

what's think!

the business manager and the general administrator may view a facility through their persistent concern for its financial status, whereas the program director may examine an institution in terms of therapeutic needs and training programs. The residents may concern themselves with the personalities of residents and the rules of living for each ward, while attendants might perceive the day-to-day life of an institution in terms of the custodial tasks before them. Similarly, one's perspectives may simply reflect the kind of training one has experienced. Some people have undergone special training in psychology and will tend to interpret people's behavior through psychological models, while the frame of reference for others may be the common social understandings about the "mentally retarded."

Truth then emerges not as one objective view but rather as the composite picture of how people think about the institution and each other. Truth comprises the perspectives of administrators, line-level staff, professional workers, outsiders, volunteers, maintenance staff, residents and family.

Just as different people may interpret the same things differently, so too may the same person interpret things differently at different times. A person's perspective on an event or an experience can change over time. The qualitative researcher is thus likely to find that her or his subjects appear inconsistent in their statements and behavior.

Your task, as a qualitative researcher, is to cut through commonsense understandings of "truth" and "reality." What appears to be false or inconsistent according to your perspective and your logic may not be according to your subjects'. And while you do not have to agree with your subjects' views of the world, you must know, accept, and present them for what they are.

RESEARCHER EFFECTS ON THE DATA

Despite their acknowledged contributions, qualitative methods are not without their critics. Most criticisms center around researchers' effects on the data they collect. While this is not the place for a detailed discussion of the central methodological issues in the social sciences, a few words should be addressed to the current criticisms of qualitative methods.

what is sieve?

Some argue that the qualitative researcher, being the sole instrument, acts like a sieve which selectively collects and analyzes nonrepresentative data. What these critics often fail to realize is that the researcher acts as a selective sieve in all forms of research. For example, those who are involved in survey research choose questions that correspond to their notions of what is important and consequently force reality into a preconceived structure. On the more positive side, the qualitative researcher employs special techniques to minimize the potential effects of bias in the data collection and analysis stages of the study. Many of these techniques are outlined in later chapters of this book.

A related criticism concerns the generalizability of the qualitative researcher's findings to other settings or subjects. In other words, how do we know that the settings or subjects we study are at all representative? Under ideal circumstances, the qualitative researcher might study a wide and varied sample of subjects. In point of fact, few researchers have the time and resources to adequately study more than a handful. Yet this problem is not as great as it appears at first. *All settings and subjects are similar while retaining their uniqueness.* This means that qualitative researchers can study certain general social processes in any single setting or through any single subject. They hope to observe and understand these general processes as they occur under specific circumstances. In a sense, then, all settings and subjects are representative of all others. At the same time, of course, some processes that appear in bold relief under some circumstances appear only faintly under others. Yet *some aspect of social life can best be studied in each setting, or through each subject, because there it is best illuminated.*[33] In his classic study *Asylums,* for example, Goffman develops a "sociological version of the structure of the self" through an examination of settings in which the self is assaulted.[34]

Finally, some critics charge that qualitative researchers elicit unrepresentative data by virtue of their presence among subjects. While they cannot help but affect their subjects' behavior, many of these effects can be minimized through the techniques discussed later in this book and especially in Chapters 3 and 5. Most importantly, however, observers or interviewers are attuned to their influence on subjects. They view themselves as they would view any other participant in a situation. They are thus able to weigh their influence when they analyze their data. And when they report their data, they should give sufficient detail concerning procedures to permit readers to similarly weigh this influence.

It is also true that most research methods employ instruments that affect subjects' behavior in uncertain ways. Webb et al. write:

> Interviews and questionnaires intrude as a foreign element into the social setting they would describe, they create as well as measure attitudes, they elicit atypical roles and responses, they are limited to those who are accessible and will cooperate, and the responses obtained are produced in part by dimensions of individual differences irrelevant to the topic at hand.[35]

Whatever the problems faced by the qualitative researcher, they are faced by other researchers as well. In few other methods, however, can the researcher actually weigh the influence of the research situation.

We admit that the criticisms of qualitative methods are not totally without reason. *Qualitative researchers must be aware of the distortions produced by their methods.* However, potential bias and distortion is the price we must pay to gain understanding of complex social settings. As Melville Dalton suggests:

> If a choice were possible, I would naturally prefer simple, rapid, and infallible methods. If I could find such methods, I would avoid the time-consuming, difficult and suspect variants of "participant observation" with which I have become associated.[36]

PHENOMENOLOGY, SYMBOLIC INTERACTIONISM, AND ETHNOMETHODOLOGY

As mentioned earlier, the phenomenological perspective is central to our conception of qualitative methodology. What qualitative methodologists look for in their research, how they conduct themselves in the research situation, and how they interpret the products of their research: all of these depend upon their theoretical perspective. Therefore, we wish to clarify what we mean by the phenomenological perspective and to discuss two major theoretical approaches, symbolic interactionism and ethnomethodology, that have become dominant forces in sociology and that fall within the phenomenological tradition.[37] In fact, the symbolic interactionists and the ethnomethodologists are currently the most vigorous supporters of qualitative methodology.

The phenomenologist views human behavior—what people say and do—as a product of how people interpret their world. The task of the

phenomenologist, and, for us, the qualitative methodologists, is to capture this *process* of interpretation. To do this requires what Weber called
verstehen, empathic understanding or an ability to reproduce in one's
own mind the feelings, motives, and thoughts behind the actions of
others.[38] In order to grasp the meanings of a person's behavior, *the
phenomenologist attempts to see things from that person's point of view.*

how the person perceives it.

Symbolic Interactionism

Symbolic interactionism stems from the works of John Dewey, Charles
Horton Cooley, Robert Park, W. I. Thomas, and George Herbert Mead,
among others.[39] Although interactionists continue to differ among
themselves as to the meaning and importance of various concepts related to symbolic interactionism, Mead's formulation in *Mind, Self and Society* represents the most comprehensive and least controversial
presentation of the perspective to date.[40]

While Mead's thoughts contain an insightful analysis of the general
processes of social interaction, the task of relating his premises to concrete and everyday terms has been left to his followers.[41] For this reason,
we will discuss the symbolic interactionist perspective as outlined by
Herbert Blumer, Everett C. Hughes, Howard Becker, and Blanche
Geer.[42]

For these theorists, people are constantly in a process of *interpretation*
and *definition* as they move from one situation to another. Some situations are familiar such as one's home, school, or place of work; others are
less familiar and may be one-encounter affairs. All situations consist of
the actor, others and their actions, and physical objects. In any case, a
situation has *meaning* only through people's interpretations and definitions of it. Their actions, in turn, stem from this meaning. Thus, this
process of interpretation acts as the intermediary between any predis-
position to act and the action itself.

Situations, or aspects of situations (the actor her- or himself, other
actors), come to be defined in different ways by different participants for
a number of reasons. One reason is that each actor brings with her or
him a unique past and a certain way of interpreting what she or he sees.
Two teachers, for example, may view the actions of a particular child
differently because of the different life experiences each has had. More-

over, people may fill different positions in a situation. (*Position* here refers to a socially defined place in a setting or an organization.) Different positions may entail different contacts or responsibilities. Thus, each position within a single situation offers a potentially different perspective. For example, a student breaks a window in a school cafeteria. The counselor might define the situation as a behavior problem; the janitor might see it as a maintenance problem; the school nurse as a health problem; and the student who broke the window as a suspension problem and, therefore, as a personal problem. Of course, all participants in a situation may define that situation in the same way; or participants at the same position (for example, counselor in the above situation) may define it differently. Additionally, other factors (the ethnic background and sex of the student, the training of the counselors) may influence participants' *perspectives.*

Since actors in a similar position generally have opportunities to communicate with one another, they may develop shared definitions of a particular situation or a category of similar situations. Sometimes definitions and meanings are shared with new members by older occupants of a position. Whatever the case, the phrase *shared perspective* refers to a definition of a situation which a number of actors hold.

From the symbolic interactionist perspective, all social organizations consist of actors who develop *definitions of a situation,* or perspectives, through the process of interpretation and who then act in terms of these definitions. *While people may act within the framework of an organization, it is the interpretation and not the organization which determines action. Social roles, norms, values, and goals may set conditions and consequences for action, but do not determine what a person will do.*

The formally presented picture of an organization influences people's behavior only to the extent that it provides fixed meanings that people use to interpret situations. For example, a college may have a grading system, a class schedule, a curriculum, and an official motto, all of which suggest that it is a place of learning and scholarly pursuits. Of course, these symbols will have some influence on how people define what they do. Yet people will act according to the meanings the organization holds for them, and not according to what some highly placed official thinks these meanings should be. For some students, the college will represent a place to meet a spouse. For many others, it is a place to get good grades in order to meet the standards for graduation.

Ethnomethodology

A great deal of controversy surrounds the influential writings of Harold
Garfinkel and his fellow ethnomethodologists.[43] For some, ethnomethodology represents nothing more than an updated version of symbolic
interactionism. For others, it represents a radical departure from other
sociological traditions. Many of the dimensions of ethnomethodology
have yet to be defined by the ethnomethodologists. In the following
discussion, then, we merely outline some of the common strains or
thoughts found in the works of several important ethnomethodologists,
including Jack Douglas, Egon Bittner, Aaron Cicourel, Roy Turner,
Don Zimmerman, and D. Lawrence Wieder, as well as Garfinkel
himself.[44]

Ethnomethodology refers not to research methods but rather to the subject matter of inquiry: how (the methodology by which) people make
sense out of the situations in which they find themselves. For ethnomethodologists, the *meanings* of actions are always ambiguous and problematic for people in specific situations. Their task is to examine the ways
people apply abstract rules and *commonsense understandings* in situations
in order to make actions appear routine, explicable, and unambiguous.
Meanings, then, are *practical accomplishments* on the part of members of a
society.

Jack Douglas has studied the process by which coroners designate
deaths as suicides.[45] He notes that this designation requires coroners to
make use of commonsense understandings ("what everyone knows") of
why people commit suicide in order to establish intentionality. Coroners
put together certain clues (for example, evidence that a person was
distressed over the loss of a job) and come up with a "suicide for all
practical purposes." In this process, however, they may ignore certain
other clues and can never establish that a person actually intended
death. Another study by D. Lawrence Wieder explores how "narcotics
addicts" in a halfway house use a "convict code" (axioms such as "do not
snitch" and "help other residents") to explain, justify, and account for
their behavior.[46] He illustrates the ways residents "tell the code," apply
maxims to specific situations, when they are called upon to account for
their actions. Wieder writes:

> The code, then, is much more a *method* of moral persuasion and justification
> than it is a substantive account of an organized way of life. It is a way, or set

of ways, of causing activities to be seen as morally, repetitively, and con-
strainedly organized.[47]

The ethnomethodologists thus "bracket," or suspend, their own commonsense assumptions to study how commonsense is used in everyday
life. Garfinkel himself has studied the commonsense or taken-for-granted rules of interaction in everyday life through a variety of mischievious
experiments (see Chapter 6 of this book).[48] Through an examination of
commonsense the ethnomethodologists hope to understand how people
"go about the task of *seeing, describing,* and *explaining* order in the world
in which they live."[49]

Our purpose in this section has been to give you some background on
different theoretical perspectives that relate to qualitative methodology
and to provide you with a general framework with which you can conduct and interpret your research. We return to the symbolic interactionist and ethnomethodological perspectives in Part Two of this book in
order to give you a clearer idea of how these perspectives can be used to
present your findings.

*   *   *

In this chapter we have attempted to give you a sense of some of the
issues that surround qualitative methods. We have been biased in our
presentation, for we believe in the potential and prospects of qualitative
methodologies. Yet we would be less than candid if we did not admit that
qualitative research is not for everyone or for every problem. Some will
find it impossible or undesirable to adopt the stance previously discussed. Others will find the methods to be incompatible with their research goals. To each her or his own.

The remainder of this book deals with data collection, interpretation,
and presentation in qualitative research. Part One includes three chapters on participant observation, one on personal documents and unstructured interviewing, and a final one on discovering methods. In Part
Two, we deal with some of the ways in which the qualitative researcher
can present his or her findings, and we offer a series of papers based on
data obtained through qualitative methods.

NOTES

1.   See Severyn T. Bruyn, *The Human Perspective in Sociology: The Methodology of Participant Observation* (Englewood Cliffs, N.J.: Prentice-Hall, 1966), pp. 2–9, 58–63; Jerry Jacobs,

Getting By: Illustrations of Marginal Living (Boston: Little, Brown, 1972), pp. 1–8; and Irwin Deutscher, *What We Say/What We Do: Sentiments and Acts* (Glenview, Ill.: Scott, Foresman, 1973), pp. 2–11.

2.   See Auguste Comte, *The Positive Philosophy,* Harriet Martineau (Trans.) (London: George Bell & Sons, 1816); Emile Durkheim, *The Rules of Sociological Method* (New York: Free Press, 1938); and Emile Durkheim, edited and translated by George Simpson, *Suicide: A Study in Sociology* (New York: Free Press, 1951).

3.   Durkheim, *Sociological Method,* p. 14.

4.   Deutscher, *What We Say.* A great deal of controversy continues to surround the use of this term. See, for example, James L. Heap and Phillip A. Roth, "On phenomenological sociology," *American Sociological Review,* **38** (June): 354–367, 1973.

5.   Max Weber, *Economy and Society,* 3 vols., Guenther Roth and Claus Wittich (Eds.), (New York: Bedminster Press, 1968). For a general discussion of phenomenological sociology, see Peter L. Berger and Thomas Luckmann, *The Social Construction of Reality: A Treatise in the Sociology of Knowledge* (Garden City, N.Y.: Doubleday, 1967); and George Psathas, (Ed.), *Phenomenological Sociology: Issues and Applications* (New York: Wiley, 1973).

6.   Jack D. Douglas (Ed.), *Understanding Everyday Life: Toward the Reconstruction of Sociological Knowledge* (Chicago: Aldine, 1970), p. ix.

7.   For a criticism of this approach, see Aaron V. Cicourel, *Method and Measurement in Sociology* (New York: Free Press, 1964).

8.   Durkheim used the descriptive studies of various anthropologists as a basis for one of his major treatises. See Emile Durkheim, *The Elementary Forms of Religious Life* (New York: Free Press, 1915).

9.   See Bruyn, *Human Perspective,* p. 9.

10.   Robert A. Nisbet, *The Sociological Tradition* (New York: Basic Books, 1966), p. 61.

11.   Early works include Nels Anderson, *The Hobo* (Chicago: University of Chicago Press, 1923); Paul Cressey, *The Taxi-Dance Hall* (Chicago: University of Chicago Press, 1932); Edwin Sutherland, *The Professional Thief* (Chicago: University of Chicago Press, 1937); W. I. Thomas and Florian Znaniecki, *The Polish Peasant in Europe and America,* 5 vols. (Chicago: University of Chicago Press, 1918–1920); Frederick Thrasher, *The Gang* (Chicago: University of Chicago Press, 1927); Clifford Shaw, *The Jack Roller* (Chicago: University of Chicago Press, 1930); Harvey Zorbaugh, *The Gold Coast and the Slum* (Chicago: University of Chicago Press, 1929); Louis Wirth, *The Ghetto* (Chicago: University of Chicago Press, 1928); William Foote Whyte, *Street Corner Society* (Chicago: University of Chicago Press, 1955); Helen and Robert Lynd, *Middletown* (New York: Harcourt Brace, 1929); W. Lloyd Warner, *The Social Life of a Modern Community* (New Haven: Yale University Press, 1941).

12.   William I. Thomas and Florian Znaniecki, *The Polish Peasant in Europe and America* (New York: Alfred A. Knopf, 1927, 2nd edition), p. 1832.

13.   Examples can be found in the works of Herbert Gans, Fred Davis, Howard S. Becker, Blanche Geer, Everett Hughes, Stephan Miller, Alvin Gouldner, Barney Glaser, Anselm Strauss, Robert Park, Aaron Cicourel, John Kitsuse, Kai Erikson, Jack Douglas, Laud Humphreys, Morris Schwartz, Arthur Vidich, Joseph Bensman, Julius Roth, Ned Polsky, Erving Goffman, Melville Dalton, Donald Roy, and others.

14.   George McCall and J. L. Simmons (Eds.), *Issues in Participant Observation* (Reading, Mass.: Addison-Wesley, 1969); and William Filstead (Ed.), *Qualitative Methodology: First-hand Involvement with the Social World* (Chicago: Markham, 1970) are the two volumes of collected essays with which we are familiar. Howard Becker's *Sociological Work* (Chicago: Aldine, 1970) is a collection of his writings, many of which deal with qualitative methodology.

15. Bruyn, *Human Perspective;* Barney Glaser and Anselm Strauss, *The Discovery of Grounded Theory: Strategies for Qualitative Research* (Chicago: Aldine, 1967); Myron Glazer, *The Research Adventure: Promise and Problems of Field Work* (New York: Random House, 1972); and L. Schatzman and A. L. Strauss, *Field Research: Strategies for a Natural Sociology* (Englewood Cliffs, N.J.: Prentice-Hall, 1973).

16. As quoted by Shaw in *The Jack Roller,* (2nd ed.) (Chicago: University of Chicago Press, 1966), p. 4.

17. See McCall and Simmons, *Participant Observation,* p. 3; and Howard S. Becker and Blanche Geer, "Participant observation and interviewing: A comparison," *Human Organization,* **XVI** (3): 28, 1957.

18. Herbert Blumer, in "Society as symbolic interaction," in Jerome Manis and Bernard Meltzer (Eds.), *Symbolic Interaction* (Boston: Allyn and Bacon, 1967), p. 148, questions "whether human society or social action can be successfully analyzed by schemes which refuse to recognize human beings as they are, namely, as persons constructing individual and collective action through interpretations of the situations which confront them."

19. See for example, Erving Goffman, *Asylums* (Garden City, N.Y.: Anchor, 1961), and Julius Roth, *Timetables* (Indianapolis: Bobbs-Merrill, 1963).

20. For writings on the history of the use of personal documents see Howard S. Becker, "Introduction" in Shaw, *Jack Roller,* 1966; Gordon Allport, *The Use of Personal Documents in Psychological Science* (New York: Social Science Research Council, 1942), Chapters 1 and 2; and Chapters One and Two in Clyde Kluckhohn's, "The personal document in anthropological science," and all of Robert Angell's, "A critical review of the development of the personal document method in sociology," both of which appear in Louis Gottschalk, Clyde Kluckhohn, and Robert Angell, *The Use of Personal Documents in History, Anthropology, and Sociology* (New York: Social Science Research Council, 1945). Interestingly enough, one of the major critiques of the use of personal documents as data comes from a "phenomenological" perspective. See Herbert Blumer, *Symbolic Interactionism: Perspective and Method* (Englewood Cliffs, N.J.: Prentice-Hall, 1969), pp. 117–27. We use the phrase "personal documents" to include data obtained through unstructured interviewing; however, we sometimes add the phrase "unstructured interviewing" for purposes of clarification and specification.

21. Becker, "Introduction," in Shaw, *Jack Roller,* 1966, p. 15.

22. C. Wright Mills, *The Sociological Imagination* (New York: Oxford University Press, 1959), p. 134. Also see Robert Coles, *Migrants, Sharecroppers, Mountaineers* (Boston: Little, Brown, 1967), p. 32.

23. Thomas Cottle, *The Abandoners* (Boston: Little, Brown, 1972), p. xvi.

24. Blumer, *Symbolic Interactionism,* p. 86.

25. Burton Blatt and Fred Kaplan, *Christmas in Purgatory* (Syracuse, N.Y.: Human Policy Press, 1974).

26. See Bruyn, *Human Perspective,* pp. 14–15; Morris S. Schwartz and Charlotte G. Schwartz, "Problems in participant observation," *American Journal of Sociology,* **60** (January): 350–351, 1955; and S. M. Miller, "The participant observer and over-rapport," *American Sociological Review,* **17** (February): 97–99, 1952.

27. Bruyn, *Human Perspective,* p. xii.

28. See Howard S. Becker, "Whose side are we on?," *Social Problems,* **XIV** (Winter): 239–247, 1967. For a critique of Becker's position, see A. W. Gouldner, "The sociologist as partisan: Sociology and the welfare state," *The American Sociologist* **3** (May): 103–116, 1968.

29. Oscar Lewis, *La Vida* (New York: Vintage, 1965), p. xii.

30. Oscar Lewis, *Five Families* (New York: Wiley, 1962), p. 1.

31. See Shaw, *Jack Roller,* 1966, p. 3.

32. We owe many of the ideas and examples in this section to Douglas Biklen.

33. E. C. Hughes, *Men and Their Work* (New York: The Free Press of Glencoe, 1958), p. 49.

34. Erving Goffman, *Asylums* (Garden City, N.Y.: Doubleday, Anchor Books, 1961).

35. E. J. Webb et al., *Unobtrusive Measures: Non-reactive Research in the Social Sciences* (Chicago: Rand McNally, 1966), p. 1.

36. Melville Dalton, "Preconceptions and methods in *Men Who Manage,*" in Phillip Hammond (Ed.), *Sociologists at Work* (Garden City, N.Y.: Doubleday, Anchor Books, 1964), p. 60.

37. Erving Goffman's dramaturgical model in *The Presentation of Self in Everyday Life* (Garden City, N.Y.: Doubleday, 1959) and the labeling perspective as summarized by Edwin Schur, *Labeling Deviant Behavior: Its Sociological Implications* (New York: Harper & Row, 1971) represent two additional perspectives although these are variants of symbolic interactionism.

38. Weber, *Economy and Society.*

39. John Dewey, *Human Nature and Conduct* (New York: Modern Library, 1930); Charles Horton Cooley, *Human Nature and the Social Order* (New York: Free Press of Glencoe, 1956); Robert Park, *Principles of Human Behavior* (Chicago: The Zalaz Corp., 1915); William I. Thomas, *The Unadjusted Girl* (Boston: Little, Brown, 1931); George Herbert Mead, *Mind, Self and Society* (Chicago: University of Chicago Press, 1934); George Herbert Mead, *The Philosophy of the Act* (Chicago: University of Chicago Press, 1938). The phrase "symbolic interactionism" was actually coined by Blumer. See Blumer, *Symbolic Interactionism.*

40. For attempts at systematic summary statements of symbolic interaction theory, see Arnold Rose, "A systematic summary of symbolic interaction theory" and Herbert Blumer, "Society as symbolic interaction," both in Arnold Rose (Ed.), *Human Behavior and Social Processes* (Boston: Houghton-Mifflin, 1962). Mead's distinction between the "I" and the "me" is crucial here. The "I," the response of an individual to the community, depends upon the "me," the ability to view one's self from the standpoint of others. See pp. 192–200.

41. See Manford Kuhn, "Major trends in symbolic interaction in the past twenty-five years," *Sociological Quarterly,* V (Winter): 61–84, 1964.

42. See Howard S. Becker et al., *Boys in White* (Chicago: University of Chicago Press, 1961); Howard S. Becker et al., *Making the Grade* (New York: Wiley, 1968); Blumer, *Symbolic Interactionism;* Everett C. Hughes, *Men and Their Work* (New York: Free Press of Glencoe, 1958).

43. See Norman K. Denzin, "Symbolic interactionism and ethnomethodology," Don H. Zimmerman and D. Lawrence Wieder, "Ethnomethodology and the problem of order: Comment on Denzin," and Norman K. Denzin, "Symbolic interactionism and ethnomethodology: A comment on Zimmerman and Wieder," in Douglas, *Understanding Everyday Life,* pp. 259–284, 285–295, 295–298.

44. Harold Garfinkel, *Studies in Ethnomethodology* (Englewood Cliffs, N.J.: Prentice-Hall, 1967); Jack D. Douglas, *The Social Meanings of Suicide* (Princeton, N.J.: Princeton University Press, 1967); Douglas, *Understanding Everyday Life;* and Jack D. Douglas, *American Social Order: Social Rules in a Pluralistic Society* (New York: Free Press, 1971); and Roy Turner (Ed.), *Ethnomethodology* (Baltimore: Penguin, 1974).

45. Douglas, *American Social Order,* pp. 106–130.

46. D. Lawrence Wieder, "Telling the code," in Turner, *Ethnomethodology,* pp. 144–172.

47.   *Ibid.*, p. 158. Wieder highlights the difference between the ethnomethodological and symbolic interactionist perspectives in this quotation. His reference to the "code" as a "*method* of moral persuasion and justification" is strictly in the ethnomethodological vein. The symbolic interactionist would tend to view it as a "substantive account of an organized way of life."

48.   Garfinkel, *Studies in Ethnomethodology,* Ch. 2.

49.   Zimmerman and Wieder, "Ethnomethodology," p. 289. For a good example of this style of work, see also M. B. Scott and S. M. Lyman, "Accounts," *American Sociological Review* V. **33**: 46–62, 1968.

PART ONE

Among the People

HOW TO CONDUCT QUALITATIVE RESEARCH

```
┌─────────────────────────────────────────────┐
│                                             │
│              CHAPTER TWO                     │
│                                             │
└─────────────────────────────────────────────┘

┌─────────────────────────────────────────────┐
│                                             │
│              Participant                     │
│              Observation                     │
│                                             │
└─────────────────────────────────────────────┘

┌─────────────────────────────────────────────┐
│                                             │
│             PRE - FIELDWORK                  │
│                                             │
└─────────────────────────────────────────────┘
```

In this chapter we discuss the pre-fieldwork stage of participant observation research: those important, but often neglected, activities in which researchers should engage before they enter the field. In the following chapter, "In the Field," we move to a discussion of the methods of data collection and intensive observation. Finally, in the last chapter on participant observation, we describe some of the techniques the participant observers can use to interpret their data.

While the following includes a description of the general methodology and specific techniques that we have employed in our own studies, we do not mean to say that there is a single best way to conduct field research. Our intention is not to establish a set of rigid principles that every researcher must follow, but rather to offer a set of guidelines and a general approach which we have found to be useful. All qualitative methodologies should leave room for flexibility.

Some researchers may prefer not to act according to our definition of participant observation given in Chapter 1 and may find it more suitable for their purposes to make single visits to a number of settings or to observe without interacting with subjects.[1] There are advantages and disadvantages to their approaches. In regard to the former, the researcher gains a general knowledge of a variety of settings at the expense of a detailed knowledge of a single setting. In regard to the latter, he or she sacrifices opportunities to question subjects for a greater sense of detachment. Still other researchers may decide to observe in a single setting for a prolonged period of time on each visit and only record a summary of their observations. Whether or not our general approach is adopted, sections of these chapters will prove to be useful to all field workers and other interested persons.

THE RESEARCH DESIGN

In contrast to most other methodologies in which the researcher's specific interests and goals are determined a priori, the research design in participant observation studies remains flexible up to and including the actual beginning of the research. *While participant observers have a methodology to follow, the specifics of their approach evolve as they proceed.*

All researchers do, of course, have some general questions in mind when they enter the field. These typically fall into one of two broad categories: one substantive and the other theoretical.

The first includes questions related to specific substantive issues in a specific setting. In a study of a mental hospital, for example, one might examine how new patients view the institution. The second category of interests is more closely tied to basic sociological problems and broader theoretical issues. Here the researcher asks questions about topics such as the nature of a certain kind of organization or the dynamics of small groups.[2]

These two categories are, of course, interrelated. Some topics are of both substantive and theoretical interest. For example, the meaning of pornographic literature in a juvenile detention home can be studied in terms of either what it tells us about the particular institution or what it tells us about social control in organizational environments.

What distinguishes participant observation and all qualitative methods from other methodologies is that *the participant observer's questions are framed in general terms.* Most practitioners of the methodology attempt to enter the field without specific hypotheses or preconceived notions. Melville Dalton writes:

> (1) I never feel sure what is relevant for hypothesizing until I have some intimacy with the situation—I think of a hypothesis as a well-founded conjecture; (2) once uttered, a hypothesis becomes obligatory to a degree; (3) there is a danger that the hypothesis will become esteemed for itself and work as an abused symbol of science.[3]

To enter a setting with a set of specific hypotheses is to impose preconceptions and perhaps misconceptions on the setting.

During the first days in the field, the observer may find that his or her ideas and areas of interest do not fit the setting. His or her questions may not be relevant to the concerns and behavior of the subjects. The participant observers will begin to formulate a new research design or new tactics and begin to ask different questions; in some cases, they will leave the setting for another.[4] In a study of a ward for the "severely and profoundly retarded" at a state institution conducted by one of the authors (see Chapters 8 and 12), the researcher entered the setting with the intention of studying residents' perspectives on the institution only to find that many residents were nonverbal and many others were reluctant to speak openly about the institution.[5] He then shifted his attention to attendants' perspectives, which proved to be a fruitful line of inquiry. The same process occurred in a study of a "hard core unemployed" job training program (see Chapter 13).[6] The researcher assumed that he would study "resocialization" in the program until he learned that factors unrelated to socialization were far more important to understanding the setting. What he thought would be his focus became a relatively unimportant part of the study.

CHOOSING A RESEARCH SITE

Any setting that meets the substantive and theoretical interests of the researcher and that is open for study might be chosen as a research site. It is relatively easy to know which setting will meet one's substantive interests; it is more difficult to choose a setting which will meet one's theoretical interests.

The observer interested in broad theoretical questions is likely to find the site she or he has chosen ill-suited to her or his interests. All settings are, nevertheless, intrinsically interesting whether or not they fulfill each researcher's theoretical concerns. In any case, it is advisable not to hold too tightly to any theoretical interest, but rather, to explore a variety of theoretical phenomena as they are suggested by one's observations in the process of data collection.

There are also geographical limitations and other practical considerations which determine which research site an observer will choose. Novices to the methodology are inclined to choose the most easily accessible sites; the choice of a setting is often decided by such factors as having a friend who knows the "gatekeeper" of an organization. It should be noted, however, that the most easily accessible settings are likely to be the most frequently visited. In such settings the researcher should expect to be responded to in a more stereotypical fashion than in other settings. And although accessibility does not necessarily make a setting less interesting, it does make it different from settings which are not as easily accessible.

One final word should be said about the choice of a research setting. For a number of reasons, *we would recommend that researchers choose settings in which the subjects are strangers to them and in which they have no particular professional knowledge or expertise.* When one observes friends or acquaintances, one is more likely to take sides or, to put it another way, to see things from only one person's perspective. One might also tend to limit what would be said in written research reports in the fear that friends or relatives might find it offensive. Experts who observe in their own domains face other problems. It is difficult for experts to hold their own beliefs and feelings in abeyance. For example, a special educator observing in a special education classroom will tend to evaluate the teacher's techniques when he or she should note and describe them. Moreover, the expert will share with participants certain commonsense assumptions, biases, and perspectives. We know one observer of "behavior modification" who, instead of describing the behavior of her subjects, characterized it as "inappropriate" or "appropriate."

OVERT VERSUS COVERT RESEARCH AND
ETHICAL CONSIDERATIONS

The participant observer can conduct fieldwork as a covert researcher, with his or her research interests hidden, or as an overt researcher.[7] There are advantages and disadvantages to both approaches. Regardless of pragmatic considerations, however, *there are serious ethical questions to be raised in regard to covert research.*[8] While there are no right answers to these questions, it is important to discuss the ethical considerations that the participant observer should take into account.

Ethical decisions necessarily involve one's personal morality. That is, one must choose among a number of alternatives or, in the case of the participant observer, among a number of responsibilities held by virtue of the researcher role. Some social scientists, such as Kai Erikson, argue that undercover research and deception jeopardize the goodwill of potential research subjects and the general public upon whom other researchers ultimately depend: "It probably goes without saying that research of this sort is liable to damage the reputation of sociology in the larger society and close off promising areas of research for future investigators."[9] These social scientists believe that researchers owe their primary responsibility to their profession. Others believe that the scientific knowledge gained through research justifies covert observation and otherwise distasteful practices.[10] Glazer describes the position adopted by Arthur Vidich in regard to a related matter:

> Vidich, himself, later acknowledged that he had been a party to deceptive assurances about the protection of identities. . . . Vidich also had little patience with the argument that some individuals had been hurt by his analysis. For him, this was the price inherent in contributing to knowledge.[11]

Still other social scientists justify covert research on the basis of the practical social benefits of such research. For Rainwater and Pittman, social science research enhances the accountability of public officials.[12] This justification is legitimate only to the extent that social science research is accessible to the public or important sectors of the public. Finally, there are those who on face value condemn the deception of subjects and who advocate a "right not to be researched."[13] Thus, some social scientists argue that researchers never have a right to harm their subjects and that the only ones who can judge whether or not the research might cause harm, even if only in the form of exposure of group secrets, are the subjects themselves.

In matters of ethics, then, the researchers must counterbalance the multiple responsibilities they have to their profession, the pursuit of knowledge, the society, their subjects, and, ultimately, themselves. Each researcher must define what is ethical.

There are a number of practical points to be made against covert research. Many covert observers find that they cannot control the anxieties that result from the fear of getting caught and the guilt of misrepresentation. Some find it difficult to relax when they must constantly guard against behavior that might reveal their research interests. There is also the real danger of being exposed and the necessity of dealing with the rapport-shattering experience of explaining one's deception to one's subjects. Perhaps the greatest disadvantage of covert research is the constraint it places on one's freedom to conduct research. The overt researcher can present her- or himself in ways that enable her or him to probe and seek information and can thus overstep the limitations that many organizations and groups place on their participants. As a member of the organization or group, the hidden observer has limitations placed on the breadth and kind of data she or he can collect.

On the other hand, there are sound arguments to be made in favor of covert observation in some cases. Since powerful groups in our society are the least likely to grant access to researchers, social science research tends to concentrate on the relatively powerless who seldom understand the purpose of research. Researchers consequently expose the faults of the powerless while the powerful remain unscathed. One might therefore propose that covert research be conducted only when dealing with powerful groups.

It is also true, as Roth argues, that the distinction between covert and overt research is an oversimplification.[14] That is, all research is to some extent secret in the sense that the researcher never tells the subjects everything. And what of researchers who observe in public places? Must they inform a crowd of people that they are being observed? Roth's arguments pinpoint the fact that there are no hard-and-fast rules for the participant observer. *Research in the field will always involve the researcher in a great deal of soul-searching and negotiation.* We have chosen to emphasize in our writing the commonly used approach, overt observation. In Chapter 6 we provide an example of a study in which covert researchers were used.

GATEKEEPERS

The participant observer normally gains access to an organizational setting by requesting the permission of those in charge. We refer to the people who have the power to grant access as *gatekeepers.*[15]

While there appears to be differential access to research settings, the new observer is often surprised at how accessible many settings are. People, it would seem, enjoy being studied. One of the authors studied the training programs for door-to-door salesmen in two companies a few years ago (see Chapter 10).[16] Although both of these companies trained prospective salesmen in the techniques of calculated misrepresentation and conning, the heads of the branch offices opened their organizations to the researcher within minutes after his request to observe them. In fact, the branch head of one of these companies gave permission over the phone after the researcher had responded to a "come on" in the newspaper used to lure trainees into the program.

Despite the ease with which the researcher gained access to these training programs, the process of getting entry frequently does take an extended period of time. This difficulty is especially apparent in large, bureaucratic organizations such as governmental agencies. This same researcher had previously sought access to a firemen's training program offered under the auspices of the United States Air Force. Officials at each of a number of levels wanted to interview him personally, and each official with whom he spoke had to ask someone else for written permission before granting permission. After three weeks, during which he had lost valuable research time, the researcher turned to the study of salesmen instead. Several weeks later he received written tentative permission to study the Air Force firemen.

Once the researcher has gained access to a setting he or she may decide to postpone the beginning of his or her study until an opportune time in the organization's schedule or history. In studying training programs, for example, she or he may want to wait for a new group to begin training in order to follow it through the entire program. In the study of other settings, such as a school, he or she may wait to enter the field at a particular phase in the calendar.

Since researchers must often wait for permission or an opportune time before they begin their fieldwork, there is often a significant interval between the initial conception of the study and the beginning of observations. In some instances, one setting does not work out for the researcher and he or she must switch to another. For these reasons, it is important that the observers allow enough time to satisfactorily complete the study. Some will allot a specific period of time for their intensive observations, such as three months in the summer, only to find that it takes almost that long to gain entry or that they must postpone their entry into the field.

Detailed field notes should be kept during the process of gaining access to a setting. As in later stages of research, notes should be recorded after telephone conversations as well as after face-to-face encounters. The data collected during this phase may prove to be helpful at a later time. The researcher will learn how persons in different positions view the organization. In the study of the institution for the "mentally retarded" mentioned earlier, for example, the researcher had the opportunity to spend time with the director of the institution during the getting-in stage. The director gave his perspective on the institution in statements such as "Nobody's perfect"; "We are overcrowded"; "We could use more money from the state." This information proved to be extremely valuable, especially when the director's perspective was compared to the perspectives of others at different levels of the institution.

The getting-in stage is also a time in which the researcher will gain insight into how clients and other outsiders are processed by the organization. *The best way to learn about the structure and hierarchy of an organization is to be handed around through it.* Finally, the notes recorded during this stage of the research serve as a reminder of any bargains the researcher made when he or she entered the research relationship. And if by chance or by fault entry is refused the notes may tell why he or she failed.

WHERE THERE ARE NO GATEKEEPERS

Much research is conducted in nonorganizational settings where the researcher does not need the permission of an official gatekeeper in order to conduct his study. Many researchers are interested in observing in public settings, such as in bars or on street corners, or in private settings, such as in homes. The observer must develop special strategies to gain the cooperation in these settings of those subjects with whom she or he plans to spend an extended period of time.

Probably the best way in which to gain the cooperation of subjects in nonorganizational settings is to establish one or two close relationships initially. In his classic study of "street corner society," Whyte sought the help of a social worker to find him an "in" among the people in whom he was interested after his own attempts had failed.[17] He was finally introduced to "Doc," who "showed him the ropes" and vouched for him with other members of the community. Liebow, a white researcher, went directly into the field and soon established a few close friendships in his study of Black street corner men.[18] Polsky advocates both of these approaches for the study of "criminals."[19] He suggests that the researcher either find someone to introduce him to a specific criminal (he notes that this is not that hard to do if one asks around) or go to where criminals spend their leisure time (pool halls, for example) and win the trust of a few of them.

While it may not be necessary for researchers to explain their purposes to those with whom they will have only one or two contacts, they would be wise to explain who they are and what they want to those on whom they will concentrate in their studies. We do not mean that observers should introduce themselves to people as researchers. *We do mean that they should identify themselves before their subjects begin to doubt their intentions, especially if they are involved in illegal or marginal activities.* Thus, Liebow explained his intentions to subjects after his first or second contact with them, and Polsky advises researchers to participate marginally with criminals and then to identify themselves.

WHAT DO YOU TELL SUBJECTS?

Some researchers are intimidated by the prospect of approaching subjects to explain the purpose of a participant observation study. A little courage and a few helpful suggestions as to how to proceed might be helpful.

One good rule to follow, with gatekeepers at the start of the research and with other persons throughout the endeavor, is to *tell the truth.*[20] Since many novices do not feel comfortable in the role of a participant observer, there is often a temptation to misrepresent themselves. They would be wise to overcome this temptation, for more often than not misrepresentation leads to embarrassment and to other difficulties as the research proceeds. However, observers need not explain their substantive or theoretical interests or their specific techniques in great detail. In fact, *it is probably unwise for researchers to volunteer elaborate details concern-*

ing the precision with which notes will be taken. If the subjects knew how closely they were going to be watched, they might become extremely self-conscious in the observer's presence. In the unlikely case that subjects ask about the nature of the data the observer is collecting, they should be told that the observer takes notes or keeps a diary.

An important point to make in explaining your purpose is that you are not necessarily interested in that particular setting or organization or in the behavior of the particular people there. Your interests are more basic and broader and concern organizations in general or organizations of the type to which you are attempting to gain access. (In certain research endeavors you might be interested in the particular setting or organization. If that is the case, follow the honesty rule.) If you are seeking access to a school, for example, you should suggest to the principal, or to the official from whom you are seeking permission, that you are interested in what *a* school is like and the nature of relationships in *a* school, rather than the nature of that particular school. Of course, you might add that there are certain aspects of that organization which make it an ideal setting to study, especially if subjects take pride in what they do. This information will tell subjects that you do not intend to view them as mere statistics.

While you may doubt your ability to adequately explain your purposes, keep in mind that many subjects will not have the background to understand the exact nature of your research. Most will be satisfied with the most general explanation of your interests. *Leave your esoteric social science vocabulary at home.* An explanation of your purpose masked in jargon may do much to scare off your potential subjects. We know of one observer who identified himself to his subjects as an "ethnographer." He later heard one subject whisper to another, "Don't make any racial jokes in front of that guy. He's an ethnographer."

Most of the people who read this book will be students. Identifying oneself as such in the field can be helpful because it is easier, and less threatening, for a gatekeeper to see the sense of a research project conducted by a student. The naïve, eager student will be an object of sympathy and will be helped and instructed. The gatekeeper, as well as other subjects, will probably assume that the student is there to learn concrete facts or tasks from "experts."

Even when the researcher is not a student, people at different levels of an organization generally make the assumption that he or she is there to learn about, or how to deal with, those at another level. For example, you may want to study the relationships between staff and inmates at a prison. The staff may think that you're interested in the inmates while the inmates will think that you're interested in the staff. In the aforementioned study of the state institution, attendants naturally assumed, without encouragement, that the researcher was there to observe the behavior patterns of the "severely and profoundly retarded." (That they would make this assumption is itself a significant piece of data.) While it is inadvisable for the observer to intentionally create false impressions, there are certain advantages to allowing subjects to maintain such misunderstandings.

The rule, then, *is to be honest, but vague or imprecise.* Present your purposes in a way that will not alarm or produce anxiety in your subjects. The explanation that you give to the gatekeeper will vary, of course, with the nature of the organization and the subjects you wish to study. It is helpful to give some thought to your approach before you have your first encounter with the gatekeeper.

THE BARGAIN

An important part of gaining access is the *bargain.* The bargain is the written or unwritten agreement between the gatekeeper, or subjects, and the researcher that defines the obligations they have to one another.[21] While the gatekeeper has access to offer, it is not always clear what the researcher has to give, if anything.

The observer may, of course, produce ideas and gain information that could be of interest to the gatekeeper. But a promise to provide such information places the researcher in a relationship of collaboration with the gatekeeper,[22] which in turn might endanger the researcher's relationships with others in the organization and create ethical problems in the protection of lower-level subjects. Researchers must make their position clear to the gatekeeper. They must explain that they are obligated to protect lower-level subjects as well as the organization and the gatekeeper. Thus, most observers are only prepared to promise the gatekeeper a very general verbal or written report on their observations, a report so general that it could in no way be detrimental to the subjects. Fortunately, most bargains do not involve even this type of obligation.

Observers should emphasize the fact that their research will not disrupt the organization or the setting. Many gatekeepers assume that social science research involves questionnaires, interviews, and other time-consuming and potentially disruptive activities. Some will therefore refuse access on the basis of the anticipated effects of the research on the subjects. This refusal is especially likely to occur in highly goal-oriented organizations where efficiency is a salient concern. The researcher must consequently promise to stay out of their way. The gatekeeper should be informed that it is as important to the quality and success of the research for the observer to minimize disruption as it is to the efficiency of the organization. Another argument that can be made in the researcher's behalf is that the gatekeeper can terminate the study at any time should the researcher become a nuisance.

Subjects are also frequently concerned with what you plan to do with the data you collect. Many will want assurances that their names as well as the names and locations of their organizations will be kept in confidentiality and that any information you gather will not be used to harm them in any way. Others will assume from certain things you say that you are bound to confidentiality. And still others will simply deny you access on the basis of their obligation to protect their employees' or clients' privacy. This last argument was made by gatekeepers of mental hygiene facilities we tried to study who were concerned less about others' privacy than about the prospect of having outsiders witness the deplorable conditions at the institutions.

Whatever the case, researchers should be clear in their own minds about what promises they make and about whether they intend to keep them. Again we move into the area of ethics. Researchers probably have no greater right to violate the guaranteed confidentiality of their subjects than physicians have a right to violate the guaranteed confidentiality of their patients. Thus, it is undoubtedly unethical, and also in bad taste, to gossip among your friends about your subjects. Yet there may be times when the researcher feels that circumstances justify the violation of the subjects' confidentiality. An observer may be witness to behavior or conditions that he or she cannot keep secret. And since researcher-subject confidentiality is not legally protected, the researcher has a *legal,* though not necessarily *ethical,* responsibility to report "criminal" acts.[23]

Observers should also take care to guard their data and field notes from all but their immediate colleagues. When the data is of a sensitive nature, the researcher would be wise to use pseudonyms for all proper names. In some cases, more extreme measures are in order for those who wish to guard their subjects' privacy. For example, Laud Humphreys destroyed all data that contained any information regarding the identities of subjects when his research became the center of public controversy.[24]

It is sufficient to say that researchers have some obligation to subjects to protect their confidentiality and to explain to them the risks they take in granting them access to the setting.

*   *   *

This chapter dealt with the pre-fieldwork stage of participant observation research. More specifically, we focused on matters related to the decisions observers must make before they enter the field and the initial contacts they must make to conduct their research. The following chapter shifts to the issues and dilemmas the observer faces in the field: "Now that you're in, where do you go from here?"

NOTES

1. Buford Junker and Raymond Gold both refer to the roles of researchers who use these approaches as "observer-as-participant" and "complete observer," respectively. See Buford Junker, "Some suggestions for the design and field work learning experiences," in Everett C. Hughes et al., *Cases on Field Work* (lectographed by The University of Chicago, 1952), Part III-A; and Raymond L. Gold, "Roles in sociological field observations," *Social Forces,* **36**: 217–223, 1958.

2. Barney Glaser and Anselm Strauss, in *The Discovery of Grounded Theory: Strategies for Qualitative Research* (Chicago: Aldine, 1967), p. 32, make the distinction between "substantive" theory and "formal" theory. This is similar to the distinction we are making.

3. Melville Dalton, "Preconceptions and methods in *Men Who Manage*" in Phillip Hammond (Ed.), *Sociologists at Work* (New York: Basic Books, 1964).

4. See Blanche Geer, "First days in the field," in Phillip Hammond (Ed.), *Sociologists at Work* (New York: Basic Books, 1964). John P. Dean et al., in "Limitations and advantages of unstructured methods," in John T. Doby (Ed.), *An Introduction to Social Research* (New York: Meredith, 1967, 2nd ed.), make the point that the participant observer has less of an investment if he started out on the wrong track than other researchers, so he tends to be more willing to junk hypotheses.

5. See Steven J. Taylor, "Attendants' perspectives: A view from the back ward," (unpublished paper presented at the 97th Annual Meeting of the American Association on Mental Deficiency, Atlanta, Ga., 1973), and "Doin' a job: Attendants and their work at a state institution" (unpublished paper presented at the Annual Meeting of the Eastern Sociological Society, Philadelphia, Pa., 1974). Also, see Robert Bogdan et al., "Let them eat pro-

grams: Attendants' perspectives and programming on wards in state schools," *Journal of Health and Social Behavior,* **15** (June): 142–151, 1974.

6.   See Robert Bogdan, "Working out failure: Measuring success in a poverty program," (unpublished paper presented at the 23rd Annual Meeting of The Society for the Study of Social Problems, New York, 1973).

7.   For a discussion of the variety of roles for field workers, see Gold, "Roles in sociological field observation." Dalton, "Preconceptions and methods," p. 68, discusses the ethical considerations of being a hidden observer. For reports of other successful hidden observing see: Donald Roy, "Quota restriction and goldbricking in a machine shop," *American Journal of Sociology,* **LVII** (March): 427–442, 1952; Donald Roy, "Banana time: Job satisfaction and informal interaction," *Human Organizations,* **XVIII** (Winter): 158–168, 1959–1960; Leon Festinger et al., *When Prophesy Fails* (Minneapolis: University of Minnesota Press, 1956).

8.   In addition to Dalton, "Preconceptions and methods," for discussions of the ethics of the hidden observer, see Kai Erikson, "A comment on disguised observation in sociology," *Social Problems,* **XIV,** no. 4: 366–373, 1966–1967; Joseph Fichter and William Kolb, "Ethical limitations on sociological reporting," *American Sociological Review,* **XVIII:** 544–550, 1953; Fred Davis, "Comment on initial interaction of newcomers in Alcoholics Anonymous," *Social Problems,* **VIII,** no. 4 (Spring): 364–365, 1961; Laud Humphreys, "Tearoom trade: Impersonal sex in public places," *Trans-Action,* **VII,** no. 3 (January): 10–25, 1970; Nicholas Hoffman, Irving Horowitz, and Lee Rainwater, "Sociological snoopers and journalistic moralizers: Comment—an exchange," *Trans-Action,* **VII,** no. 7 (May): 4–10, 1970.

9.   Kai Erikson, "A comment on disguised observation in sociology," in William J. Filstead (Ed.), *Qualitative Methodology* (Chicago: Markham, 1970), p. 254.

10.   Apparently few social scientists would carry this belief to its logical extension. Thus, Lofland, who justified his own covert research among an Alcoholics Anonymous group, writes, "The 'research' activities of Nazi Germany taught us (or should have) very well that there are definite moral limits on what can be done in the name of science." See John Lofland, *Deviance and Identity* (Englewood Cliffs, N.J.: Prentice-Hall, 1969), p. 301. Also see John Lofland, "Reply to Davis' comment on 'initial interaction,' " *Social Problems,* **VIII,** no. 4 (Spring): 365–367, 1961.

11.   Myron Glazer, *The Research Adventure: Promise and Problems in Field Work* (New York: Random House, 1972), p. 133.

12.   L. Rainwater and D. J. Pittman, "Ethical problems in studying a politically sensitive and deviant community," *Social Problems,* **XIV** (Spring): 365–366, 1967. See also, J. F. Galliher, "The protection of human subjects: A reexamination of the professional code of ethics," *The American Sociologist,* **VIII** (August): 93–100, 1973.

13.   Edward Sagarin, "The research setting and the right not to be researched," *Social Problems,* **XXI,** no. 1 (Spring): 52–64, 1973.

14.   Julius Roth, "Comments on 'Secret observation,' " in Filstead, *Qualitative Methodology,* pp. 278–280.

15.   See Howard Becker, *Sociological Work: Method and Substance* (Chicago: Aldine, 1970).

16.   Robert Bogdan, "Learning to sell door to door," *The American Behavioral Scientist,* **XVI,** no. 1 (Sept.–Oct.): 55–64, 1972.

17.   William Foote Whyte, *Street Corner Society* (Chicago: University of Chicago Press, 1955).

18.   Elliot Liebow, *Tally's Corner* (Boston: Little, Brown, 1967).

19. Ned Polsky, *Hustler's, Beats and Others* (Garden City, N.Y.: Doubleday, 1969).

20. See John Dean, Robert Eichorn, and Lois Dean, "Establishing field relations," in Doby, *Social Research.*

21. Of course others, such as funding agents, may be part of the bargain.

22. This may also be a promise that the researcher cannot keep since there can be no assurance that the research will provide useful information.

23. See Paul Nejelski and Kurt Finsterbuch, "The prosecutor and the researcher: Present and prospective variations in the Supreme Court's Branzburg Decision," *Social Problems,* **XXI,** no. 1 (Spring): 3–21, 1973.

24. As reported in Glazer, *Research Adventure,* p. 110.

CHAPTER THREE

Participant Observation

IN THE FIELD

In this chapter we consider the fieldwork stage of participant observation research. Our discussion can be logically divided into two aspects.[1] The first relates to social interaction: the ways observers should conduct themselves in the presence of subjects. The second aspect deals with data collection: the means by which observers can elicit and record the data necessary to understand a setting or some important part of it. We begin with the observer's "first days in the field."[2]

ENTERING THE FIELD

Participant observers enter the field with the hope that they can establish with subjects relationships characterized by trust and a free and open exchange of information. Ideally, researchers are perceived as neutral figures who have no special alliances with any particular subjects and no relationships outside of the setting that might harm the subjects. They conduct themselves in such a way that they eventually become an unobtrusive part of the scene, people whom the participants take for granted and whom they consider to be nonthreatening. Many of the techniques used in participant observation correspond to everyday rules about inoffensive social interaction; skill in this area is a prerequisite for doing meaningful fieldwork.

Researchers remain relatively passive throughout the course of the fieldwork, but especially during the first days in the field. Observers who dive into the field are unlikely to establish the kinds of relationships conducive to free and easy data collection. Thus, participant observers must "feel out the situation," "learn the ropes,"[3] and "come on slow." They have to be exposed to their subjects so that the subjects can become familiar with them, develop trust in them, and feel at ease in their presences. *A good rule to follow in the initial stage of the fieldwork is not to challenge the behavior or statements of the subjects or to ask questions that are likely to put them on the defensive.*

Researchers who are disruptive to the setting or intimidating to the subjects, are likely to be asked to leave. At the very least, they will alienate those on whom they depend for information.

Different subjects will exhibit different degrees of receptivity to the observer. For example, although the gatekeeper may open the organization to you, others may resent your presence or the fact that they were not consulted. In such a situation it is important for you to contact other subjects, explain your interests, and ask their permission to observe.[4] In a study of school teachers' use of media (see Chapter 11), for example, the researchers interviewed each teacher individually in order to explain the research and to guarantee anonymity prior to beginning the project. Subjects should be informed in subtle ways also that what they tell you will not be reported to others. Some researchers may want to start at the bottom of an organizational structure and get approval to observe at each successive level of the hierarchy. While this route may not ensure entry, it will give proper homage to subjects at each level.

When first entering the field, researchers are often overwhelmed by the amount of information they receive. One way to regulate the flow of information is to limit each period of time spent in the setting. Initial observation periods of an hour or less may prevent observers from being overwhelmed. As they become more familiar with the setting and adept at observation skills, they can increase the length of time spent observing.

Research conducted in the field is especially exciting early in the study. The observer often doesn't want to leave the setting for fear of missing something important and leaves the field drained of energy and filled with so much information that he or she never gets a chance to record it. Observations are only useful to the extent that they can be remembered and accurately recorded. *Don't stay in the field if you will forget much of the data or if you will not have the time to write your field notes.*

FEELING UNCOMFORTABLE

During the first days in the field, the researcher inevitably feels uncomfortable. People generally shun unnecessary interaction with strangers in their everyday lives. Witness the behavior of people in elevators, waiting rooms, and other public settings. Researchers and nonresearchers alike are embarrassed to approach strangers and introduce themselves. However, it is essential for researchers to interact, and they must, therefore, learn to overcome or handle their feelings.

It is necessary at times for researchers to lower their defenses and to approach subjects. The only way to get to know what's on subjects' minds is to talk with them, and if, as frequently happens, they do not come to you, then you must go to them. In a study of a training program for the "hard core unemployed" (Chapter 13), a program coordinator unsuccessfully attempted to deny the researcher access to the setting.

The coordinator kept his distance from the observer for two months until the observer finally asked to meet with him to discuss the program. They talked for seven hours. Had the researcher not directly approached him, an important perspective would have been lost to the study.

An advantage that researchers have is that their subjects probably consider them people who are interested in but uninformed about what is going on in the setting. It is thus appropriate for them to ask general and straightforward questions. Visitors are generally expected to possess a degree of naïveté concerning the affairs and activities of the setting. Researchers in a school, for example, would not be expected to be competent in areas related to educational procedures, teaching, and standardized testing.

At other times, it might be advantageous for researchers to place themselves in awkward positions. They may, for example, solicit invitations to participate in unofficial activities, such as coffee breaks, by being with subjects at the right times. In our society, people are embarrassed to do things without extending invitations to others to participate. Observers must often seize such opportunities whether they think that the subjects want them there or not. On the first day of the research conducted at the state institution, by simply being around them at the end of their shift, the observer received an invitation to go to a local bar frequented by attendants.

In any case, *all observers are faced with embarrassing situations in the field.* Take comfort in the fact that others have faced what you face and that *you will feel more comfortable in the setting as the study progresses.*

BEING FORCED INTO ROLES

Observers will often find that their subjects do not completely understand their purpose for visiting settings even though they have carefully explained it to them. In some instances, the subjects will understand their purposes but will still not know how to deal with them. Many subjects consequently place researchers into categories commonly given to outsiders. The personnel in schools, mental hospitals, and other such institutions, for example, are familiar with volunteers and tend to force observers into the trappings of that role, especially if the observers are students or women. Observers may be asked to sign the volunteer book on each visit and may be assigned to certain clients.

Researchers would be wise to control how subjects define them and to resist being forced into relationships, modes of dress, and patterns of behavior that are not conducive to carrying out research. One observer was forced into a tutoring relationship with a boy in a detention home despite the fact that he had carefully explained his interests to the home's director. Needless to say, it was extremely difficult for him to collect the kind of data in which he was interested. Do a great deal of thinking before you accept roles such as that of the volunteer.

DON'T LET SUBJECTS TELL YOU WHOM, WHAT, OR WHEN TO OBSERVE

While observers cannot concentrate on all aspects of a setting, they should be familiar enough with everything to know what they are missing. It is therefore important for them to resist all attempts by their subjects to place constraints on whom, what, or when they observe.

Everyone, it seems, attempts to present her- or himself in the best possible light in the presence of strangers. It is only natural that subjects will react to observers in this manner. They will show them those aspects of the setting in which they are seen in a favorable light and hide, or at least downplay, those aspects in which they are not.[5] In many organizational settings, an official is appointed to give tours to visitors. Although these tours may be valuable in certain respects, tour guides tend to offer a biased and selective view of the setting. Official tour guides in institutions, for example, will often show visitors only the best wards or the model inmates, and will discourage visitors from seeing other wards and speaking with other inmates. Tour guides and others in these settings sometimes place pressures on visitors not to talk to inmates at all. Don't assume that what the tour guide shows and tells you is all there is to see and hear.

Observers must also resist subjects' attempts to schedule their time for them. We know one novice who contacted a detention home in order to set up a time to begin his observations. The supervisor with whom he spoke told him that he wouldn't be interested in visiting the home that day or the next since the boys would just be making Halloween decorations. He then suggested which times of the day would be best for the observer to "see something going on." The observer allowed himself to be forced to choose from a limited number of alternatives when he should have made it clear that he was interested in a variety of activities and times.

It is important for researchers to select their own places and times to observe. They must be able to observe the setting on all days of the week and at all hours of the day. They should also be present during special events or activities. To do otherwise is to obtain a limited view of the setting. Therefore, don't hesitate to subtly confront subjects who try to structure your observations.

ESTABLISHING RAPPORT

While the settings that researchers enter are different as a result of their being there, they should attempt to minimize the effects. *Observers must conduct themselves in such a way that the events that occur during their observations do not significantly differ from those which occur in their absence.* It is therefore essential for researchers to win the trust and confidence of their subjects; that is, to establish rapport with them.

The goal of researchers is to blend into the setting they observe. They hope to become natural, although neutral, parts of the scene. Dress is chosen with this consideration in mind. If your subjects dress casually, then you should also. Where dress distinguishes whose at different levels of an organization, you should dress either as those with whom you want to identify or in a neutral style. In a study of an institution where administrators wear jackets and ties, lower-level staff wear a certain kind of uniform, and inmates wear another type of uniform, casual dress might be appropriate. If you are especially interested in gaining the confidence of administrators, you might dress more formally. However, you should not wear anything in which you feel uncomfortable or unnatural. Don't imitate dress or speech patterns if you cannot feel at ease with them. To do so might give subjects the impression that you are trying to mimic them.

There are instances in which observers wish to tell their subjects specific things by their clothing. They may, for example, want to let them know that there are important differences between them. In a study of drug addicts, Polsky made a point of wearing a short-sleeved shirt and an expensive watch, both of which would let any newcomer know that he wasn't an addict.[6]

As mentioned earlier, observers "come on slow" during the first days in the field. Although they do not allow their subjects to push them around or to tell them what to observe, they remain passive, relating to people in a nonthreatening manner. It is important for subjects to know that the observer is the type of person to whom they can express their feelings without fear of disclosure or negative evaluation.

Observers frequently become the people with best comprehension of what everyone in the setting knows and thinks. This information is best kept to oneself. To display too much knowledge of the situation makes subjects aware of one's presence and causes them to withdraw. Thus, observers should be careful not to reveal or discuss certain things that subjects have told them even if they were not related in private. And they should be sure to let the subjects know that what they say will not be shared with others. On the researcher's second visit to the state institution, for example, one attendant casually asked, "Did you tell (director) about the boys here on this ward?" The observer quickly answered, "No, I didn't even tell him where I was. I don't tell people on the outside about the institution so why should I tell him about all of you?" This conversation proved to be a crucial step in gaining the trust of this particular attendant.

The more that subjects think that the observer knows about a certain area the less free they are to offer their own opinions. For this reason, the researcher should not show off his or her competence or knowledge. Let your subjects speak freely and say what's on their minds. You will find that many subjects hold beliefs that are inaccurate if not patently absurd. Don't go out of your way to correct these beliefs. You will only succeed in making people self-conscious in your presence.

Probably the easiest way for observers to gain rapport with their subjects is to establish what they have in common with them. The casual exchange of information is often the vehicle through which observers can break the ice. And once the ice is broken, they can move on to other things. In the "hard-core" job training study, for example, the researcher got to know his subjects through conversations about fishing, children, sickness, past jobs, and food. It is also natural for subjects to want to know about the observer's interests and out-of-situation activities, especially as the study progresses. They will spend hours in interaction with the subjects and will ask them hundreds of questions. If they want subjects to be open with them, they must be willing to reciprocate on some level.

Another way for observers to establish rapport is to participate in activities with subjects. Of course, *they limit their participation until they have gained a feeling for the setting and an understanding of how their participation will be received.* In some settings, such as a structured elementary school classroom, researchers might not participate at all. And in others, such as the recreation room of a detention center, they might actively participate.

Observers may learn that they will not be accepted until they participate. In some settings, observers will find that they must share a meal or a drink with their subjects before they can gain their confidence. In other settings, they will find that other behavior is required. We know one researcher who conducted a study of an infant ward at a state school for the "mentally retarded." The ward contained 40 infants and was understaffed. The members of the staff were initially abrupt in their responses to the observer and did their best to ignore him. The situation became increasingly uncomfortable until one day the researcher offered to help the two attendants feed the infants. As he began to feed the first child the attendants opened up and began to share their concerns and complaints with him. And for the first time they invited him to join them for refreshments in the staff room.

The researcher in the state institution study mentioned earlier participated in a variety of activities with attendants, some of which involved the violation of institutional rules. The attendants would pass the time pitching nickels in the ward dayroom on some occasions and would slip to a back room to drink beer on others. The observer joined in both of these activities. This participation solidified the rapport between researcher and subjects. The attendants felt that they could trust the observer since he too had been involved in marginal activities. One, in fact, stated that in order to be accepted, it was necessary to drink beer on the ward. That way, "you couldn't say nothin' cause you was doin' it too." The observer also smoked cigarettes on the ward with the attendants and a few of the residents. They would warn each other of the approach of a supervisor. The attendants came to feel that the observer was someone who was on their side and someone around whom they could freely discuss their superiors.

Of course, researchers who participate in marginal activities with one group of subjects run the risk of shattering their rapport with another group. Had the observer been caught drinking beer on the ward, for example, the administrators would have lost no time in asking him to leave the setting.

Finally, observers can only establish rapport with their subjects if they pay proper homage to their routines. All people like to do things in certain ways and at certain times. Observers must be careful not to disrupt these routines. Polsky offers advice on how to observe the criminal in his natural setting: "If he wants to sit in front of his TV set and drink beer and watch a ballgame for a couple of hours, so do you; if he wants to walk the streets or go barhopping, so do you; if he wants to go to the racetrack, so do you; if he indicates (for whatever reason) that it's time for you to get lost, you get lost."[7] We know of one observer who, in a study of a hospital, came late to two staff meetings and then asked the physicians, who were pressed for time themselves, to reschedule the staffings to suit his schedule. Needless to say, it was a long time before he was welcomed into the setting.

Many researchers find that, regardless of their efforts to establish rapport, certain subjects resent their presence in the setting. Racial or social class differences sometimes divide observer and subject. Whatever the situation, researchers should attempt to win all subjects over to a position of receptivity. *Don't assume that hostile subjects will remain hostile as the study progresses.* Even the most hostile may soften over a period of time. When subjects realize that you are getting to know other subjects and their points of view, they will probably want their points of view to be known, often as a matter of protection. You should, therefore, provide reluctant subjects with opportunities to change their reactions to you. Continue to be friendly and to approach them without pushing them into interaction.

DEVELOPING RELATIONSHIPS

In the ideal situation participant observers develop close and honest relationships with all of the participants in the setting in which they conduct their research.[8] As mentioned earlier, however, researchers must usually win the confidence of one or two subjects in order to be accepted by others or to gain access to the setting. In settings such as prisons that are characterized by distrust or danger, for example, it may be necessary for observers to have a key figure vouch for them before they can be trusted by others. Many observers also tend to attach themselves to anyone who appears to be friendly when they feel threatened or unsure in the initial stages of the research.

Observers will sometimes cultivate a close relationship with knowledgeable subjects.[9] Most researchers have one or more "key informants" upon whom they can depend for a deep understanding of the situation and who are willing to share their knowledge. Since observers spend a limited amount of time in the setting, key informants can also give them a sense of the history of the setting and can provide them with information concerning events that occur when they are not there.

While it may be necessary or convenient to concentrate on one or two subjects, especially in the beginning of the study, researchers who do so run certain risks. In the first place, there is the danger that they may obtain a selective view of the setting. It is wrong to assume that all participants will have the same perspectives. Thus, observers may gain a firm knowledge of one subject's perspective at the expense of gaining a knowledge of others. For this reason, researchers would be wise to avoid contact with one or two people exclusively.

In the state institution study, the "ward charge," or supervising attendant, tended to monopolize the observer's time on each of his visits. As the research progressed, the attendant began to repeat himself, telling the same stories and presenting the same views on every observation session. It wasn't until the observer scheduled his visits on this attendant's days off that he had the opportunity to establish rapport with several other important participants in the setting and to hear their perspectives.

The observer in the hard-core unemployed job training study faced similar problems with one of the staff members who was particularly friendly to the researcher and openly expressed his views. The observer was forced to temporarily withdraw from this relationship, however, when he found that it was too exclusive. The relationship was reestablished after he had had the opportunity to learn the views of others.

Since each training program in this study lasted four weeks, the researcher had to establish rapport with new trainees several times. He "came on slow" during the first few days of each training session. Since the trainees were attempting to form friendships within the group, the researcher decided not to seek close relationships initially. Instead, he passively observed while the trainees heard lectures, viewed films, and participated in simulated work tasks. When, on the third day of each session, the trainees settled down to a routine, he approached them individually and attempted to spend equal time with each. By the time that the trainees had gotten to know each other and were spending time socializing, the observer had established rapport with many of them. The rest usually accepted him when they saw the others doing so.

Observers who jump into close relationships with one or two subjects also face the danger that these subjects may not be respected participants in a setting. It is often difficult to find out who is an outsider and who is central to a group until one has spent a considerable amount of time in the setting. And if researchers attach themselves to an unpopular person or an authority figure, they may find that they are regarded as an extension of that person and that others are reluctant to share information with them. In a factory, for example, an observer would not want lower-level workers to see him or her as an arm of a foreman or of management.

As a general rule, then, *researchers should hold back from developing close relationships with individual subjects until they have a good grasp of the nature of relationships in the setting. Where it is essential for them to establish rapport with a selected few subjects initially, they must be willing to withdraw from those relationships as circumstances demand.*

OBSERVING IN SETTINGS CHARACTERIZED BY CONFLICT

All organizations are characterized by conflict and disagreement to some extent. In those settings in which there is a high level of conflict, researchers find themselves in delicate situations.[10] While they may not be expected to engage in open combat, people in the setting may vie for their allegiance. Their informants on both sides of the conflict will want a measure of support in exchange for the information they give them.[11] At the same time, observers cannot be openly supportive of both sides at once. To offer support to everyone is to lose everyone's confidence.

Probably the best way for observers to deal with such situations is to lend a sympathetic ear and an occasional nod of the head. Don't give your subjects the impression that you're taking sides. And, if possible, you should spend equal time with both of the parties in the conflict. Observers often walk a tightrope and must be able to sense when they are off-balance.

Even observers who have established themselves as neutral insiders may be called upon in times of conflict to give advice or mediate relationships. While this situation allows them to collect rich data, it also places them in difficult positions. In their attempts to advise subjects, they may use knowledge that was related to them in confidence, thereby alienating certain subjects and raising ethical issues. Perhaps more important, however, is the fact that observers who advise influence the setting in unknown ways. Their advice results in behavior that would not have occurred were they not there.

Although it may be difficult to conduct research in a setting characterized by conflict, conflict is an important aspect on which to focus in all studies. It is during such periods that people most freely offer their perspectives. Conflict results in new perspectives, new procedures, and new coalitions. To see the dynamics of their creation is a significant research experience that often yields rich data and deep understanding.

HOW MUCH SHOULD THE RESEARCHER PARTICIPATE?

Researchers often find themselves drawn into increasing participation in the activities of their subjects. In some settings, the observer will be expected to demonstrate friendship and goodwill through participation. In others, subjects will attempt to involve the observer in their own marginal activities as a protection against disclosure. Thus, the attendants in the state institution research invited and expected the observer to participate in activities such as drinking beer and pitching nickels.

As mentioned earlier, such participation may be a prerequisite to establishing rapport. The researcher who remains completely passive and aloof will find that subjects are reluctant to share information. At the same time, *the observer must remember that his or her primary purpose is to collect data. Any participation that interferes with the ability to do so should be avoided.* We know an observer who, on his first day in the field at a teachers' lunchroom, overheard his subjects express a desire to have a sensitivity training workshop. Since he had previously led a number of such workshops, he immediately offered to help them. Needless to say, he was forced to abandon his role as a researcher.

The researcher walks a thin line between active participant and passive observer.[12] While the researcher will have to weigh factors such as the nature of the setting, the goals of the research, and her or his own disposition in order to determine an appropriate level of participation, there are a few general rules that we have followed and that might prove to be helpful.

First, don't try to compete for esteem in the formal or informal status hierarchy in the setting. It is unnecessary and probably undesirable for the researcher to be regarded as "one of the boys." It is sometimes difficult for the observer to remove him- or herself from the competition for status. He or she, as does everyone, has a self-concept to defend and wants to tell as many good jokes as the next person or wants to be thought of in a special way by the opposite sex.

"Rapping" was a common pastime among the trainees in the job training study (Chapter 13).[13] Here, rapping, also called "playing the dirty dozen" and "joking," refers to a competitive verbal exchange the object of which is to "put down" another person by the clever use of phrases with double meanings. The observer found himself to be the object of trainees' jokes and, after a few days of observation, was encouraged by them to engage in verbal exchanges regarding his potency as a lover and his capacity as a drinker. Although he gradually began to participate in these exchanges and developed joking relationships with a number of women, he soon realized that he lacked the ability to perform well on this level. At first, he saw his inability to rap well as a barrier to conducting his study. He soon learned, however, that this inability was an asset. As the program progressed, the trainees came to spend more and more time rapping. The themes of the rapping sessions were nearly always the same and failed to provide any new understandings. Since the observer had so little ability at rapping, he was not always forced into these exchanges and could concentrate on other themes. It is, of course, preferable to remain a researcher by choice and not by default.

Where involvement is essential to acceptance, then by all means participate. Where involvement means competition for status, withdraw. The latter form of involvement exposes the researcher to the hostility of her or his subjects and interferes with her or his ability to observe.

Second, don't be afraid to let subjects know that there are differences between you. Polsky suggests that researchers should know where to draw the line before entering the field and that after establishing what they have in common with their subjects they should point out their differences.[14] This procedure may save later embarrassment. Many observers are reluctant to confront subjects and are exploited by them. Thus, Polsky offers the following example: "I have heard of one social worker with violent gangs who was so insecure, so unable to 'draw the line' for fear of being put down, that he got flattered into holding and hiding guns that had been used in murders."[15]

Finally, don't lose sight of the ethical issues raised by your participation. Subjects will sometimes try to involve researchers in activities that violate their sense of ethics. On occasion, the attendants in the state institution study physically and verbally abused the residents under their charge. At times, they exerted subtle pressures on the observer to participate in these activities. While the researcher did not usually confront the attendants on these occasions, he acted as if he had not heard them or had misunderstood them.

There are times when the observer may feel ethically bound to participate, or to intervene, in the activities of his or her subjects, even though such intervention may affect rapport. Many researchers believe that to passively observe behavior is to condone it. One observer recently visited a facility for the "mentally retarded" and saw a physician treat residents in a manner that she considered inhumane. In a belligerent tone, the researcher challenged the physician, who responded with a hostile diatribe on moralistic do-gooders and his views on the "mentally retarded," his job, and the facility. Although unwittingly provoking rich data, the observer did not have the opportunity to return to the facility and may have closed that setting to other researchers. Others prefer to remain passive in such situations. Thus, one researcher, while conducting a study of a juvenile gang, passively observed the brutal beating of a young girl by a gang member. He admitted that it was difficult to sleep that night, but argued, "What could I do? I was just an observer. It wasn't my place to intervene." The latter observer took a pragmatic approach while the former opted for an ethical one.

The researcher must learn that certain normally appropriate behavior is inappropriate for the observer. He or she should participate only to the extent necessary to establish rapport unless he or she feels ethically bound to do otherwise. Beyond that, he or she must control active involvement.

LEARNING THE LANGUAGE

An important aspect of observation is learning how subjects use language.[16] *Researchers must start with the premise that words and symbols used in their world may have different meanings in the world of their subjects.*[17] They must also be attuned to new words and words used in contexts other than those with which they are familiar.

People who spend a prolonged period of time together inevitably develop shared symbols which are more or less unique. An individual family, for example, will have special symbols and special meanings for certain words in addition to the meanings shared by the rest of society. Ethnic, class, and other groups will also have their own sets of verbal and nonverbal symbols. Thus, Wallace provides a glossary of selected terms and their meanings on "skid row."[18] His glossary includes such items as: *beanery,* a cheap restaurant; *dead one,* a retired hobo; *dingbat,* the lowest type of tramp; *jack,* money; *slave market,* street corner employment office. Similarly, Giallombardo offers the argot, or special language, used in a women's prison: *bug house,* an institution for the "mentally insane" or for "mentally defective" delinquents; *butcher,* a prison doctor; *flagging,* older inmate attempting to involve a younger one in homosexuality.[19] The existence in itself of a particularly specialized vocabulary indicates some sort of separation of a group from the "mainstream" of society. As a general rule, then, the more specialized the vocabulary, the greater the isolation of the group.

The vocabulary used in a setting may provide important clues to how participants define situations and other people and to how different segments view and relate to each other. In the job training program studied by one of the authors, the staff and the trainees used special terms to refer to each other. These terms were indicative of the distrust that prevailed in the setting. For example, some of the staff used the phrase "professional trainees" in reference to people who had been involved in other job training programs at other times in their lives. The implication was that these trainees were not serious in their desire to find full-time employment and were exploiting the program for their immediate gain. Some of the trainees, on the other hand, referred to the staff as "poverty pimps," a phrase which suggested that the program organizers were living off the plight of others.

Certain assumptions may be built into the vocabulary used by persons in a group or setting. In mental hygiene facilities, for example, staff members often take it for granted that the setting is "therapeutic" for residents. Thus, any activity in which residents participate is referred to as "therapy." "Milieu therapy" may mean nothing more than that a group of people are left to wander around in a room. Similarly, the phrase "on-the-job training" was used by staff in the job training program to refer to the first three weeks of employment after the completion of the training program. In point of fact, no special learning activities were conducted during this period. New employees who had not participated in the training program performed the same tasks as those who had. In the state institution study mentioned earlier, a number of assumptions lay behind the metaphors attendants used to characterize residents. Terms such as "kids" and "boys" implied that adult residents were childlike and incompetent; and words and phrases such as "vegetable," "low-grade," "pine-box case," and "the thing" implied that residents were subhuman and incapable of change.

Many observers, especially those with some professional training, are trapped by esoteric vocabularies and professional jargon. Terms like "schizoid," "paranoid," "manic-depressive," and "mentally ill" have little concrete meaning and are based on psychiatric assumptions and ideology rather than scientific knowledge.[20] The uncritical researcher will often accept these labels without examining the assumptions of the labelers. School psychologists, teachers, and administrators sometimes use an elaborate pseudopsychological vocabulary that may reflect social class and racial bias.[21] Thus, a lower-class black child who cannot read, or who is disruptive, is often referred to as "educable retarded," "cultural-familial retarded," or "emotionally disturbed" while a middle-class white child with the same behavior might be called "learning disabled" or "minimally brain-damaged."

People in certain settings also require a special vocabulary to build lines of action in those settings. Calling a person a "low grade" or a "mongoloid" may allow psychiatrists or attendants to act toward that person in certain ways. Or calling a child "emotionally disturbed" may allow school administrators and teachers to deny that child his or her right to an education.

The observer must examine vocabularies as a function of the assumptions and purposes of their users and not merely of the characteristics of the persons or objects of reference. This fact applies even to seemingly clear-cut words. A person who is described as "nonambulatory" might be thought of as one who is unequivocally unable to walk. Yet, in an understaffed hospital or nursing home "nonambulatory" might be used to refer to persons who could walk if they had some minor assistance.

Carefully study your subjects' vocabularies. What do words and phrases mean? Who uses what words? What commonsense assumptions do they reveal? In what contexts are terms applied? Under what circumstances are certain words used? How are terms applied to persons or things? What criteria are used to categorize someone or something? The researcher must directly or indirectly question subjects on the meanings of the terms they use. Of course, some meanings will have to be inferred by the observer from the subjects' behavior. For example, as one researcher has hypothesized,[22] it may be difficult for construction workers to verbalize the fact that it is a sign of acceptance into the group for a worker to have his spouse insulted by others.

Let us add a cautionary note at this point. *The true significance of subjects' verbal and nonverbal symbols can only be determined in the context of their other behavior and after an extended period of observation.* There is a danger of imputing to subjects meanings that they did not intend. People use many, if not most, words without much thought to the implications and merely because they have learned the words through associations with other people. For this reason, Polsky warns against the assumption that a person's vocabulary necessarily reflects her or his beliefs, feelings, or motives:

> I have seen it seriously argued, for example, that heroin addicts must unconsciously feel guilty about their habit because they refer to heroin by such terms as "shit," "junk," and "garbage." Actually, the use of any such term by a heroin addict indicates, in itself, nothing whatever about his guilt feelings or the lack thereof, but merely that he is using a term for heroin traditional in his group.[23]

While the words that people use may lend important insight into their assumptions and the meanings of their behavior, it is naïve to presume that the intricacies of a social setting can be revealed solely by its participants' vocabulary.

Researchers would be wise to avoid using their subjects' vocabulary and speech patterns unless and until they feel comfortable with them and have mastered them. They otherwise run the risk of appearing foolish or, even worse, condescending. As the study progresses, the researcher will pick up some of the subjects' words and word usages. Probably the best advice that can be given is for the researcher to use them as they come naturally.

There will be instances in which it is inappropriate for the observer to use his subjects' vocabulary at all. Among certain groups, for example, members have terms to refer to each other which would be offensive if used by an outsider. It is quite one thing for a Black person to refer to another as "nigger" in jest or in anger, and quite another for a white observer to do so; quite one thing for a gay person to refer to another as a "fag," and quite another for a straight observer to do so; quite one thing for a feminist to refer to another as "sister," and quite another for a male observer to do so. In other instances, the researcher may choose not to use the appropriate terms despite the fact that it is conspicuous. The observer at the state institution, for example, found it offensive to refer to residents in certain ways and did not use many of the terms used by attendants.

Observers should also avoid words that are comfortable for them but that their subjects are likely to misunderstand or to find pretentious. State things simply. It is unlikely that most subjects will be impressed by a large vocabulary, and, even if they are, they will only be more self-conscious and less candid in the researcher's presence.

ASKING QUESTIONS

While participant observers enter the field with some broad questions on their mind, they must allow themes and information to emerge before pursuing their own areas of inquiry. In other words, *observers ask questions in such a way as to enable the subjects to talk about what is on their minds and what is of concern to them without forcing them to respond to the observers' interests, concerns, or preconceptions.* Observers who do otherwise risk certain dangers. Their subjects may, for example, anticipate their interests and respond accordingly. That is, they will only "tell them what they want to hear" and never discuss their real concerns. Or they may be offended by the observer's questions. We know of one group of observers who, on a tour of a mental hygiene facility, questioned a supervisor about a ward's "time-out," or isolation, rooms: "Are they allowed to go to the bathroom?" "Do they still get meals when they're in there?" The supervisor was infuriated by the implications of these questions, and shot back, "What do you think we are here—sadists?" There are certain questions which are too sensitive to ask until the observer has won the confidence of subjects, and the only way for the observer to know which issues are especially sensitive is to sit back and listen.

In the initial stages of the research, the observer asks questions in a nondirective and unobtrusive manner. Use the phrases with which you usually initiate conversations: "How are you doing?"; "What's up?"; "How do you like it here?" Such questions allow subjects to respond in their own way and with their own concerns. If, on the other hand, you ask questions such as "What do you like least about this place?" or "Don't you ever feel guilty about what you're doing?" you not only risk offense but also force subjects to relate to your frame of reference. You should also choose words that support your subjects' definitions of what they do. One researcher referred to the "funeral business" on her first observation session at a funeral home. This seemingly innocuous phrase contradicted the director's view of his work as a profession and not merely a business.

The observer's questions should be framed in sympathetic terms: he or she must look at things from the subjects' perspective. Once she or he has a sense of how they view their world, questions can be phrased sympathetically and without revealing his or her own feelings or point of view. It was not uncommon for the attendants at the state institution to straitjacket or to otherwise restrain residents. The observer was always careful to ask questions in ways that would not intimidate the attendants: "Does he always give you problems?" Had he asked questions which required attendants to justify their actions—"What is the institution's policy on restraint?"; "Why do you always jacket people?"—he may have lost their goodwill and candor.

While the observer generally remains passive during the first days in the field, she or he does encourage subjects to talk about the important topics that they themselves raise. Encouraging gestures and verbal responses that indicate your interest—"Is that right?" and "That's interesting."—are usually sufficient to keep someone on the track. And small signs of sympathy— comments such as "I know what you mean."; "That's rough."; "I follow you." and gestures such as nodding the head—demonstrate support and encourage continuation. Conversely, you should be less responsive when subjects raise irrelevant or trivial topics such as discussions about the weather.

The observer also presses subjects for clarification on their remarks. *Don't take it for granted that you understand the full implications of what your subjects say.* Use phrases such as "What do you mean?"; "I don't get you."; and "I don't follow you.". Moreover, you should continually restate your subjects' statements according to your own understanding and ask for confirmation.

Many observers become impatient in the early stages of the fieldwork. Some bombard their subjects with a multitude of questions and allow, or even encourage, them to skip from one topic to another. Others try to force their subjects to talk about significant issues when they would prefer to engage in small talk. These researchers lose sight of the fact that they must gain their subjects' trust and confidence before they can expect them to share their knowledge and feelings. For this reason, the observer should aim for his or her subjects' acceptance when he or she first enters the field. If in order to gain this acceptance, one must sit back and listen to idle talk for a few sessions, then one should be willing to do so.

As the research progresses, the observer can alter the strategy used to elicit information.[24] She or he may, for example, find it desirable to ask specific questions of certain subjects or to set up semiformal interviews with subjects toward the end of the fieldwork stage. She or he might also change the structure of the questions by asking subjects to respond to hypothetical situations or by directly challenging their views or behavior. At what point the observer will use these strategies depends on the setting and the nature of the relationship with subjects. In the state institution study, the researcher was able to question one attendant about the abuse of residents on the second visit to the ward without causing offense. With other attendants, however, he was never able to freely raise the issue of abuse.

Once themes, concerns, and perspectives have emerged from the setting, observers begin to explore specific hypotheses. Thus, they try to find out which subjects hold which beliefs and under what conditions by asking each subject similar questions both when they are alone and when they are with others. They may even solicit subjects' reactions to hypotheses or may ask them to verify information they gave in the early stages of the research.

FIELD TACTICS

There are certain tactics that the researcher can use to probe for information that is difficult to obtain. The nature of these tactics usually depends on the individual observer and the setting in which the study is conducted.

The researcher at the state institution developed specific ways to gain access to information in an unobtrusive manner. For example, he frequently visited the ward late at night, after the residents had been sent to bed and when the attendants had the time to engage in long conversations, and at shift changes, when accounts of the days' events and the most recent institutional rumors were given to one set of attendants by another. The observer obtained access to ward records by asking attendants specific questions about residents and past ward events that he knew that the attendants couldn't answer without consulting their files. Finally, he probed sensitive issues, such as the abuse of residents or the use of residents as ward workers, by presenting questions in a joking way. Of course, this last tactic was only used with certain attendants and after the researcher had become a trusted participant of the setting.

One field tactic that almost any observer can use is eavesdropping. Many observers have strong internalized feelings about listening in and may refrain from doing so on ethical grounds. Yet, there are times when researchers cannot help but overhear remarks that are not intended for them, especially when they are present when someone happens to make or receive a phone call. And there are other times when the subtle eavesdropper gains illuminating data that could not otherwise have been obtained. Researchers would probably be wise to overcome their anxieties and take advantage of such situations unless they feel ethically bound not to do so.

FIELD NOTES

Systematic and analytical participant observation depends upon the recording of complete, accurate, and detailed field notes.[25] Field notes should be recorded after each and every observation period, as well as after more casual contacts with subjects outside the setting (meeting with subjects by chance in the street or conversations over the phone, for example). Although the most intensive note-taking occurs during the fieldwork stage of the research, observers should record notes during the pre-fieldwork stage and formal analysis stage if and when they have contact with subjects.

Since field notes provide the data of participant observation, researchers should strive to produce the most comprehensive field notes possible. To do this requires a tremendous amount of self-discipline, if not compulsion. Observers will often spend up to six hours recording notes for every one hour in the field. They will find themselves trying to cut corners: to postpone the recording of notes, to only record the highlights, or not to record them at all. "Nothing happened today that was very important" is a common rationalization. Yet the observer's consciousness should be such that everything that occurs in the field is a potentially important source of data.[26] Even "small talk" can lend insight into subjects' perspectives, and may cause a reinterpretation in the observer's understanding of the setting when viewed in context at a later time. Moreover, seemingly insignificant events may prove to be important when examined together at the end of a study.

Probably the best way for observers to force themselves to rigorously record the field notes is to have someone else read them after each session. This outside reader can draw attention to any omissions or contradictions in the notes and can press for elaboration on unclear points.

Observers must develop a level of concentration sufficient to enable them to commit to memory everything they see, hear, smell, think, and so on. After they have left the field, they transcribe what is in their memories onto tapes, which are later typed, or directly onto paper. Included in the notes are descriptions of subjects (their appearance, gestures, and expressions), events, conversations, and the observer's own feelings, opinions, and working hypotheses. The sequence and duration of events and conversations are noted. The fabric of the setting is described in detail. In short, the field notes represent an attempt on the part of the observer to record on paper everything that she or he can possibly remember about the session.

SPECIFIC HINTS IN RECALLING DATA

Although precise data recollection may seem like a difficult, if not impossible, task to some, novice observers will be amazed by the accuracy with which they can recall specific details through training, experience, and concentration. Some observers use the analogy of a switch to describe the ability they have developed to remember people, conversations, and settings. That is, they can "turn on" the intensive concentration they need to observe and to recall. This analogy is a good one if for no other reason than that it sets the tone for the goal of other observation skills.

Individuals vary both in the amount that they can remember after a given observation session and in the specific techniques that are most facilitative of data recollection. Most researchers will, however, find the following suggestions to be helpful in recalling conversations and other details.

1. *Look for "key words" in your subjects' remarks.* While you should strive for accuracy in your field notes, it is neither possible nor necessary to remember every word that your subjects use. You can, however, concentrate on and commit to memory certain key words or phrases in every one of your subjects' sentences or sets of related sentences that will enable you to recall the meanings of their remarks. And it is with meanings that you are concerned. This process is not as difficult as it may sound. You will learn that certain words and phrases naturally stand out in your mind. In the state institution study, for example, the researcher could easily remember words such as "low grade," "dining room boys," and "bung hole." Other, more common, words, such as "boring," "pay day," and "zoo" in the state institution study, for example, may be somewhat more difficult to remember but can be recalled with concentration and effort. Once you have identified meanings with key words, you will be able to reconstruct complete sentences from your notes by using what you know of the subjects' grammatical constructions and speech patterns.

2. *Concentrate on the first and last remarks in each conversation.* Conversations generally follow a logical sequence. That is, a certain question elicits a certain response; a certain remark provokes another; a certain topic leads to a related one. If you can remember how a conversation was initiated, you can frequently follow it through to the end in your own mind. And even when conversations do not follow a logical sequence, when remarks "come out of nowhere," the anomalies will often be simple to recall. Thus, you will find that the substance of long monologues, which usually produce an inordinate amount of anxiety in the novice observer, is retrievable.

3. *Leave the setting as soon as you have observed as much as you can accurately remember.* While this point has already been made, it bears repeating. New observers should probably not spend periods of more than one hour in the setting until they have a good sense of their powers of recollection or unless events occur that will never reoccur. As their ability to remember improves, they can, of course, spend more time in the field. Many observers are tempted to remain in the setting longer than

they should. If the session has been productive, they are eager for more. If it has been unproductive, they reason that something must soon happen. It is wise to avoid this pitfall.

4. *Record your notes as soon after the observation session as possible.* The longer you wait between observation and recording, the greater the data loss. Try to schedule your observation sessions in such a way that you can record your notes immediately afterwards.

5. *Don't talk to anyone about your observation session until you have recorded the field notes.* Many, if not most, researchers are unable to resist the temptation to recount the events of the day to co-workers and others before they have recorded their notes. You should resist this temptation as much as possible. Otherwise you run the risk of clouding your memory and of decreasing your ability to recall other events accurately. Of course, once you have recorded your notes, you may be able to recall additional data by discussing the day's events with someone else.

6. *Draw a diagram of the physical layout of the setting and attempt to trace your movements through it.* In a sense, walk through your experience. Doing this is an invaluable aid to help you recall specific events and to give others who might read your notes a frame of reference. A diagram of the seating plans can be helpful in a similar way. The seating plan forces you to recall who did what and to describe less conspicuous subjects.

7. *Once you have drawn the diagram and traced your movements, outline the specific events and conversations that occurred at each point in time before you record your field notes.* Doing this will enable you to record events in the proper time sequence as well as allow you to recall specific details. Your outline does not have to be elaborate. It need only contain key words, the first and last remarks of each conversation, and other reminders.

The observer in the state institution study taped his outline on the way home from the observation site, which was located a substantial distance away. He let conversations and events flow freely from his mind at this time. Later, when the outline was transcribed, he organized events according to the temporal sequence in which they occurred. The final product of this effort, the field notes, contained a detailed and concise account of the day's events. You will find that the time you take to construct your outline is well worth it in terms of the accuracy and clarity it adds to your notes.

8. *Pick up pieces of lost data after your initial recording session.* Observers often recall events or conversations days or even weeks after they have

recorded their field notes. These pieces of data should be incorporated into the notes. This problem will be minimized, however, if the researcher carefully outlines his or her notes before recording them.

TAPING AND TAKING NOTES
IN THE FIELD

While most observers who conduct the type of fieldwork described in this chapter rely on their memories for data collection, some researchers prefer either to carry a tape recorder with them into the field or to take notes in the presence of subjects. We would advise against the use of either of these two practices, at least in the initial stages of the research. The goal of the researcher is to minimize the effects of his or her presence. He or she hopes to win the confidence and candor of subjects to the greatest extent possible. Taping and note-taking can only interfere with the ability to do so.[27]

It is true, as some argue, that the researcher who tapes in the field increases the accuracy of field notes and saves the time it takes to record observations. Yet, the accuracy the trained and experienced researcher gains with the use of a tape recorder is probably illusory. Since such an observer already understands the substance and meanings of subjects' remarks, a verbatim transcript may offer little more than the precise wording of those remarks.

The effect of a tape recorder on observers' rapport with their subjects will, of course, depend upon many factors. In some settings, subjects will gradually come to accept the observer and to freely express their views. In others, they will never come around. For example, it is doubtful that all of the attendants in the state institution study would have been as willing to offer their perspectives had they known that their words were being recorded on tape. Some, in fact, took months of cultivation before they reluctantly shared beliefs and information with the observer even in the absence of a tape recorder. In any case, researchers would be wise to trust their memories and powers of concentration until they "feel out the situation." If they find that they cannot remember important conversations, they can resort to the use of a tape recorder later. And by that time they will have gained the trust of the subjects or at least the knowledge of which subjects and situations should be taped.

There are very few instances in which it is advisable to take notes in the field. Note-taking reminds subjects that they are under constant surveillance and informs them of the researcher's prime areas of interest. Moreover, note-taking probably adds little accuracy to the data of the skilled observer. One of the few times when notes can be taken without negative effects occurs in a situation, such as a classroom or a lecture, where others are taking notes. Even under these circumstances, however, the researcher should exercise discretion.

Some observers, during long sessions in the field, go to a private place, such as their car or a restroom, to jot down key phrases that will help them later to recall events. Others feel ill-at-ease spending long periods of time in the bathroom. As long as the observer can take such notes inconspicuously, to each his or her own.

THE FORM OF THE NOTES

For the purposes of clarity and later data retrieval, observers should adopt a standard form for their field notes. Although each observer will use a different form, every set of notes should contain the following items:

1. *Start each set of notes with a title page.* The title page should include such information as the date, time, place of observation, and the date and time the notes were recorded. Some observers also title each set with some phrase that indicates the nature of the data the set contains: "The Ward Xmas Party" or "The Monday Before Final Exams," for example.

2. *Include your diagram of the setting at the beginning of your notes.* Number each of your movements in the setting and indicate the page of your notes on which that movement is described. This will serve as an easy reference when you want to check specific events and will provide readers of your notes with a useful point of reference.

3. *Leave margins wide enough for your and others' comments.* These margins will also enable you to code your notes in the data analysis stage of the research.

4. *Form new paragraphs often.* Begin a new paragraph when the topic changes, when a different party enters a conversation, and at other appropriate places. This procedure not only facilitates reading but also helps when you are coding your notes.

5. *Use quotation marks to record remarks as often as possible.* It is not necessary to have a flawless reproduction of what was said. What is important is capturing the meaning and approximate wording of remarks. If you can't recall the exact wording of a dialogue, you should paraphrase: "John said something like—I've got to go home. Bill agreed and John walked out." Some researchers use quotation marks to signify exact recall, apostrophes to signify less precision in wording, and no markings to signify reasonable recall.[28]

One final note: record your field notes on ditto masters if you have access to a duplicating machine. You will then have extra copies which can be shared with others or used for data analysis in the post-fieldwork stage of your research.

RECORD YOUR OWN REMARKS
AND ACTIONS

Participant observers should carefully record their own behavior as well as the behavior of subjects. They must be able to examine their influence on the setting and the meanings of subjects' remarks and actions in the context in which they occurred. Thus, in some instances, observers will find that solicited statements must be interpreted differently than unsolicited ones. And in other instances, they will find that subjects' remarks are meaningless, or at least misleading, when viewed apart from the questions which elicited them.

Many observers are reluctant to record their actions and statements in the fear that they will reveal their blunders or failings or in the belief that what they say and do is unimportant.[29] You would be wise to avoid these fears and beliefs unless you are willing to sacrifice an understanding of all of your data.

OBSERVER'S COMMENTS

In addition to an account of the researcher's behavior in the field, *the field notes should include a record of her or his feelings, interpretations, preconceptions, and future research plans.* These should be clearly distinguished from descriptive and factual data through the use of parentheses and the designation "O.C." for "Observer's Comment."

It may be difficult for those trained in "objective research" to accept the researcher's own feelings as an important data source. Yet, the participant observer must be able to empathize with subjects, to experience vicariously their experiences, and to share their sufferings and joys. To stand back and deny one's feelings in the name of objectivity is to refuse to take the role of the other person.[30]

What you feel may be what your subjects feel or may have felt in the past. Your first impressions may be the same ones that others have had. You should use your feelings, beliefs, preconceptions, and prejudices to help you develop hypotheses. The following comments are excerpted from field notes in the state institution study.

> (O.C. I feel quite bored and depressed on the ward tonight. I wonder if this has anything to do with the fact that there are only two attendants working now. With only two attendants on, there are fewer diversions and less bantering. Perhaps this is why the attendants always complain about there not being enough of them. After all, there is never more work here than enough to occupy two attendants' time so it's not the fact that they can't get their work done that bothers them.)

> *   *   *

> (O.C. Although I don't show it, I tense up when the residents approach me when they are covered with food or excrement. Maybe this is what the attendants feel and why they often treat the residents as lepers.)

In the following excerpt from the job training study conducted by one of the authors, the observer reflects upon one of his first encounters with a trainee after having spent the initial stages of the research with staff members:

> I approached the two trainees who were working on assembling the radio. The male trainee looked up. I said, "Hi." He said, "Hi" and went back to doing what he had been doing. I said, "Have you built that (the radio) right from scratch?" (O.C. After I said this I thought that that was a dumb thing to say or perhaps a very revealing thing to say. Thinking back over the phrase, it came across as perhaps condescending. Asking if he had built it right from scratch might imply that I thought he didn't have the ability. He didn't react in that way but maybe that's the way people think of the "hard core" unemployed out at the center. Doing well is treated with surprise rather than as standard procedure. Perhaps rather than expecting that they are going to produce and treating them as if they are going to produce, you treat doing well as a special event.)

The observer thus gained a possible insight into staff members' definitions of trainees through a reflection on his own remark.

The researcher also notes any special ideas and interpretations or potential areas of interest in the "Observer's Comments." These comments serve as a reminder of topics to pursue later. The comment below is taken from the field notes from the state institution research:

(O.C. Many residents on this ward collect and hoard seemingly insignificant things. This is similar to what Goffman writes about in institutions of this kind. I'll have to start looking into this.)

The following comments are excerpted from field notes of a teacher training program study:

(O.C. Although I feel Jim has a pretty good understanding of my goals, he is trying hard to find something for me to do. I hope the issue is clear that I'll just be around listening and reflecting. Roles such as group facilitator and assistant supervisor are too binding and biasing for my role as an observer. Jim certainly seems to need help with his own feelings of incompetence but I must resist the temptation to be any more than reflective with him.)

*   *   *

(O.C. Although Dr. Bridge sounds sincerely interested in the study, I wonder if the 30 minutes interview he scheduled for me at such an inconvenient time was an attempt to brush me off.)

In sum, the "Observer's Comments" contain all subjective feelings or impressions and speculative interpretations which the researcher thinks are important to note. They can prove to be an invaluable aid in directing the researcher's attention to important topics and in developing hypotheses.

DESCRIPTIONS OF SETTINGS AND ACTIVITIES

The setting in which you conduct your research should be described in detail in your field notes. *You should be able to capture the "essence" of the setting in your description.* Are the walls painted? What color are they? Is the plaster broken? Do the floors shine? What objects are in the room? What is on the bulletin board? Do sounds carry in the room? Are there any special smells in the setting?

You should be careful to use descriptive and not evaluative words when record-ing descriptions in your field notes. A stove covered with grease must be characterized as just that and not as disgusting or nauseating. Similarly, record activities and events in descriptive terms. You would not report that people were engaged in occupational therapy, but rather that they were engaged in activities, such as coloring or caning chairs, which cer-tain people referred to as "occupational therapy."

Your own interpretations and evaluations should be included in your "Observer's Comments." You can then compare your impressions with those of others. Witness the following excerpt from the state institution study:

> A strong smell of feces and urine mixed with antiseptic permeated the air as I entered the smaller dormitory. (O.C. I find the smell to be repulsive, so much so that I immediately want to leave. Yet the attendants do not seem to mind the smell. Some claim to have gotten used to it. Others never mention it. I wonder if this reflects the difference between myself and them or the fact that I am a newcomer to the ward compared to them.)

Although you need to fully describe a setting only once in your notes, you should be sensitive to any changes that occur. Some aspects will change daily. Others which you would expect to change will not. In any case, a change may represent a major event. A change in the seating pattern in a teachers' lunchroom, for example, may reflect a change in social relationships in the school.

You will find that an accurate description, as well as a diagram, of the research setting will give you important insight into the type and inten-sity of activities which occur and the nature of participants' perspectives. Different aspects of the ward at the state institution conveyed the staff's and administration's assumption that the residents were either childlike, destructive, or subhuman.[31] Furniture was constructed of metal, heavy wood, or hard plastic. The television was mounted high on the wall. There were no curtains or decorations on the ward with the exception of three pictures of cartoon characters and one of a pair of hands folded in prayer. Beds were pushed together and lacked pillows and sometimes sheets. Residents and attendants used different water fountains. The residents' bathroom, in contrast to that of the attendants, had no toilet stalls, seats on the toilets, toilet paper, mirrors or soap. Of course, some, if not most, aspects of many settings will not be significant. You should nevertheless note and question the meaning of everything you observe.

DESCRIPTIONS OF PEOPLE

People, like settings and activities, *should be carefully and accurately described in the notes.* Keep in mind the fact that people convey something about themselves and make assumptions about others on the basis of clothing, accessories, and general appearance.[32]

Marginal members of a setting do not, of course, need to be described in as much detail as more central members. For example, one would only casually mention the appearance of a mail carrier unless it were relevant to the way subjects react to him or her or to an understanding of the setting.

You should note the characteristics of individuals that lend insight into how they define themselves or how they will be defined by others. Describe in detail the aspects of a person's appearance that indicate age, social class, and demeanor. What color is her or his hair? Is it well-groomed? What is the condition of his or her teeth? What kind of clothes is she or he wearing? Are the clothes stylish? Do they fit? Are they well-pressed? Is he or she wearing any accessories? How tall is she or he? What kind of build does he or she have? What is her or his posture like? How does he or she walk? These and other questions should be answered in the field notes. Moreover, subjective impressions should be included in "Observer's Comments." Note the description in the following excerpt of a man coming to a door-to-door training session.

> The door leading from the corridor opened and a man paused for a moment and tiptoed in. (O.C. He looked surprised when he opened the door, like he didn't expect to see all the people. His tiptoeing seemed to be an attempt not to cause any excess noise. His carriage was one of "I'm imposing.") He was approximately 5′ 7″ and had a deep brown suntan. (O.C. It looked like he was tan from working outside.) His skin was leathery. His hair was black and combed back. It had a few streaks of gray and he was slightly bald in front. He was maybe 45 years old. He was thin. His clothes were cleaned and well-pressed and fit him well. A set of keys was hanging from his belt on a key ring in back. He had on dark brown flannel straight-leg trousers with a light tan stretch belt with the buckle worn on his hip. He had on a dark brown plaid sport shirt with a button down. He was wearing well-polished loafers and had on black horn-rimmed glasses.

As your research progresses, you will notice that certain characteristics differentiate your subjects according to their status in the setting. In some cases, the signs of status will be quite obvious. Thus, some employees in certain organizations wear work clothes or uniforms while others wear dresses or pantsuits or coats and ties. Hats, stripes or bars on uniforms, and name plates may also be important indicators of a person's position. In other cases, signs that indicate status will be subtle and will strike the observer only after an extended period of time in the field. In one study, for example, some women employees carried their handbags with them wherever they went. It took the researcher several observation sessions to realize that these women held inferior positions in the organization and, unlike others, were not provided with lockers. Similarly, attendants are distinguished from residents in many "total institutions" by the heavy key rings which hang from their belts. Certain residents in the state institution study tried to appear to be attendants by hanging keys on strings from their belts.

You must constantly question the meanings of subjects' clothing, accessories, and appearance. Do not assume that differences among people in these areas serve realistic purposes. You might observe that certain men in an organization carry attaché cases. Whether these men have more work than others or not would be a matter to be explored.

People, as settings, should be described in specific and nonevaluative terms. Words such as "bashful," "shy," and "aggressive" should be relegated to an "Observer's Comment." You should not describe behavior with words such as "daydreaming" or "bragging." It is one thing to say that a person looks off into space and quite another to say that he or she daydreams. The only place to interpret behavior is within the parentheses of an "Observer's Comment."

RECORD DIALOGUE ACCESSORIES

One's gestures, nonverbal communications, tone of voice, speed of speech, and general speech patterns tell much about the meanings of one's words. We can all recall instances in which people said "no" in such a way that they implied "yes." Dialogue accessories are thus extremely important to understanding interaction and should be included in the field notes. The following comments and descriptions are typical of those that might accompany remarks in your notes:

Joe loosened his tie and said, . . ."

*　　*　　*

Mary looked down the hall and gestured with her index finger to come closer. (O.C. I interpreted her gestures to be a concern that someone would hear what she was going to say.) In a low voice she said, ..."

*   *   *

As Joe spoke, the sound of his voice got louder and louder and he began pointing his finger at Paul. Paul backed up a step and turned red.

*   *   *

Bill raised his eyes to the ceiling as Mike walked past. (O.C. I interpret this to be a ridiculing gesture.)

You should also try to capture accents when you record your subjects' remarks. Even if you have difficulty writing words phonetically, you will find it simple to portray a person's accent once you have identified a pattern in his or her speech. For example, some people leave the final "g" off of words ending in "ing" when they speak: "goin'," "doin'," "fightin'."

RECORD WHAT YOU DON'T UNDERSTAND OR THINK YOU MAY HAVE MISUNDERSTOOD

Observers often encounter phrases or conversations that they do not understand. This material is sometimes difficult to recall precisely and many researchers tend to omit it from their notes. Such an omission is a mistake. *Even the most incomprehensible remarks may become understandable when viewed in the light of later conversations or events.* In the state institution research, for example, attendants made frequent reference to "bung-holing," a word which the observer did not understand. It was only later that he learned that this was an institutional term for homosexual anal intercourse.

There are also times when the observer recalls conversations or words which appear to be out of context or inappropriate. Such data should be recorded as is. You should trust your ability to remember what was said. Don't try to reconstruct what you heard to make it read better in your notes. After all, people say the oddest things at the oddest times. Of course, data of this nature are less reliable than other data. The observer would not base any hypotheses on this material in the absence of supporting evidence.

OTHER DATA

While field notes provide the central data in participant observation research, *other research methods may be used in conjunction with fieldwork in order to gain a greater understanding of the setting.*[33] The researcher should, however, forego any method which would disturb the setting or destroy rapport with subjects. Subjects usually lose most of their self-consciousness after the observer has spent a prolonged period of time in the field. For the researcher to try to administer a formal questionnaire or a sociogram at this point could only make them conscious of their subject status.

As mentioned earlier, observers can conduct open-ended interviews toward the end of the fieldwork.[34] They will then have the trust of their subjects and enough "inside information" to make their questions poignant and relevant to the interests of subjects. They might also decide to conduct follow-up interviews with subjects after they have left the research setting or to interview persons who are outside the setting but related to it.

Although it is probably advisable for researchers to record open-ended interviews in the same manner in which they record their regular observations, they may decide to tape record at least some of the interviews if, of course, this will not intimidate the subjects. They are the best judge of the approach at this point.

Another important source of data is written records such as official documents or publications, memos, correspondence, contracts, salary schedules, files, attendance records, evaluation forms, and diaries. These records should be viewed not as objective data, but rather, as expressions of the people who write and keep them. They can also alert the researcher to potentially fruitful lines of inquiry. Since materials of this nature may be considered sensitive and confidential, observers would be wise to wait until they have been accepted by subjects before asking to see them. And even then they should ask casually and at an appropriate time. If there is any doubt whether or not to ask to see such material, it is best to wait or to find another way to gain access to them.

The researcher might use other kinds of records in order to gain an historical perspective on the setting. The historical records of an organization, local newspapers, history books, retired members, and local historical societies may be valuable data sources. The observer in the job training study made frequent use of such data in his research. He not only inspected materials relevant to the formation of that program in local newspapers and in interviews but also researched materials on the local and national history of poverty and unemployment programs. Through an historical perspective, the observer can view the setting in the context of its past and in relation to other settings. Moreover, participants' perspectives are often better understood when seen in the light of past events.

Finally, the observer can collect data on a single phenomenon from a variety of independent sources. In the job training study, the researcher gathered data on trainees' success in job placements, on the perspectives of personnel managers in the plants that hired them, on the views of the training program director and staff, and on the reports that were sent to the state. He was also able to compare and examine the discrepancies between official attendance records and his own.

BOUNDARIES OF A STUDY

During the first days in the field, researchers familiarize themselves with the setting. At this time they are concerned more with a general knowledge of the various aspects of the setting than with specific hypotheses. As the study progresses, they learn that limited time and resources restrict the scope of the study. They must decide on the dimensions and focus of the research: on what is most important and meaningful to pursue.

Probably the first decision the observer must make in this regard concerns geographical boundaries. Should he or she focus on one ward in a hospital or several? Should he or she visit subjects in their homes or in other settings? Should he or she pursue subjects who have left the setting? Although there are no clear-cut answers to these questions, remember that you cannot study everything. Once you have a general knowledge of a setting or organization, concentrate on one or a few parts of it. The beginning observer would be wise to select a rather small setting with no more than eight to twenty-five subjects and to master it first.

There are other boundaries which the researcher can and should place on the study. The observer may pursue certain themes as they emerge in the data by placing her- or himself in relevant situations or by asking subjects relevant questions. In a study of a mental hospital, for example, one could focus on the inmate status system or on the techniques of inmate control. And in other institutional settings, one could study the meanings of time or death.[35]

You might find it helpful to temporarily leave the field after the initial stages of the research or at other junctures. Doing so will allow you time to clear your mind, to see things in perspective, and to set your priorities. When you return to the field, you can pursue important topics and themes. A break from the intensive observation that the research requires may also give you a second breath and the endurance needed to continue the study.

Some participant observers prefer to work in teams in order to broaden the base of their research. In this approach, a number of individual observers visit a number of different, but similar, settings or visit a few settings at different times. The basic techniques of participant observation remain the same in team research with the exception that field tactics and areas of inquiry are developed in conjunction with others.[36]

THE AMOUNT AND DISTRIBUTION OF TIME DEVOTED TO A STUDY

The participant observer will never reach a point when he or she can state conclusively that a study is complete. There will always be new themes to explore and new areas to investigate. Yet most researchers arrive at a stage when the hours spent in the field yield diminishing returns. When your research goals are fulfilled, your questions are answered, and your data become repetitive, you should leave the field or at least discontinue the *intensive* observation phase of your research. Other obligations may, of course, force you to conclude your research before you reach this stage. Take heart in the fact that you still will have gained important insight into some aspect of social behavior.

Studies may last anywhere from a few weeks to well over a year. The study of door-to-door salesmen (Chapter 10) was completed in only three weeks. In this study, however, the researcher observed daily and focused on one specific aspect: techniques of persuasion that were taught to sales trainees. The job training program study lasted three months, during which time the observer made daily visits to the setting and yielded over one thousand pages of field notes. The observer also visited the training center before and after the intensive observation stage of the research and conducted 90 interviews with trainees, plant personnel managers, and others. In the state institution study, the observer made weekly or biweekly visits to the setting for a period of over one year.

In most instances, researchers should spend at least several months in a setting regardless of the frequency of their visits. This length of time enables them to view the dynamics of change in the setting and lessens the likelihood of their observations being conducted at an unrepresentative time.

*   *   *

At the conclusion of the field work phase of the research process, the observer will presumably have collected hundreds, or even thousands, of pages of "raw" data, the recorded observations of subjects' words and behavior. He or she will be faced with the question: "What does it all mean?" While there is no easy answer to this question, there are some techniques he or she can use to begin to address it. The following chapter turns to a discussion of some of these techniques.

NOTES

1.   J. Lofland, "Editorial introduction—analyzing qualitative data: First person accounts," *Urban Life and Culture,* **3** (October): 307, 1974.

2.   Morris and Charlotte Schwartz, "Problems of participant observation," *American Journal of Sociology,* **LX** (January): 343–354, 1955. They discuss the passive role as only one role on a passive-active continuum.

3.   Blanche Geer et al., "Learning the ropes: Situational learning in four occupational training programs," in Irwin Deutscher and Elizabeth Thompson (Eds.), *Among the People* (New York: Basic Books, 1966).

4.   For a general discussion of how officers react to being observed by researchers or being interviewed in an organizational study, see Chris Argyris, "Diagnosing defenses against the outsider," *Journal of Social Issues,* **VIII,** no. 3: 24–34, 1952.

5.   See also Samuel Wallace, *Skid Row as a Way of Life* (New York: Harper Torchbooks, 1968). Wallace describes the "tour guide" skid rower who will talk to any social scientists willing to pay the price and who will tell the kinds of stories he thinks people want to hear.

6.   Ned Polsky, *Hustlers, Beats and Others* (Garden City, N.Y.: Doubleday, Anchor Books, 1969), p. 128.

7.   *Ibid.,* p. 129.

8.   For a discussion of gaining access to functioning orgnizations and developing favorable research relations during the process, see Robert Kahn and Floyd Mann, "Developing research partnerships," *Journal of Social Issues,* **VIII,** no. 3: 4–10, 1952.

9.   For a discussion of closer relationships with subjects and the effect on the study, see S. M. Miller, "The participant observer and 'over-rapport,' " *American Sociological Review,* **XVII**: 97–99, 1952.

10.   See Donald Roy, "Role of the researcher in the study of social conflict," *Human Organization,* **XXIV** (Fall): 262–271, 1965.

11.   Peter Blau, *Exchange and Power in Social Life* (New York: Wiley, 1964).

12.   See Raymond Gold, "Roles in sociological field observation," *Social Forces,* **XXXVI**: 223, 1958.

13.   For the use of the term in the black ghetto see: Thomas Kochman, "Rapping in the black ghetto," Rainwater, L., *Soul* (Chicago: Aldine) 51–77, 1970. Also see: John Horton, "Time and cool people," *Trans-Action,* **IV,** no. 5 (April): 6, 1967; Ulf Hannerz, *Soulside: Inquiries into Ghetto Culture and Community* (New York: Columbia University Press, 1969), p. 84–87, 129–135; Roger D. Abrahams, "Playing the dozens," *Journal of American Folklore,* **LXXV**: 209–220, 1962. The use of the term today by American youth is somewhat different from its ghetto use in that in some sense it stands for an "honest" exchange of "important" ideas.

14.   Polsky, *Hustlers, Beats and Others,* p. 127.

15.   *Ibid.,* p. 128.

16.   See Howard S. Becker and Blanche Geer, "Participant observation and interviewing: A comparison," *Human Organization,* **XVI,** no. 3: 28–32, 1957, for a discussion of "learning the language."

17.   See Irwin Deutscher, *Notes on Language and Human Conduct* (Syracuse, N. Y.: Maxwell Graduate School of Social Sciences and the Youth Development Center, mimeographed, 1967) and Severyn T. Bruyn, *The Human Perspective in Sociology* (Englewood Cliffs, N. Y.: Prentice-Hall, 1966), pp. 212–214.

18.   Wallace, *Skid Row.*

19.   Rose Giallombardo, *Society of Women: A Study of a Women's Prison* (New York: Wiley, 1966).

20.   For a critical look at the vocabulary and rhetoric of psychiatry, see the works of Thomas Szasz. For example, *Ideology and Insanity* (Garden City, N.Y.: Doubleday, 1970), and *The Myth of Mental Illness* (New York: Hoeber-Harper, 1961).

21.   See Aaron Cicourel and John Kitsuse, *The Educational Decision-Makers* (Indianapolis: Bobbs-Merrill, 1963), Chap. 4.

22.   See Jack Haas, *From Punk to Scale: A Study of High Steel Ironworkers* (University Microfilms, 1970).

23.   Polsky, *Hustlers, Beats and Others,* pp. 123–124.

24.   See Anselm Strauss et al., *Psychiatric Ideologies and Institutions* (New York: Free Press, 1964), pp. 26–27.

25.   See the Appendix for an example of field notes.

26.   Of course, experienced observers and those who have spent a considerable amount of time in a single setting can selectively omit trivial material from the field notes. The point is that we often do not know what is important early in a research project and, for this reason, we must be alert to anything and everything that might possibly be significant.

27.   See Polsky, *Hustlers, Beats and Others,* p. 121.

28.   George McCall and J. L. Simmons, *Issues in Participant Observation: A Text and Reader* (Reading, Mass.: Addison-Wesley, 1969, p. 74.

29.   Arthur Vidich, "Participant observation and the collection and interpretation of data," *American Journal of Sociology*, **LV**: 354–360, 1955, emphasizes the importance of the researcher's "self-objectification."

30.   Herbert Blumer, "Society as symbolic interaction," in Jerome G. Manis and Bernard Meltzer (Eds.), *Symbolic Interaction: A Reader in Social Psychology* (Boston: Allyn and Bacon, 1967), pp. 146–147. These ideas are the methodological extension of the social theory presented by George Herbert Mead. See his *Mind, Self and Society* (Chicago: University of Chicago Press, 1934), and *The Philosophy of the Act* (Chicago: University of Chicago Press, 1938).

31.   For an excellent discussion on the historical perceptions of the "mentally retarded," see Wolf Wolfensberger, *The Origin and Nature of Our Institutional Models* (Syracuse, N.Y.: Human Policy Press, 1974), pp. 2–24.

32.   See Erving Goffman, *The Presentation of Self in Everyday Life* (Garden City, N. Y.: Doubleday, 1959).

33.   For a discussion of the importance of using a variety of research methods and a variety of data bearing on the same research problems, see Eugene J. Webb, et al., *Unobstrusive Measures: Non-Reactive Research in the Social Sciences* (Chicago: Rand McNally, 1966), Chap. 1.

34.   See Becker and Geer, "Participant observation."

35.   See for example, Julius Roth, *Timetables* (Indianapolis: Bobbs-Merrill, 1963), and Barney Glaser and Anselm Strauss, *Awareness of Dying* (Chicago: Aldine, 1965).

36.   The observation team is commonly used in conducting research. For examples, see Howard S. Becker et al., *Boys in White* (Chicago: University of Chicago Press, 1961) and *Making the Grade* (New York: Wiley, 1968).

CHAPTER FOUR

Participant Observation

WORKING WITH DATA

In the preceding chapters, we described the process by which the participant observer locates a setting, enters the field, and gathers data. In this chapter, we describe some of the ways in which the observer can begin to analyze his or her data in the post-fieldwork stage of the research. Here we deal with the mechanics of analysis. Our purpose is to offer guidelines which we have used and which you may find helpful.

When we speak of "data analysis" we mean the techniques you can use to make sense out of and to learn from the hundreds, or even thousands, of pages of recorded statements and behavior in your field notes.[1] More specifically, *"data analysis" refers to a process which entails an effort to formally identify themes and to construct hypotheses (ideas) as they are suggested by data and an attempt to demonstrate support for those themes and hypotheses.*[2] By *hypotheses* we mean nothing more than propositional statements that are either simple ("attendants distrust professionals at the institution") or complex ("attendants misinterpret residents' behavior because they lack empathy for the residents"). The purpose of hypotheses, as we use them, is to sensitize one to the nature of behavior in a setting and of social interaction in general: to help one understand phenomenon that were not previously understood.

Unlike practitioners of most other methodologies, the participant observer seeks merely to demonstrate the plausibility of his or her hypotheses and not to "test" or to "prove" them. The latter terms have more meaning in the context of quantitative research models where hypotheses are formulated and examined according to certain formal or statistical procedures. And while the observer can perform such procedures on data, the scores obtained will neither prove hypotheses nor greatly increase understanding.[3]

Although data analysis is often a time-consuming and painstaking process, the particular techniques to be followed and the amount of time spent depend upon the quantity of field notes and the research goals. In those instances in which the research is aimed at only a cursory understanding, data analysis need not be intensive. Some researchers, for example, find it suitable for their purposes to quickly read through their data, make note of apparent themes, and select exemplary quotations to illustrate these themes when they report their studies. In most instances, however, the researcher will spend weeks, or even months, going over his or her data in a systematic attempt to understand and interpret it. Some researchers devote as much time to data analysis as they do to data collection.

WHEN SHOULD THE ANALYSIS START?

In a sense, *data analysis is an ongoing process in participant observation research.* Observers note important themes and formulate hypotheses throughout their studies. They pursue the broad questions and areas of interest that were on their minds when they entered the field.[4]

As the research progresses, observers refine certain hypotheses and discard others by holding them up to experience. They may introduce leading questions that will encourage subjects to talk about areas related to hypotheses. Or they may ask specific and direct questions once they have gained the confidence of subjects.

In the job training program study, the observer had an early hunch that men trainees clearly differentiated "women's factory work" from "men's factory work." The hunch came after one of the staff personnel had reported the following to the observer: "when the men saw women doing the work [soldering] on the assembly line, they didn't want any part of it." Since this sex differentiation would have important implications for the potential success of the program and for the meanings of work, the researcher pursued his hunch on later visits to the setting. He found that, although men and women differed in the types of work they valued, men did not reject certain work as "women's work." For example, they expressed little pride in doing physical labor and openly avoided jobs that were dangerous or "too hard." The observer dropped his earlier hypothesis and turned to the pursuit of others.

While the participant observer explores themes and hypotheses throughout the course of her or his study, *it is during the post-fieldwork stage of the research that he or she concentrates most on the analysis and interpretation of data.* At this time, when all of the evidence is in, so to speak, she or he refines hypotheses and examines the conditions under which they hold true.

Once observers have collected what they consider to be sufficient data to understand those aspects of settings in which they are interested, they leave the field to engage in a period of intensive analysis. Of course, many observers need a month or so to read, contemplate, or rest before they tackle the difficult task of data analysis. Moreover, practical considerations, such as the amount of time it takes to transcribe taped field notes, may force the researcher to postpone analysis. We mention this rather mundane point because it is all too often forgotten. Some observers establish unrealistic schedules for the completion of their research and underestimate the time and energy a participant observation study demands. At the conclusion of their fieldwork, they find themselves swamped with other obligations that they have neglected.

In any case, *the observer would usually be wise to begin analysis soon after he or she has left the field.* At this time the data are fresh and exciting. And if he or she wishes to return to the setting to pick up loose pieces and to clarify any points, this can be done while rapport is intact and informants are accessible. The researcher may even solicit the comments of key informants during data analysis as a check on the validity of her or his work.[5]

There are, nonetheless, instances in which the observer should postpone analysis. Since personal attachments and biases often develop during the course of the research, the observer often needs a chance to create some distance between her- or himself and the setting in order to see the data from a wider perspective. Certain things are easier to recognize and to treat objectively after a period of time has elapsed. However, this is not a concern for most new observers, who generally conduct rather limited studies and are not deeply involved in the setting.

DISCOVERING THEMES AND FORMULATING HYPOTHESES

The researcher will already have developed some clear ideas and hypotheses in regard to the meaning of his or her data by the time he or she concludes his or her observations. In the intensive analysis stage of the research he or she refines his or her ideas and hypotheses, and searches the data for new ones. Some hypotheses will be modified. Others will be subsumed under broader ones.

Since certain themes remain hidden from the researcher and certain hypotheses emerge only when the data are viewed in a certain manner, *the participant observer must examine data in as many ways as possible* in order to understand the general significance of a setting. Although there is no precise formula which will enable the researcher to construct hypotheses and to recognize themes, the following suggestions should be helpful.

1. *Read your field notes.* Collect all of your data (field notes, Observer's Comments, and other materials) and read through them carefully. Almost everything is potentially important, depending upon the researcher's purpose. Seemingly minor details may provide a clue to understanding broader aspects of the setting. For example, the observer at the state institution noticed that many attendants had relatives who worked as attendants on other wards. This casual observation led to the hypothesis that attendants' perspectives on their jobs, their supervisors, and the residents under their charge were supported and reinforced in off-the-job situations as well as on-the-job ones. Write notes to yourself recording themes and hypotheses as you read through your data.

You should also be alert to topics that your subjects either intentionally or unintentionally avoid. In a study of a "delinquent gang," one would expect youths to talk about the moral or legal implications of their acts. The fact that youths did not discuss these implications would be a fruitful line of inquiry.

As an added check, *have someone else read over all of your data.* An outside reader can sometimes better capture those subtle aspects of the setting that elude the involved observer.

2. *Code important conversation topics.* You will find that certain topics occur and reoccur in the conversations of your subjects. Each of these topics should be noted and coded. You are thus beginning to assemble everything that was said about an important aspect of the setting. In the state institution study, the researcher coded such conversation topics as "attendants' training," "pay," "programming for residents," "cleaning the ward," and "supervisors." Note that at this point in time the coding categories are relatively objective and unambiguous: people either said something about training, for example, or they didn't.

Once you have read through your data and gained a sense of which topics are important, you should assign a number, letter, or other symbol to each of these topics. Duplicate your field notes and code this copy by putting the number corresponding to each topic next to the relevant paragraphs in the margin of your notes. This task will be facilitated if, as mentioned earlier, you have frequently formed new paragraphs when you recorded your data.

Cut the duplicate by paragraphs and place them into manila folders according to coded topic category. You can make additional copies of the paragraphs or sentences that pertain to more than one coding category. In any case, the original copy of the notes should be left uncut. And each paragraph that is cut from a copy should be identified with the page number of the field notes from which it was taken. This will enable you to consult the original copy of the notes for the context of the paragraph or the stage of the fieldwork in which it was recorded.

After the coding process has been completed, the data should be read, sorted, and examined for patterns. You are likely to learn that themes which were once obscure will be clearly illuminated.

3. *Construct typologies.* Typologies, or classification schemes, can be useful aids in forming hypotheses and discovering themes. Read over your data. Make note of how your subjects classify people and behavior and of the differences between and among subjects that allow them to be classified. The researcher in the state institution study in the analysis stage of his research constructed several typologies that led to the generation of important hypotheses. One typology concerned attendants' perspectives on different residents. Residents were viewed as either "dopes," "pets," "workers," or "bastards" (troublemakers). The observer went on to relate this classification to the differences in treatment received by different residents. And this led to hypotheses about attendants' broader perspectives on their work. Another typology related to the length of time each attendant had worked at the institution, which, in turn, was

compared, among other things, to the respective attendant's everyday behavior. The observer concluded that there was little relationship between the two and was thus able to discard the commonsense distinction between "old-line" and "new-line" workers in such settings.

Since the purpose of typologies, as described here, is merely to sensitize you to subtle aspects of the setting that you may have otherwise overlooked, they need not be rigid or precise. Use them freely. Examine your data in a variety of ways.

4. *Read the literature pertinent to your interests and your research setting.* After and perhaps during the intensive observation stage of the research, the observer consults the professional literature. He or she compares findings reported in the literature with what is beginning to appear in his or her data and looks for unanswered questions which the study might address. And when she or he finally begins to write papers or articles he or she relates it to what has been written in the past.

The researcher also utilizes the concepts, models, and paradigms of others. In the research conducted at the state institution, the observer made frequent use of ideas found in the literature on deviance, total institutions, work, and mental illness and retardation in addition to that on general theoretical issues. These ideas helped him to formulate hypotheses and to put things in perspective.

Finally, what one sees, hypothesizes, and subsequently reports depends upon one's theoretical assumptions. Theory provides an explanatory or interpretive framework that enables the researcher to make sense out of the morass of data and to relate data to other events and settings. For this reason, it is important for the researcher to expose her or himself to different theoretical perspectives during the intensive analysis stage of the research.

In Chapter 1 we briefly described and mentioned the importance of symbolic interactionism and ethnomethodology. In order to give you a clearer idea of how you might use these perspectives in your own studies, we would now like to offer a series of illustrative questions that you can apply to your data.

While you should use these to explore how people see their world, don't push your data into the frameworks that the questions suggest. Use them if, and only if, they apply to your data and coincide with your interests.

Following the symbolic interactionist perspective, one would be concerned with how subjects define the situations in which they find themselves. More specifically, one would ask the following questions:

"How do various subjects define their settings, the various aspects of these settings, and themselves?" This question would be directed toward individual definitions or perspectives and group definitions or shared perspectives and could lead to a typology of subjects based on how they view their world.

"What is the process by which definitions develop and change?" One would explore actors' backgrounds and positions, objects (including other people) present in a setting, and communications between actors.

"What is the relationship between the various definitions held by different subjects?" This question would allow one to examine the basis of consensus or conflict in a setting.

"What is the relationship between actors' perspectives and their behavior?"

The ethnomethodologist, as you may recall, is interested in how meanings are accomplished in specific situations. The ethnomethodologist would thus ask questions of the following nature:

"What are the abstract meanings of different actions?" One would examine how people think and speak about actions apart from the situations in which those actions occur.

"What are the specific meanings of different actions in specific situations?"

"What are the commonsense assumptions held by actors?" You would explore what people take for granted in their everyday lives.

"How do actors account for, or explain, their actions?" One would try to see how people apply abstract meanings in ambiguous situations. In short, how do people make their actions appear orderly, rational, and in accordance with the rules?

These are, of course, only two of the many possible theoretical perspectives one might use to interpret one's findings. Use the perspective or approach most compatible with your interests and theoretical assumptions.

WORKING WITH HYPOTHESES

After the researcher has formulated hypotheses, he or she turns to an analysis of the extent to which they are supported by data and the conditions under which they hold true. In the course of this process, he or she modifies or converges certain hypotheses and discards or develops others.

The observer constructs a new coding scheme once she or he has formulated basic hypotheses. He or she assigns a number to each hypothesis and codes and sorts his or her data (statements, behavior, Observer's Comments, and written documents) in the manner described above. The exact number of hypotheses the researcher seeks to analyze will of course, depend upon the quality and quantity of the data and his or her own interests and goals. The observer in the job training program study coded his data into over 150 categories. The researcher at the state institution, on the other hand, analyzed his data according to approximately 50 coding categories. This coding scheme included such hypotheses as "attendants distrust professionals at the institution"; "attendants discount IQ as an indicator of intelligence"; and "cleanliness and order, minimizing work, and controlling residents' behavior are attendants' dominant concerns in their work." Note that some of the researcher's hypotheses may subsume others. One could argue, for example, that attendants' distrust of IQ stems from their distrust of professionals. The observer's coding categories, then, will not necessarily be mutually exclusive. Showing the relationship between hypotheses in order to achieve an integrated picture or model is your ultimate goal.

Unlike many other researchers who enlist "hired hands" to code their data, *participant observers typically code and analyze their own data* for several reasons.[6] In the first place, hypothesis creation is a neverending process in participant observation research. As observers code their data they gain an even deeper understanding of the setting they have researched. In the second place, participant observers must call upon their own experience and judgment to make sense out of data which is ambiguous and subject to varied interpretations. Coding, then, entails far more than the routine assignment of numbers to "True/False," "Agree/ Disagree" responses on a survey questionnaire. And while observers themselves will face ambiguity when they attempt to analyze data, they can be aware of and take into account this ambiguity when they report their findings.

In any case, *the participant observer should have some sense of the criteria he or she will use to code certain statements and behavior as supportive or nonsupportive of some hypotheses and not of others.* He or she will make use of such criteria and commonsense assumptions anyway,[7] and specifying them makes them consistent and open to his or her scrutiny and that of others. Let us take the hypothesis "attendants discount IQ as an indicator of intelligence." The researcher in the state institution study accepted data of the following nature as supportive of this hypothesis: direct statements ("You can't trust IQ,"; "IQ don't mean shit."); sarcastic rhetorical questions ("And you mean to tell me that his IQ is under 20?"); and dogmatic statements made in reference to how to understand residents' behavior ("You can't understand 'em unless you're up here all the time."). Conversely, statements and behavior of the following nature were coded as nonsupportive: direct statements ("You can always know what they'll do if you know their IQ."); explanations of residents' behavior based on IQ ("Oh, the reason he does that is that his IQ is only 20."); explanations of attendants' behavior toward residents based on IQ ("We can do that to him 'cuz his IQ is only 15."); and attempts to ascertain residents' IQ before taking certain actions ("I don't know if trying to teach him anything will do any good. Let me check his IQ."). Observers will not, of course, know which criteria are relevant until they have become sufficiently familiar with the contents of their field notes. And, in some instances, some criteria will be determined after they have already begun to code their data. What is ultimately important is for researchers to be able to understand their rationale for having coded certain data in one way and not another at the conclusion of the analysis stage of their studies.

On the following pages, we will discuss some of the ways in which participant observers can analyze and increase their understanding of their data. Accept them for what they are: helpful devices. Use them if and when they are appropriate and feel free to create your own.

1. *Do the data support the hypothesis?* Once the observer has coded and sorted the data by hypothesis he or she should examine the extent to which the items in each coded category support the respective hypothesis. This process entails nothing more than making a distinction between and comparison of supportive (positive) and nonsupportive (negative) items. One would, of course, expect to find a relatively greater number of supportive items than nonsupportive items. Yet the existence of nonsupportive items is not in and of itself sufficient cause to discard an hypothesis.[8] In view of the fact that coding procedures and criteria are by nature imprecise and impressionistic, it is not unreasonable to learn that some items contradict others. Moreover, people are often inconsis-

tent in what they say and what they do as they move from one situation to another.

In any case, the observer should carefully scrutinize all nonsupportive items. He or she may find that what appears to be a contradiction is not one at all. The researcher at the state institution formulated one hypothesis that in effect stated that attendants viewed residents as total incompetents. He subsequently found that this view was only expressed in certain circumstances: when the attendants sought to account for the lack of programming they offered residents. This realization led to the generation of an alternative hypothesis, one that paid proper attention to the situational nature of attendants' perspectives.

While certain researchers have developed statistical operations that the observer can use on data, the observer must always depend upon his or her individual judgment and ability to account for the existence of inconsistencies in order to conclude that a specific hypothesis is supported by the data. Perhaps the only valid advice to offer is that you should be able to state your degree of confidence in each hypothesis when you write up your findings. And in the event that you have little confidence in a particular hypothesis don't be afraid to discard it completely.

2. *Solicited or unsolicited statements?* Although observers should allow their subjects to voice their own concerns, they must in the course of their studies probe certain areas and ask certain questions in order to obtain information. By doing so, they will in some instances alert subjects to their position and elicit what they think they want to hear or what will put them in a favorable light. In others they will obtain answers to questions which are not on subjects' minds and which are irrelevant to their actual concerns. Therefore, it is important that the observer scrutinize and compare solicited statements, responses to questions or remarks, with unsolicited, or volunteered, statements.[9]

After the items in each coded category have been sorted according to whether or not they support the respective hypothesis, they should be sorted according to whether or not they were solicited.[10] Of course, some items, such as descriptions of behavior, will not be relevant and can be put aside. Different proportions of solicited to unsolicited statements will require different interpretations. One might have to modify an hypothesis if all of the supportive items had been solicited or if solicited and unsolicited statements contradicted each other.

While solicited and unsolicited statements should be treated differently, they are equally valuable. They lend insight into how people view things different situations.

You should also examine your data for the different kinds of questions in relation to a specific topic that evoked different responses. You may find that one type of question elicited one type of answer and that another type of question elicited something different.

3. *Observer's influence on the setting.* Researchers cannot help but influence the settings they observe.[11] Especially during the first days in the field subjects are artificial in many of their actions. They remain cautious in their words and deeds and may even try to "put the observer on." In the state institution study, for example, one attendant admitted the following to the observer at the conclusion of his first day of observation:

> Yea, we didn't do a lot of things today that we usually do. Like if you wasn't here we woulda snitched some food at dinner and maybe hit a couple of 'em around. See, before we didn't know you was an ok guy.

Later in the study another attendant reported the following to the observer:

> We usually know when someone's comin'—an hour or so beforehand. They let us know when someone's comin' so we can put some clothes on 'em—make sure they're not bare-assed or jerkin' off when someone comes up here. I had some visitors up here today. . . . They asked me a bunch of questions. I answered em, but I wasn't gonna overdo it. You know? I wasn't gonna tell 'em everything.

People, it would seem, attempt to present themselves well before strangers. And as new faces become familiar ones, everyone's behavior changes.

When analyzing data, the researcher must consider the effect his or her presence had on the setting. Was the atmosphere artificial when he or she first entered the field? Did it return to normal at some point in time? How did her or his behavior and the subjects' perception change their behavior?

You should, if you can, list the stages of your research in terms of the degree to which you were accepted by subjects.[12] For example, the observer at the state institution noted four temporal stages according to his rapport with and acceptance by the attendants: (1) Outsider: treated cautiously; (2) Frequent Visitor: attendants spoke freely, but remained guarded in much of their behavior; (3) Casual Participant: attendants spoke and acted freely; and (4) Accepted Participant: accepted by attendants and identified as "one of their own." While such schemes are admittedly artificial and dependent upon the observer's selective perception, they can be used to provide an added check on data.

Once you have distinguished these stages in your own study, you can sort the items in each coded category according to the stage of the research at which they were recorded. The nature of your data is likely to have changed as you moved from one stage to another. You may even be able to conclude that contradictory statements can be explained by your influence on the setting.

Again, practically all data, no matter how "artificial," are valuable. What is important is to be able to interpret and understand them in context.

4. *In the presence of whom?* Just as the observer influences what a subject may say or do, so too do other participants of the setting. You should be alert to the differences between what subjects say and do when they are alone and when they are in the presence of others.[13]

Each category should be sorted according to this aspect. One might find, for example, that teachers express different thoughts on the value of audiovisual equipment in the presence of school administrators or "instructional technologists" than in the presence of other teachers. Or one might find that they say one thing when alone and quite another when they are with others.

5. *Direct statement or indirect inference?* Observers code items that both directly and indirectly support or contradict their hypotheses. They would be wise to carefully analyze and summarize both the direct and indirect evidence in the intensive analysis stage of their research.

In regard to the hypothesis "control is a dominant concern among attendants," the observer in the state institution study coded items that were direct ("You can't give them everything they want or you won't be able to control them.") and indirect (residents forced to sit quietly throughout the day). If he had found that direct statements supported the hypothesis but that indirect statements and behavior did not, he would have a variety of options open to him. He could discard the hypothesis; he could conclude that attendants say one thing and do another; or he could decide to reevaluate the criteria he used to code his data. For example, he might consider the possibility that certain observations were related to something other than control or that when attendants speak of "control" they mean something other than what the observer understands by that word.

One would certainly hope that the hypotheses would be supported in a variety of ways. When that support is not there, the observer must go over his or her data in depth again in an attempt to seek a new understanding.

6. *Who said and did what?* The observer will sometimes make generalizations about all subjects on the basis of what one or a few of them said or did. For example, a "key informant" may speak so much about a certain topic that it appears throughout the notes despite the fact that no one else addressed it. For this reason, the researcher should pay special attention to the source of the data on which he or she bases conclusions.

Sort the data for each hypothesis according to individual subjects or sets of subjects if you have observed different groups or in different settings. If you learn that all subjects express a certain perspective or do things the same way, fine. If not, you can speculate on the reasons why some are different or at least qualify your findings with "some of the subjects" or "most of the subjects."

7. *Were the subjects telling the truth?* The participant observer is often faced with the possibility that his or her subjects may not have told the truth when they related their feelings or reported past incidents.[14] He or she may find that subjects contradict themselves from one day to the next. In the research conducted at the state institution, for example, an attendant could on one occasion state, "These here are all low grades," and on another, "Yea, they're dumb like a fox."

Yet the fact that people do not always "tell the truth" does not mean that their intention is to lie, if by lying we mean conscious deception. As previously emphasized, people are inconsistent. Their perspectives, feelings, and beliefs change as they move from one situation to another. Even "objective" incidents are perceived selectively. Thus, Dean and Whyte note, "*The informant's statement represents merely the perception of the informant, filtered and modified by his cognitive and emotional reactions and reported through his personal verbal usages.*"[15]

Accept as a fundamental premise the concept that there is no truth, only perspectives and deceptions. Once you have identified a deceptive statement as such by an intuitive process that entails an examination of a subject's motivations, you should separate that statement from the rest of your data and analyze it as an additional key for understanding what is important in the eyes of your subjects. When it is clear that there has been a deliberate attempt to deceive, it is also clear that the subject matter of that deception is important in a way that other subject matter is not.

OBSERVER BIAS

An issue that is often raised in regard to participant observation research is whether the researcher has allowed his or her own biases to color the findings.[16] To an extent, the observer cannot avoid bias. Since data, including that collected by quantitative methods, are never self-explanatory, the researcher must necessarily draw upon his or her own knowledge and experience to make sense out of what he or she has recorded.

Although a certain amount of bias is unavoidable, there are several ways in which the researcher can minimize its effects. Some researchers maintain a record of both their own biases and the processes by which they reach their conclusions throughout the course of their studies. This record enables them to *discount* their findings: to understand them in context.[17] Stronger safeguards may be found in the use of teams of observers to conduct research or in the use of colleagues to read and comment on field notes and research reports.

In any case, the researcher should ask her- or himself a series of questions as he or she concludes the study. Has he or she presented likeable subjects in a favorable light and unlikable subjects in an unfavorable one? Has she or he overidentified with the subjects' view of the world?[18] Or has he or she smugly dismissed subjects' perspectives without first having understood them? In short, an understanding of one's data requires some understanding of one's perspectives, logic, and assumptions.

*   *   *

The preceding three chapters have been concerned with the three stages of participant observation research: pre-field work, work in the field, and working with data. We have tried to expose the reader to the problems and promises of participant observation. Hopefully, we have instilled in the reader, and especially the novice, an excitement for this type of research and a desire to "go to the people."

In the remainder of Part One, we focus our attention on other qualitative research methods. The next chapter looks at personal documents and unstructured interviewing. Those who are specifically interested in participant observation are encouraged to skip to Part Two, and particularly to Chapter 7, which deals with the presentation of findings, before moving to Chapters 5 and 6. Following this order will avoid a break in continuity and allow the reader to follow the research process from the initial conception of a participant observation project to the final research report.

NOTES

1. For accounts of how different researchers have analyzed their data, see Fred Davis, "Stories and sociology," *Urban Life and Culture* **3** (October): 310–316, 1974; Jacqueline P. Wiseman, "The research web," *Urban Life and Culture* **3** (October): 317–328, 1974; Sherri Cavan, "Seeing social structure in a rural setting," *Urban Life and Culture* **3** (October): 329–346, 1974; and Julius A. Roth, "Turning adversity to account," *Urban Life and Culture* **3** (October): 347–361, 1974.

2. See Barney Glaser and Anselm Strauss, *The Discovery of Grounded Theory: Strategies for Qualitative Research* (Chicago: Aldine, 1967). Also see Barney Glaser, "The constant comparative method of qualitative analysis," *Social Problems*, **XII**: 436–445, 1965.

3. See A. Circourel, *Method and Measurement in Sociology* (New York: Free Press, 1964).

4. See Blanche Geer, "First days in the field," in Philip Hammond (Ed.), *Sociologists at Work* (New York: Basic Books, 1964).

5. See William Foote Whyte, *Street Corner Society* (Chicago: University of Chicago Press, 1955, 2nd ed.).

6. Julius Roth, "Hired hand research," *The American Sociologist* (August): pp. 190–196, 1966. Harold Garfinkel, *Studies in Ethnomethodology* (Englewood Cliffs, N. J.: Prentice-Hall, 1967), pp. 18–24, offers many insights into general problems involved in coding procedures.

7. See Howard S. Becker et al., *Making the Grade: The Academic Side of College Life* (New York: Wiley, 1968), pp. 121–128.

8. Not all qualitative methodologists would agree with this statement. For example, see the discussion of "Analytic Induction" by Florian Znaniecki, *The Method of Sociology* (New York: Farrar and Rinehart, 1934); W. S. Robinson, "The logical structure of analytic induction," *American Sociological Review*, **XVI**: 812–818, 1951; Alfred R. Lindesmith, S. Kirson Weinberg, and W. S. Robinson, "Two comments and rejoinder to 'The logical structure of analytic induction,' " *American Sociological Review*, **XVII**: 492–494, 1952; and Ralph H. Turner, "The quest for universals in sociological research," *American Sociological Review*, **XVIII**: 604–611, 1953.

9. See Howard S. Becker, "Problems of inference and proof in participant observation," *American Sociological Review*, **XXIII**: 652–660, 1958; and Howard S. Becker et al., *Boys in White* (Chicago: University of Chicago Press, 1961). We have drawn heavily from the fine work of Becker and his colleagues in this section. Also see George J. McCall, "Data quality control in participant observation," in George J. McCall and J. L. Simmons, *Issues in Participant Observation: A Text and Reader* (Reading, Mass.: Addison-Wesley, 1969), pp. 128–141.

10. For clarification, you may want to summarize your data in table form.

11. See Chris Argyris, "Diagnosing defenses against the outsider," *Journal of Social Issues*, **VIII**: 24–34, 1952; Morris S. and Charlotte Green Schwartz, "Problems in participant observation," *American Journal of Sociology*, **LX**: 343–354, 1955; and Arthur J. Vidich,

"Participant observation and the collection and interpretation of data," *American Journal of Sociology,* **LX**: 354–360, 1955.

12.   See Robert Janes, "A note on phases of the community role of the participant observer," *American Sociological Review,* **XXVI**: 446–450, 1961; and Severyn T. Bruyn, *The Human Perspective in Sociology: The Methodology of Participant Observation* (Englewood Cliffs, N. J.: Prentice-Hall, 1966), pp. 206–207.

13.   See Becker, "Problems of inference and proof," and Becker et al., *Boys in White.* There is massive evidence that the setting and the presence of different people make vast differences in what people say and do. See Irwin Deutscher, *What We Say/What We Do* (Glenview, Ill.: Scott, Foresman, 1973).

14.   See John P. Dean and William Foote Whyte, " 'How do you know if the informant is telling the truth,' " *Human Organization,* **XVII** no. 2: 34–38, 1958. Also see McCall and Simmons, *Participant Observation,* pp. 114–115, for a summary of Vidich and Bensman's points.

15.   Dean and Whyte, "How do you know," p. 34.

16.   See Vidich, "Participant observation."

17.   Deutscher, *What We Say,* pp. 5–6.

18.   See S. M. Miller, "The participant observer and 'over-rapport,' " *American Sociological Review,* **XVII**: 97–99, 1952; Herbert J. Gans, *The Urban Villagers* (New York: Free Press, 1962), pp. 336–346; Bruyn, *Human Perspective,* pp. 229–230; and McCall, "Data quality control," pp. 132–133.

CHAPTER FIVE

Personal Documents and Unstructured Interviewing

This chapter treats personal documents: what they are, how to collect them, and how to interpret them. We use the phrase *"personal documents" to refer to an individual's descriptive, first-person account of the whole or a part of his or her life or an individual's reflection on a specific event or topic.*[1] More concretely, we discuss such materials as autobiographies, diaries, letters, and long open-ended interviews that are recorded verbatim.[2] The chapter begins with a short discussion of different types of personal documents and moves on to discuss how to collect them with an emphasis on one type: data obtained through open-ended interviewing.

TYPES OF PERSONAL DOCUMENTS

Solicited Versus Unsolicited

It is useful, for our purposes, to think of all personal documents as being either solicited by the researcher or unsolicited. Solicited personal documents are those that are produced at the request of the researcher. This kind is illustrated by the person who "tells his or her own story" to a researcher in a series of open-ended interviews. Unsolicited documents, on the other hand, are created by the subject either for his or her own use (a personal diary) or at the request of some other party (student compositions). In solicited personal documents, the researcher actively participates in the production of the document and must consequently employ special techniques and procedures. In unsolicited personal documents, the researcher makes use of documents that already exist. His or her task is confined to the selection, location, analysis, and presentation of such documents.

The Motivation of the Author *or Subject*

Personal documents also differ according to the motivation of the person producing them. A person may write an autobiography for a number of reasons: to gain a sense of immortality, to teach others, to gain understanding of self, to justify actions to others, for monetary gain, for esthetic enjoyment, to influence the actions of others, or simply because they were coerced into writing.[3] *Different motivations will obviously produce documents with different thrusts.* An autobiography written for a popular audience, for example, would most likely stress the more entertaining and "salable" aspects of one's life at the expense of the mundane and truly personal. *All personal documents are valuable,* however, once the researcher has taken the motivations into account. If nothing else, they reveal what the author thinks that others will find exciting or entertaining.

Comprehensive Versus Limited

As suggested earlier, personal documents may encompass a person's entire life or may focus on a single incident, time period, or theme. Differences according to this dimension usually determine how the materials are used. Life histories are generally presented in a long narrative as an autonomous source of understanding, while more limited personal documents are merged together to provide a composite picture of a specific topic or to supplement participant observation data.

Edited Versus Complete

Personal documents may be presented either in their original form or, more likely, in an edited and reorganized version. In some instances they may be used selectively to illustrate a point a researcher is making.

Anonymous Versus Authored

The author, or subject, of a personal document may reveal or conceal his or her name from the reading audience. For a number of reasons, we feel that *it is best to use pseudonyms and fictitious names for researcher-induced documents.* In the first place, most people will tend to be more guarded and less candid in their recollections, opinions, and accounts if they know that their names will be revealed. In the second place, the use of pseudonyms precludes the possibility that a person will use documents as vehicles for self-aggrandizement or retribution against others. In the third place, authored personal documents may cause unforeseen embarrassment to the author or to others and raise certain ethical, if not legal, implications for the researcher. In spite of these apparently sound points, many excellent and intimate personal documents have been published that have used the authors' real names.

Forms

In addition to the distinctions we have already made, personal documents can be classified according to their "commonsense" forms. The *intimate diary* is probably the most revealing and private type of personal account. Some have suggested that the spontaneously produced and continuously written diary is the *sine quo non* of personal documents in terms of intimacy and self-exploration. Anne Frank, in the introduction to her own diary, wrote:

> I hope I shall be able to confide in you [the diary] completely, as I have never been able to do in anyone before. . . .[4]

The intimate diary is an excellent source of data because of the level of intimacy and because it contains reflections on one's immediate experiences.

Although the diary is epitomized by the stereotype of the adolescent girl who withdraws to the quiet of her room to remove her diary from her hiding place and to bare her soul, there are other types of valuable ongoing personal documents. People in business or on trips, for example, often maintain *logs* of their activities and movements. These records are sometimes accompanied by reflections on events and places and notations on meetings and money spent. And while they cannot approach the intimate diary in completeness and depth, they can provide an important source for understanding how people structure, and comprehend their worlds.

Some people also keep ongoing *developmental records* of the progress of their children.[5] In these documents, parents reflect upon a specific person in their lives, their child, and give us an insight into their definitions of development, parenthood, and childhood.

Another source of personal documents, and one that has been largely neglected by social scientists, is *private letters.* Since a letter often represents an attempt of the author to share with intimates things that he or she has experienced, it can lend important insight into the perspectives of people and the nature of their relationships. The soldier on the battlefield, the grandparent thousands of miles from his or her family, the urban migrant—all share their sadness and their joy through letters.

Less personal forms of communication can also reveal an individual's view of the world. *Memos,* for example, are an available and potentially valuable form of document. Even *public letters,* such as letters to the editor and the "Dear Abby" variety, show how people understand issues and problems despite the fact that their authors are generally less spontaneous and more guarded than in other forms of correspondence. Note, however, that the nature of those letters that are selected for publication are not necessarily representative of all of the letters which an editor or journalist receives. In fact, they probably tell us as much about the editor or journalist as they do about their authors.

Another less spontaneous form of personal documents is *solicited compositions* or short narratives that cover a specific topic. These may or may not be created specifically for the researcher. Few people will ever forget the "what I did over the summer" type compositions annually written on the first day of elementary school. The strength of such solicited compositions lies in the fact that they are focused on a single event or topic and may be assembled for analysis.

Autobiographies, both solicited and unsolicited, represent another form of personal documents. Here the author writes a comprehensive account of his or her entire life or a major part of it. The researcher may, in the case of solicited autobiographies, facilitate the endeavor by giving the author some direction. In the classic study *The Jack Roller,* for example, Shaw asked Stanley, the author, to write his own story with the aid of a list of crucial events in his life.[6] When Shaw found the account to be inadequate in detail, he directed Stanley to areas that were in need of further elaboration.

The last form of personal documents we discuss are those in which the subjects tell their story to researchers in an *open-ended interview.* Note that we refer here to an essentially unstructured interview where researchers attempt to capture the words of their subjects and not merely a summary of responses. A personal document is no longer a personal document when the wording of the material passes from the subject's control to that of the researcher.

In this section we have attempted to present neither an exhaustive list of the forms of personal documents nor a precise classification scheme. We have intended, rather, to give the reader an idea of what we mean by personal documents.

HOW TO COLLECT PERSONAL DOCUMENTS

How to Obtain Documents

The researcher who seeks to examine unsolicited personal documents is faced with the single, although often difficult, task of locating such materials. While there are literally millions of personal documents "waiting to be found," *the researcher will amost always have to imaginatively and aggressively search them out.* Thus, one who is passive in this endeavor is likely to remain empty-handed.

One of the simplest and most effective ways to locate personal documents is to place an ad in the paper describing the kinds of materials you want and the uses to which they'll be put. Thomas and Znaniecki, in their classic study, *The Polish Peasant*, ran ads in the newspaper to find letters to Polish immigrants in one of the first attempts to employ personal documents in social science research.[7] You may be surprised to find that many people would rather put their letters and memorabilia to some useful purpose than burn them. Some people will even be willing to share with the researcher such intimate documents as a diary. After all, diaries are sometimes written with the expectation that someone, preferably unknown to the author, will read them at some future time.

You might also be able to obtain documents from people who receive a large volume of mail in their everyday work. Newspaper editors, celebrities, and "advice to the lovelorn" columnists undoubtedly receive more mail than they know what to do with and may be willing to share some of it with you if they realize it will be used for research purposes. Many local historical societies also maintain files of letters and documents that make extremely interesting reading. Even organizational files may contain personnel forms, dossiers, and biographical information that reveal how people define themselves or their positions. Finally, friends and acquaintances may be able to provide you with an adequate supply of personal documents.

In addition to interviewing, which will be discussed at length in the next section, there are a number of ways to collect solicited personal documents. Some of these, such as composition writing in a class, were suggested in our previous discussion. Others require a bit of imagination on the part of the researcher. Allport, for example, ran a competition for the best essay on "My life in Germany before and after January 30, 1933" for a study reported in 1941.[8] He received 200 manuscripts averaging 100 pages in length in response to this competition.

Personal Documents Collected Through Interviewing

We have touched on only a few ideas of how to obtain and solicit personal documents. We would now like to discuss at length one particularly important way to collect personal documents; namely, in-depth interviewing for the purpose of constructing autobiographies. Our purpose here, as in the chapters on participant observation, is simply to familiarize you with one approach to collecting data: we want you to see how we do it. While we discuss interviewing for autobiographies the points we make will be helpful to other forms of open-ended interviewing.

Remember, as we said at the beginning of this book, *research is a craft*. To be a successful researcher is to be something more than a technician. You must create technique rather than slavishly follow procedures. What we share with you in the following pages is what has worked for us and what seems congruent with our conception of social science research and our own ethics.

We illustrate the points we make with our own experiences in extended interviewing. We mention studies conducted with two subjects: Ed Murphy and Jane Fry. The former is labelled "mentally retarded" and has spent a good part of his life in state schools. Jane Fry defines herself as a "transsexual" and has been in and out of several psychiatric facilities.[9] A segment of her autobiography is included in Chapter 9.

While our illustrations are drawn from people on the margins of society, people whom most sociologists would call deviant, the techniques that we have used are no different from those that would be used with any so-called typical person. We faced neither special rapport problems nor a reluctance to participate on the part of our subjects. Our subjects confirmed our position that all people have at least one important story to tell—their own—and that they want to share it with others.

How to Choose a Subject.   Although everyone does have at least one good story to tell, some people have better stories and make better research partners than others. For example, the many hours of interviewing, which research of this kind entails, requires a firm commitment on the part of the subject to see the project through to its end. Moreover, it is essential that the subject have free time to devote to the interviewing. The practical demands on some people's lives preclude participation in a venture of this nature.

Another, less concrete, criterion that you may use to select subjects is their ability and willingness to verbalize their past and present experiences and feelings. People simply do not have an equal ability and willingness to make vivid the details and meaning of their lives. And while a good interviewer may be able to bring out the best in subjects, he or she cannot perform miracles on people who are not free with their words. Casual conversations with an individual prior to the beginning of a project can, of course, give you a fair idea of what kind of subject he or she will make.

Another obvious criterion that you may apply in choosing research subjects is whether or not they are the "kind" of people in whom you are interested. As a student of society, you may be interested in people who are marginal in their life styles or who have had certain experiences. Take note, however, that people are not always what they appear to be. The "kind" of person a subject is may have little relevance to the kind of life he or she leads. And as you get to know any person, aspects of her or his life that you never imagined existed may come to the forefront. Thus, we are familiar with one research project conducted among people who had recently dropped out of college. What the researcher found was that this fact played an insignificant role in the lives of the "dropouts!"

Finally, you would be wise to avoid the selection of a subject with whom you have a professional or otherwise special relationship. If you are a clinician, for example, stay away from your own clients. Since the professionals in most professional-client relationships have certain rewards and punishments at their disposal, clients have a major stake in fostering impressions that are in their own best interests. You might also avoid anyone who could potentially be your client. Professionals, after all, operate under certain assumptions and predispositions which color their interpretation of what potential clients say and do. In short, it is difficult for them to take certain people's perspectives seriously.

It should also go without saying that close friends or relatives make poor subjects. Here the problem is that the researcher may overidentify with the perspectives of his or her research partner. If nothing else, you should at least take these considerations into account when you choose a subject and later try to interpret the meanings of his or her words.

How to Find a Subject. Most subjects are not "found," but rather, emerge in the course of the researcher's everyday activities. Once you have developed a certain frame of mind, you will find yourself measuring people according to their appropriateness as subjects: "Now that person would make an excellent subject."

Of course, the social scientist who lives his or her life in limited circles, in the university setting, is less likely to find the "right" kind of subject. *It is through involvement in other communities that one establishes the kind of reputation and contacts necessary to meet and recruit ideal research partners.*[10] It is also in other communities that one can familiarize oneself with the places and symbols of a potential subject's life.

Ed Murphy worked at a local branch of the Association for Retarded Children when we first met him. He was recommended to one of the authors as a guest speaker for a course in architecture and social science. Ed was articulate in his presentation. Students in the course were being asked to design a living center for the "retarded" and he was there to tell them what he thought appropriate. His words revealed the obvious: that "they," the "retarded," want the same things that other people want in a living situation and that to think that "they" needed a specially designed residential facility was the concretization of our own preconceived notions of what the "retarded" are like. In fact, the word "retarded" lost meaning as Ed spoke.

We kept in touch with Ed after that experience. Since we were familiar with the institutions where he had lived and the organization where he worked, we had a number of things in common and had frequent opportunities to run into him. Ed was more than an acquaintance when we finally began the project.

The same author first met Jane Fry when she came to speak to a class taught by a friend with a group from a gay liberation project. Jane's presentation, as Ed's, was striking in the insight it provided and in the vividness of her description of her life. It wasn't until some time later that the author met Jane at a meeting at a local crisis intervention center and through that meeting and others solidified their relationship. By the time that he finally approached her to participate in the research project he had strong feelings that she would make an excellent subject and she had a strong trust in him.

How to Approach a Subject.   It is perhaps more sensible to *allow the research project to gradually evolve as a mutual undertaking* than to directly approach a potential subject with the frightening question, "Do you want to write your autobiography with me?" *Come on slow;* tell potential subjects that you think they have something important to say:

> You've had some interesting experiences and you tell about them in an interesting way. I bet that your autobiography would make good reading.

Later, after you have given the potential subject a chance to think about the project, you can approach the matter directly. Most people will be flattered by the prospect of their stories being the subjects of research projects.

Explain the nature of the research. Assure subjects that their only task will be to tell about their own life and experiences. If your prospective subject is interested, schedule a time and place to meet to work out the details. If, on the other hand, he or she is uninterested or skeptical, you can try to coax him or her, but, as suggested earlier, only at the risk of beginning a project that will never come to a satisfactory conclusion.

We followed the above approach in our research with Ed Murphy and Jane Fry. We met with them a few times before we seriously raised the idea of the project. Interestingly enough, both had privately contemplated the idea of writing their autobiographies before we had ever approached them. Jane, in fact, had attempted to write her life story several years earlier, only to have abandoned the project after having written a few pages. Both Ed and Jane were enthusiastic about the endeavor at the end of our first serious discussion with them.

Issues to Discuss at the Early Stages of the Project.   During the early stages of the project, the researcher should attempt to clarify any issues that may be on the subject's mind or that may arise later as a source of misunderstanding. These issues should be formally addressed at a special meeting between the researcher and the subject.

Don't be overpowering. Allow your subjects to speak their concerns.

Remember that *it is at the beginning of the project that the tone of your relationship is established.* If you want a free and open relationship, you should be prepared to give subjects a say in how you will conduct the project.

The following topics would seem to be the most easily misunderstood and, consequently, the most important to clarify: (1) your motives and intentions; (2) anonymity; (3) final say; (4) royalties; (5) the overall plan; and (6) the logistics of getting started.

1. *Your motives and intentions.* Most potential subjects will wonder what you hope to get out of the project. There may even be fears and suspicions that the final product will be used to their disadvantage. In order to deal with these concerns, you should openly discuss your motives and intentions early in the project. It is usually enough just to raise these matters to put your subjects' minds at ease, especially if they already know you. In any case, you should, as in participant observation research, strive to be open and honest.

If you are a social scientist, your motivation for entering the project will probably have something to do with a desire to present your subject's views and experiences to others, to develop understandings of people and situations that you did not understand before, to create social change, and to make some contribution to your field or to advance professionally. If you are a student you will have similar or additional motives. Tell your subject these things. Most subjects will be able to identify with educational and academic goals and will be more than willing to be partners in that kind of a project.

Although you yourself will probably be unclear on the final outcome of the endeavor, you should explain to your subject your expectations. If you intend to make it a term project or if you hope to be able to publish a book or papers on the basis of the research, discuss where you think the work will appear and whose name will be on the title. Thus, in most instances, you would explain that the work would not, in most probability, be published commercially, but rather, for a limited audience. You should also mention that you neither intend nor expect to make a large profit through the materials you produce.

Be optimistic in regard to the outcome of the project. Tell your subject that you would not be willing to spend the time that the research will require were it not for the hope that something important would come of it. You should not, however, be so optimistic that you create unrealistic expectations in your subject. Mention the potential difficulties you may face in finding a publisher and in seeing the project through to the end. Most potential subjects will be willing to accept the uncertainty if there is any likelihood that the project will come to something.

After this discussion, your subject will probably still be unclear on certain points. However, you will have taken a step toward developing the open and trusting relationship which the project will require.

2. *Anonymity.* As mentioned earlier, anonymity is an important issue in autobiographical research. This topic should be raised with the subject in the preliminary stages of the research. Some subjects will, of course, want their names to appear in print. If the subjects have strong feelings in this regard, you would probably be wise to go along with them. And if they do not, you should disguise the names of people and places in any written materials. In the research conducted with Jane Fry, it was initially understood that her name would appear in any published works. As the project progressed, however, the potential difficulties led to a mutual agreement to substitute Jane's name with a pseudonym.

3. *Final say.* One way to strengthen subjects' confidence in you is to offer them the opportunity to read and discuss with you any written materials before they are sent to publishers for consideration. Some researchers go as far as to give their subjects final veto power over what is or is not published. In our own research, we have guaranteed subjects the right to review and comment upon any written works. In most instances, who has the final say will not be a major issue. Assuming that the researcher and subject have developed a relationship characterized by openness and trust, both the researcher's fear that the product of so much effort will be rejected by the subject and the subject's fear that he or she will be grossly misrepresented by the researcher are probably unfounded. Yet this is a potentially explosive matter and should be clarified at the beginning of the project.

4. *Royalties.* While the subject of royalties from published works may appear trivial or farfetched to researchers at first, they should discuss the matter with their subjects before they begin their work on projects. Such mundane matters are often the source of suspicion and hard feelings. In the spirit of partnership, we share royalties with subjects, with them receiving the larger percentage. Our partners, like many autobiographical subjects, have been poor and, to put it plainly, have needed the money. And since they have neither had their names appear in print nor have received professional credit, they deserve far more than we do

in terms of material gain. Of course, the research partners may decide to donate any money that may accrue from the project to a non-profit organization.

The researcher should at some point consider consulting a lawyer about royalties. What the subject gets should be a matter of legal contract and not of charity. Moreover, even small royalty checks may produce more problems than benefits for subjects. If, for example, subjects receive public assistance, royalties can affect their eligibility status. With the aid of a lawyer, special trust funds can be set up to get around these kinds of problems.

As our earlier discussion might indicate, we think it unwise to pay subjects to be interviewed. Remember that the endeavor should approximate a research partnership rather than an employer-employee relationship.

5. *The overall plan.* You should clarify to your subject the process you intend to follow—the overall plan—in the beginning stages of the research. For example, you should explain such matters as whether or not the interviewing sessions will be taped, who will transcribe the tapes, and who will bear the expenses of having them transcribed. We have always borne such expenses ourselves or have taken out loans to be repaid with the first royalties.

The subject can also be given some idea of how you intend to structure the interview, how long and how much time the process will take, and how you intend to work with the data. Thus, you would explain how the subject's words will be presented and edited.

6. *The logistics of getting started.* Finally, you should work out any additional matters in regard to the logistics of getting started. You will, for example, have to find a convenient meeting time and place. In the research conducted with Ed Murphy and Jane Fry, we chose to do the interviewing in our private office after working hours. This setting allowed us to work without interruption and in a comfortable atmosphere, both of which are important to the success of a project.

Once you have mutually decided on a place and time to work, set up a number of appointments and get working. If you find that the place or time is inconvenient, change to others. Always be sensitive to your subject's schedule and preferences.

The Researcher-Subject Relationship. We have already emphasized our position that *the interviewer-subject relationship should consist of a partnership.* Unlike participant observation research, the project belongs to both the researcher and the subject in autobiographical studies.

In this type of research, interviewers are far less concerned with concealing their own feelings and positions. After all, since the subject is expected to bear his or her soul—to open up completely—there has to be some exchange. *It is probably unfair and undoubtedly counterproductive for the researcher to completely hold back his or her own feelings.* At the same time, it is probably unwise for him or her to offer an opinion vehemently on everything that comes up. Somewhere between total self-disclosure and total detachment lies the "happy medium," which the researcher should strive to meet. Perhaps the best advice is to hold back in the interview and open up some in other situations. If researchers believe that they have had an influence on what subjects have to say, they should weigh that influence at the conclusion of their studies.

The researcher should also be willing to participate sometimes in the everyday life of the subject. This contact enhances rapport and familiarizes you with the persons and places in the subject's life. Although the here and now, the mundane, is an important part of everyone's life, people are often too close to their everyday experiences to reflect upon them. A knowledge of that life on the part of the interviewer can facilitate discussion and stimulate questions on areas that might otherwise have been ignored.

The researcher may also choose to play an advocacy role in the lives of his or her subjects both during and after the interviewing. As mentioned earlier, one's subject is likely to be one of society's "underdogs," powerless by virtue of his or her socio-economic status or label. The researcher, on the other hand, is likely to be secure and powerful in his or her position at a university. For this reason, the researcher can and, we think, should advocate on behalf of the subject where necessary and desired. When Jane Fry was discriminated against by a junior college, for example, one of the authors found a lawyer for her and put her in contact with a mental health rights group.

The Interview Situation.   There are actually few exact rules which may be offered to help interviewers in their research.[11] If you understand your goals, your subject, and the interview situation, there is wide latitude in what you can do. What is ultimately important is not your procedures, but rather, your frame of reference:

My job . . . is to bring alive to the extent I possibly can a number of lives . . . entrusted to a person like me, an outsider, a stranger, a listener, an observer, a doctor, a curious . . . fellow who one mountaineer described as 'always coming back and not seeming to know exactly what he wants to hear or know.'[12]

Our goal in this section, then, is modest. We simply tell you what we have done. If you have the proper frame of reference, some of the following suggestions may be helpful.

Frequency and Length of the Interviews. Your interviews should be long enough to adequately cover the topics that are raised but not so long that either you or the subject is fatigued. In general, it takes some time to get started, to get the dialogue to center on important topics. Once you are on a certain topic, such as high school, let your subject talk her- or himself out. You should, therefore, allocate rather large periods of time for each interview. Anything less than one hour is too short. You need at least two hours or more to explore any topic in depth. And anything longer than about four hours will probably burn the subject out. You can, however, go longer if you take a long break, perhaps for lunch, after a few hours.

The amount of time an interview takes will, of course, vary from day to day. Schedule a three- to four-hour block of time. If the interview is not particularly productive, you can always end early.

The frequency with which you conduct your interviews will be determined by your time schedules and your general inclinations. With unlimited time you could probably interview daily. In order to preserve some continuity in the sessions, we would suggest that you meet no less than weekly. It is too difficult to pick up pieces when you are not interviewing regularly.

Whatever the case, you should be flexible and sensitive to how the interviews are progressing. When, as often happens, the interviews become monotonous, you should be prepared to take a week or two off. It is also a good idea to talk about how the project is going on a weekly basis.

Recording Interviews. Although we earlier advised the participant observer to rely on memory to gather data (Chapter 3), we would advise the interviewer to use a tape recorder whenever possible. In the first place, the interviewer's data, unlike the participant observer's, consists almost entirely of words, words, we might add, that come throughout the interview and that are overwhelming in volume. The interviewer cannot sit back to watch for awhile and is deprived of the lapses in conversations that the participant observer enjoys. It is entirely possible that without electronic recording equipment many of the most important autobiographical studies would never have been undertaken. Thus, Oscar Lewis wrote in his introduction to *The Children of Sanchez,* "The tape recorder, used in taking down the life stories in this book, has made possible the beginning of a new kind of literature of social realism."[13] In the second place, the interviewers are involved with people who have a fair understanding of the nature of the project and, indeed, are partners in it. Since they know that their words are being weighed, they are unlikely to be alarmed by the presence of a tape recorder. In the third place, the interview situation is already artificial in the sense that the subjects are not going about their everyday activities in their everyday setting. They are thus continually reminded of their status as subjects. And, finally, the interviewer and subject have an extended period of time in which to develop rapport and mutual trust and in which to become accustomed to a tape recorder. Note that participant observers must interact with a number of subjects, some of whom never completely trust them.

The foregoing remarks should not make us lose sight of the fact that most people's memories are better than they suspect and that the interviewer can forego the use of a tape recorder if subjects have strong feelings about it. We ourselves have relied on our memories and participant observation techniques to record the substance of brief, one-hour, interviews. Others, such as Thomas Cottle, regularly conduct interviews without the use of a tape recorder.[14]

If the interviewers do decide to tape record their subjects' words, they should attempt to minimize whatever negative effects its presence might have. Use either a small and quiet recorder or place it out of sight. The microphone should be unobtrusive and sensitive enough so that the subject does not have to speak directly into it. Finally, you should use a tape recorder that will accommodate long-playing tapes. There are few things as disruptive to the flow of a conversation as having to constantly check and turn over the tapes on a recorder.

A final note of caution: *make sure that your equipment is functioning properly before each session.* One can only imagine the frustration one would feel were several hours of exciting dialogue lost due to malfunctioning of the equipment.

How to Structure the Interview.   During the first few meetings especially, the interviewer must take care to allow the subject to speak her or his concerns and at his or her own speed. He or she is most likely to be self-conscious at this point in time and most guarded in his or her personal feelings and experiences. *You would be wise to solidify your relationship with the subject before you probe sensitive and painful periods of his or her life.*

Probably the best way to begin the first interview is to question your subject about areas that he or she already mentioned and that you know she or he is willing to discuss. Let the subject take over from there. If he or she wants to offer opinions rather than to describe experiences, allow this. If he or she wants to talk about what you consider to be an insignificant part of his or her life, let that occur. In the first few interviews with Ed Murphy, the interviewers questioned him about his life at a state institution. Ed had previously discussed his experiences at the institution in front of classes of students and was most comfortable with this topic. He was, however, initially reluctant to open up on certain aspects of his institutionalized life. The researchers waited patiently until they had established the kind of relationship in which they could confront him with this reluctance before pressing him on these aspects.

As the project progresses, you will find that the periods of your subject's life have been related out of sequence and that many topics have been raised but not fully discussed. This discovery should not be a source of concern as long as you make note of what has and what has not been covered. After each session, for example, you should write down what was discussed in depth and what was casually mentioned. You should also, at some time, ask your subject to write a chronology of the events in his or her life. You can later structure the interviews in such a way as to cover all of these topics. In the research with Ed Murphy, the interviewers prepared a rough agenda before each meeting.

Jane Fry was asked to write a detailed chronology of her life, which was used to provide a framework for the interviewing and a mechanism to keep track of what had been covered. During the last few interviews, Jane and the researcher actually went over the chronology point by point and reviewed what had been discussed in an attempt to discover any forgotten items.

Create an Atmosphere Conducive to Openness.   The interviewer must be able to create an atmosphere in which the subject feels comfortable enough to talk freely and openly. In the preceding section, for example, we suggested that the interviewer must be responsive to the sensitivities of the subject in order to develop a relationship of trust. To probe aggressively into aspects of people's lives that are painful for them to discuss is both callous and counterproductive.

A free and open atmosphere is something that must be created by the researcher. For this reason, we offer the following suggestions that, even though they are related to inoffensive social interaction, are all too often forgotten by the researcher in the attempt to solicit information.

1. *Don't interrupt.* Even if she or he is relatively uninterested in the topic, the interviewer, like the participant observer, should sit back and listen to what the subject has to say. Once there is a convenient break in the conversation, you can gently change the subject. A good way to do this is to refer to something that was previously mentioned:

> You said something a few days ago when we were talking. Could you tell me more about it?

When the subjects do say something important, let the conversation flow.[15] Encourage them to continue with sympathetic gestures and relevant questions. And don't repeatedly interrupt or take them on tangents just because they mention something in which you are interested. You should explore each topic and it's sociological implications fully before you move to anything else. You can always make note of something and return to it later.

2. *Pay attention.* Although a tape recorder can capture everything that your subject says, you should resist the temptation to not listen during your interview sessions with the subject. After all, a major part of the subject's motivation to enter into the project was her or his belief and your assurances that he or she had something important and interesting to say. And if you want him or her to maintain a commitment to the endeavor, you had better support this belief by paying proper attention to every word.

There are, to be sure, other reasons for being a good listener. A good listener can structure the conversation: ask the right questions and solicit information about topics that haven't been covered. Perhaps the most important point is that to pay attention is to learn while you listen and to experience things in a new and different way. Cottle expressed this best when he wrote:

> If there is a rule about this form of research it might be reduced to something as simple as pay attention. Pay attention to what the person does and

says and feels; pay attention to the scene, the streets, rooms, textures, color and lighting; pay attention to what is evoked by these conversations and perceptions, particularly when one's mind wanders so very far away; and finally, pay attention to the responses of those who might, through one's work, hear these people. Paying attention implies an openness, not any special or metaphysical kind of openness, but merely a watch on oneself, a self-consciousness, a belief that everything one takes in from the outside and experiences within one's own interior is worthy of consideration and essential for understanding and honoring those whom one encounters.[16]

3. *Be nonevaluative.* As subjects begin to share more and more experiences and feelings with the interviewer, as they begin to let down their "public front," they inevitably become self-conscious in the interviewer's presence. They typically preface or conclude intimate conversations with such statements as: "You must think I'm terrible for doing that," and "This makes me sound like a real weirdo."

If, as is hoped, the subject is to continue to share these experiences and feelings with the interviewer, to regard her or him as a confidant, then the interviewer must make a conscious effort to refrain from negative statements about the subject's behavior or worth as a human being. Encouraging people to open up and then demeaning them with the very information you solicit causes them to withdraw from the relationship or, at the very least, to relate only those things that they think you will consider admirable.

Perhaps the best way to control yourself in this respect is to attempt to understand your subjects for what they are and not to judge them in your own mind. You should communicate this position to your subjects. Tell them that your intention is not to criticize or to judge, but rather, to understand. You should also reassure your subjects that they are "all right" in your eyes, especially after they have revealed something very personal or embarrassing. Throughout the conversation, intersperse comments like: "I know what you mean," "That's happened to me," "I've often wanted to do that myself," and "A friend of mine did the same thing."

If you find that you cannot condone something and must state your position, do so gently and empathically. Voice your disagreement, but add that you can understand her or his opinion.

4. *Be reflective.* In general, interviewers must examine themselves and, in particular, the meaning of their words and gestures. They must guard against smugness. And while they should be sympathetic and empathic to subjects, they should also carefully avoid "patronizing

actions, undue cordiality or ingratiation."[17] Robert Coles strikes at the heart of the matter when he observes:

> Somehow we all must learn to know one another. . . . Certainly I ought to say that I myself have been gently and on occasion firmly or sternly reminded how absurd some of my questions have been, how misleading or smug were the assumptions they convey. The fact is that again and again I have seen a poor, a lowly, an illiterate migrant worker wince a little at something I have said or done, smile a little nervously, glare and pout, wonder a little in his eyes about me and my purposes, and through his grimace let me know the disapproval he surely has felt; and yes, the criticism he also feels, the sober, thought-out criticism, perhaps not easily put into words. . . .[18]

Probing. The interviewer, like the participant observer, must probe for the details of the subject's life and experiences. Although he or she should not pressure the subject to talk about sensitive areas, she or he should encourage her or him to offer specific descriptions of specific events. It is through such descriptions that the inner life of the subject is revealed and through such descriptions that a story "comes alive."

The researcher will find that what is sufficient detail for everyday conversation is inadequate for the interview. Unlike most people with whom the subject comes into contact, the researcher is concerned with the mundane, the day-to-day struggles and experiences, as well the highlights, the periods of intense suffering and intense joy. Also unlike most people, *the researcher cannot take for granted commonsense understandings and assumptions that most people use in their daily interactions.* Indeed, it is the task of the researcher to reveal and examine these understandings and assumptions. In the research conducted with Ed Murphy, for example, the interviewers probed both the meaning of being "retarded" and the subtle understandings people use to classify others as "retarded."

Probably the best way to solicit detailed descriptions is to constantly follow up your subject's remarks with specific questions:

> Can you describe what the place looked like?
> How did you feel at that time?
> Can you remember what you said then?
> Can you give me an example of that?
> What do you mean by that?
> I'm still not clear on that. What happened exactly?

You should continue to probe until you have a clear picture in your own mind of people, places, experiences, and feelings in your subject's life.

There are other ways in which interviewers can stimulate subjects to detail their life experiences. As mentioned earlier, they can ask subjects to write a chronology of their lives. A variation of this technique was used in the interviewing conducted with Ed Murphy. On several occasions, Ed, along with the interviewers, outlined a "typical day" at different times in his life. He described his activities from the moment he got up until the moment he went to sleep.

A subject's personal letters, pictures, and other memorabilia can also be used to help her or him describe experiences in adequate detail. Such materials can spark memories and allow the subject to recall old feelings. In addition, they can be examined as a source of understanding in and of themselves.

Ask subjects for any and all letters, school papers, and other documents that they might have stored away. Most subjects will be willing to share these with you. Jane Fry, for example, freely showed the interviewer personal documents and short narratives written during critical periods of her life. Some of these documents were eventually incorporated into her autobiography.

Although a skillful and probing interviewer can maximize subjects' ability to recall the details of their past, there are instances in which subjects simply cannot remember experiences or periods of their lives. One would not, for example, expect anyone to be able to describe one's infancy. While you will have to be satisfied with a rather incomplete picture of those years of a subject's life, however, there are questions you can ask in order to collect data about this period.

How does your family describe you as a baby?
When you get together with your brother do you ever talk about when you were kids?
What kind of stories do you tell?
Do your parents ever talk about your birth?

Questions of this nature stimulate open discussion and can solicit information about what people consider to be important in childhood.

Finally, what people remember in detail and what they forget can itself be important data. Does a subject remember the good times and forget the bad ones? Does he or she gloss over the painful and embarrassing experiences? These are questions which researchers must ask themselves throughout their projects.

Telling the Truth.   *While the interviewer does not search for "truth" in his or her subject's words she or he should be alert to purposeful distortions of facts and events.* You should, as a matter of course, question the motivation behind a subject's remarks. In the early stages of the interviewing, for example, you might expect the subject to want to place him- or herself in a favorable light. As you develop a mutual trust and feeling of partnership in the project, you would expect the subject to be more open and honest with you. Trust, however, is seldom enough. You as a researcher have an obligation to check your data and to share your checks with potential readers.

You should examine your subject's story carefully for inconsistencies. Whether or not you conclude that the subject consciously distorted his or her account of an event or an experience, you will gain insight into his or her view of the world. In the research conducted with Jane Fry, the interviewer casually and inoffensively checked the validity of Jane's remarks. Jane frequently skipped from one topic to another; and since she unwittingly covered the same incidents on two or three different occasions, the researcher could compare different versions of a number of experiences. The interviewer also had the opportunity to meet and question people whom Jane had known at different times in her life and to visit many of the places she mentioned in her story and to consequently compare her impressions with his. Finally, the interviewer spoke with a number of people who had gone through the same experiences as Jane. For example, he extensively questioned a Navy officer on the accuracy of Jane's account of life in the Navy.

You should, of course, protect your subject's confidentiality when you speak to others. And you should advise your subject of your actions. It is one thing to explain your intentions and concerns to your subject, and quite another to have someone report back to him or her that you were secretly checking up on his or her story.

If you do indeed find contradictions in your subject's story, gently confront him or her with the evidence:

> Maybe you could explain something for me. Last time you said this, but what you say now doesn't go along with that. I don't get it.

Suspected lies often turn out to be misunderstandings or honest changes in a subject's perspective.

Losing Rapport During the Project.   As with any relationship, tensions can arise between you and the subject during the course of the project. A subject may miss or come late for interviews or may want to end them early. Either of you may become bored with the interviews. Or you might find an increased reluctance on the part of the subject to talk about certain topics. Ed Murphy, for example, became less willing to talk openly as the topic of conversation moved from his institutional experiences to his early childhood and family experiences. He would dismiss questions with an abrupt "That's not important" or "I don't want to talk about that now." Even more distressing, however, was Ed's tendency to talk around certain painful topics. He would conveniently misinterpret uncomfortable questions and give inappropriate answers.

You must remember that your relationship with the subject is one of give and take. If, on a particular occasion, you find a subject to be reluctant to speak about a certain topic, you should respect his or her feelings. If, however, you find a subject to be repeatedly reluctant to talk about a topic, you should confront him or her directly. With Ed Murphy, for example, we assured him that our questions and certain topics were important:

> I think it is important to know about your family life. A lot of families try to shelter a child who is labeled retarded. I think you should tell about your feelings and experiences.

While Ed continued to be uncomfortable with some issues, he did eventually open up on several key topics.

Be sensitive to your subject's low spots and feelings. When you believe that something is wrong, clear the air and explain your concerns to your subject. If your relationship with the subject continues to be tense, you should be prepared to take a break from the interviewing.

Length of the Project.   The precise length of the project will depend upon such factors as the age of the subject, the subject's ability to remember and to detail events, the frequency of the interviews, and your research goals. In most instances, however, a complete autobiographical study will take at least 50 to 150 hours of intensive interviewing. These hours should be spread over a substantial period of time, with a probable minimum of four months, in order to minimize the chance of interviewing the subject at an atypical period of his or her life.

When you have covered all of the periods outlined in your subject's chronology and when the amount of new information and insight gained in each interview begins to significantly decrease, you should take a break for a week or two. Read through your data and think up new questions. If you find that the subject continues to repeat her- or himself after you resume the interviews, you will know that you have reached the end of the project.

In some studies, personal factors and pragmatic considerations will force you to conclude the project. Thus, a subject may lose interest or may become pressed for time. In the interviewing with Jane Fry, the project ended when she had to leave town.

Multisubject Interviews.   In our discussion so far we have focused on the single subject, multiinterview research project. The researcher can, however, vary the research approach to include a number of subjects interviewed at different times. Oscar Lewis, for example, combined the techniques of participant observation and open-ended interviewing to conduct autobiographical studies on a number of related people in their own settings.[19]

For those who have the time and resources, multisubject interviewing is undoubtedly a worthwhile project. The multisubject approach allows the researcher to view the relationships between and among people and the differences in their perspectives. If, however, you have limited time and resources, you might be wise to concentrate on one subject and to first understand his or her perspective before you expand your study to encompass others.

Although researchers who interview a number of subjects together would essentially follow the interviewing techniques outlined in this chapter, they must create special strategies for establishing rapport with all of their subjects. They would, for example, be careful to avoid even the appearance of favoritism.

Maintain a Journal of Your Impressions and Observations.   The fact that you may tape record your interviews does not obviate the need to write down your impressions and observations after each interview session. *You should,* like the participant observer, *make note of emerging themes, subjective feelings, and your own behavior:*

> That's the third time she's raised that topic on her own. It must be important to her. I'll have to look into this in the future.

*   *   *

> Somehow we were both bored tonight. We just wanted to get the interview over with. Maybe this was because of the topic or maybe we were both tired today.

*   *   *

> I think I was a bit too aggressive tonight. I wonder if he just said those things to keep me off his back. I'll have to keep this in mind when I go over the conversation.

Such notes both help you guide future interviews and provide a frame of reference when you later try to interpret your data.

Since a tape recorder can only capture words, *you should also record any striking nonverbal expressions* made during an interview. A subject's gesture, such as a grimace, a smile, or a blush, may be essential to understanding the meaning of his or her words when you later try to interpret the data. What would later appear to be sincerity, for example, may actually have been sarcasm.

Finally, *you should maintain a record of any conversations with the subject apart from the interview session.* A subject is often likely to be more relaxed and open outside of the interview. Ed Murphy, for example, would frequently get into involved topics during breaks and informal contacts with the interviewer. Such data are clearly important and should be compared with that collected in the interview situation.

WORKING WITH DATA

Personal Documents

Personal documents, like participant observation data, can be coded and examined according to themes or the researcher's hypotheses. We would suggest that researchers use the techniques outlined in Chapter 4 to analyze their data when appropriate. They would be concerned for example, with such issues as whether the data supported their hypotheses and, if so, under what conditions. Of course, matters like the influence of the observer and the presence or absence of others would be irrelevant in the analysis of unsolicited personal documents.

In order to give you a clearer idea of how you might go about the analysis of letters, diaries, and other personal documents, let us examine a letter quoted in Goffman's *Stigma* which is rich in sociological understanding and compassionate in human terms.[20] Assume, for the time being, that the following were one of a number of letters from disabled, or "stigmatized," persons in the researcher's possession:

Dear Miss Lonelyhearts—
I am sixteen years old now and I dont know what to do and would appreciate it if you could tell me what to do. When I was a little girl it was not so bad because I got used to the kids on the block makeing fun of me, but now I would like to have boy friends like the other girls and go out on Saturday nites, but no boy will take me because I was born without a nose—although I am a good dancer and have a nice shape and my father buys me pretty clothes.
I sit and look at myself all day and cry. I have a big hole in the middle of my face that scares people even myself so I cant blame the boys for not wanting to take me out. My mother loves me, but she crys terrible when she looks at me.
What did I do to deserve such a terrible bad fate? Even if I did do some bad things I didn't do any before I was a year old and I was born this way. I asked Papa and he says he doesnt know, but that maybe I did something in the other world before I was born or that maybe I was being punished for his sins. I dont believe that because he is a very nice man. Ought I commit suicide?
Sincerely yours,
Desperate

The researcher would begin to identify themes in the data, and, subsequently, to create hypotheses in regard to the lives of the stigmatized.[21] He or she might, for example, code his or her data according to the following categories, among others. First, despair is a pervasive theme among the stigmatized (the crying, the mention of suicide, the signature itself). Second, a stigma has different meanings for a person at different times in his or her life. ("It was not so bad" when she was a little girl, but now that she has reached adolescence, when other girls have boy friends and go out on Saturday nights, it is unbearable.) Third, a stigmatized person is defined by that stigma. (The fact that she may be a good dancer, have a nice shape, and wear pretty clothes doesn't get her dates.) Finally, stigmatized persons, and people generally, try to make sense out of the inexplicable. ("What did I do to deserve such a terrible bad fate?") In the course of the analysis, the researcher might refine some of these hypotheses, discard others, and construct still others.

One final note of caution: *examine personal documents in the context in which they were produced.* While "Desperate's" letter contains a sensitive and soulful expression of her feelings, for example, you should be alert to the possibility that she may not always feel what she expresses in that letter. One could argue that people only write letters to "Miss Lonely-hearts" when they are most depressed or introspective, or that only certain kinds of people keep diaries. *A personal document, then, reflects what one person thinks and feels at one point in time and in one context.*

Unstructured Interviewing

The interviewer can analyze data in either one of two basic ways. One method is to code data in terms of themes and hypotheses in the manner previously described. The researcher would weigh such factors as whether or not the data was solicited: whether or not he or she had "put words in the subject's mouth." One would usually take this approach for multisubject interviews, especially if a limited amount of time were spent with each subject.

Another way in which to analyze and to present data is in terms of a cohesive life history. Here the researcher codes the subject's words according to certain phases or periods in his or her life, what many qualitative researchers call a person's *career. The concept career refers to the sequence of occupational and nonoccupational positions a person fills through his or her life and the changing definitions of self and the world he or she holds at various stages of that sequence.* In the life of a "retarded" person, for example, one might look at how the meaning of being "retarded" changes as that person moves through infancy, early childhood, high school, and finally adulthood.

We have adopted the latter approach in our research. In the Jane Fry study, her story was coded according to such categories as "High School," "Life in the Navy," "Entering the Psychiatric Ward," "The Present," and "Reflections and the Future." Note that these were Jane's own categories: the way she told her story and conceptualized her life.

Also in our research, we have presented our subjects' stories in autobiographical form, that is, in their own words. Our comments, interpretations, and analysis have been relegated to the introduction or conclusion of our subjects' stories. One could, of course, present a subject's story along with one's interpretations, as have Robert Coles and Thomas Cottle.[22]

Probably the best way to start to write your subject's life history is to read carefully through all of the data. As mentioned above, you should code the stages of your subject's life as he or she sees them. These will eventually provide the basis for chapters in your subject's autobiography. Certain topics, such as current events or sports, may not be relevant to your interests and can be put aside. After you have coded the data, cut and separate the various coding categories. You should, of course, keep an uncut copy of the interview transcripts for reference purposes.

As you begin to piece together your subject's story, you will need to decide which materials and phrases to include and in what form. You should probably omit repetitious phrases and words as well as expressions like "ah" and "you know." However, you should include your subject's characteristic speech patterns, grammatical constructions, and mispronunciations. In some instances, you may have to add a word or two to make a statement understandable. For example, an answer to a question may be meaningless unless you incorporate the question. As a general rule, *you should make the story readable without interpreting or changing the meaning of the subject's words.*

You will also find that the transcripts of your interviews contain two or more accounts of various *events* or *experiences*. In most cases, you can combine the different versions to provide the fullest possible description. If, however, you find that the versions contradict each other or if you are unclear on certain topics, you should return to your subject for elaboration and clarification. Note that *contradictions in a subject's perspectives should not be a source of concern.* People can honestly see and feel different things at different times. If your subject can explain the contradictions, fine. And if not, you should call the reader's attention to those contradictions in the final autobiography.

You should take other considerations into account when you write your subject's story. You would probably be wise, for example, to omit any words or statements that may have been "put in the subject's mouth." You should also be clear in your own mind whether a subject's description of his or her feelings about an experience reflects a current perspective or a perspective at the time it occurred.

*   *   *

Until now, we have been attentive to the logic and procedures of two qualitative research methods: participant observation and personal documents. In the next chapter, we consider examples of other ways in which qualitative research can be conducted. Our goal in Chapter 6, as opposed to the preceding chapters, is to encourage creativity and innovation in field methods. We would again advise the reader who is specifically interested in personal documents to skip to Chapter 7 on the presentation of findings.

NOTES

1.   For definitions see John Madge, *The Tools of Social Science* (Garden City: Anchor Books, 1965), p. 77; Ruth Shonle Cavan, "Interviewing for life-history material," *The American Journal of Sociology,* **XXXV:** 101, 1929–1930; Gordon W. Allport, *The Use of Personal Documents in Psychological Science* (New York: Social Science Research Council, 1942), p. xii; Robert Angell, "A critical review of the development of the personal document method in sociology 1920–1940," in Louis Gottschalk, Clyde Kluckhohn, and Robert Angell, *The Use of Personal Documents in History, Anthropology and Sociology* (New York: Social Science Research Council, 1945), p. 177. Note that most of the finest works on personal documents were written in the period 1920–1950. This demonstrates social scientists' neglect of these materials as sources of data in recent years.

2.   For a discussion of how personal documents differ, see Allport, *Personal Documents.*

3.   See *ibid.,* Chap. 5, for a discussion of motivation.

4.   Anne Frank, *The Diary of a Young Girl* (New York: Doubleday, 1952).

5.   A good example of this kind of document is Joseph Church, *Three Babies* (New York: Random House, 1966).

6.   Clifford Shaw, *The Jack Roller* (Chicago: University of Chicago Press, 1930).

7.   William I. Thomas and Florian Znaniecki, *The Polish Peasant in Europe and America* (New York: Alfred A. Knopf, 1927, 2nd ed.).

8.   Allport, *Personal Documents.*

9.   The complete autobiography of Jane Fry can be found in Robert Bogdan (Ed.), *Being Different: The Autobiography of Jane Fry* (New York: Wiley, 1974).

10.   Seymour Sarason makes some important points regarding why social scientists should become involved in the community. Seymour Sarason, *The Psychological Sense of Community* (San Francisco: Jossey-Bass, 1974), Chap. 10.

11. For general discussions about autobiographical interviewing see: Clyde Kluckhohn, "The personal document in anthropological science," in Gottschalk, Kluckhohn, and Angell, *Use of Personal Documents,* pp. 109–133; Thomas Cottle, "The life study: On mutual recognition and subjective inquiry," *Urban Life and Culture,* **III,** no. 3 (October): 344–360, 1973; and Cavan, "Interviewing," pp. 100–115.

12. Robert Coles, *Migrants, Sharecroppers, Mountaineers* (Boston: Little, Brown, 1967), p. 39.

13. Oscar Lewis, *The Children of Sanchez* (New York: Vintage, 1961), p. xii.

14. See, for example, Thomas Cottle, *The Abandoners* (Boston: Little, Brown, 1972), p. xvi.

15. See Kluckhohn, "Personal document," p. 122.

16. Cottle, "Life study," p. 351.

17. *Ibid.,* pp. 344–360.

18. Coles, *Migrants,* p. 29.

19. See Lewis, *Children of Sanchez,* and Oscar Lewis, *La Vida* (New York: Random House, 1965).

20. Erving Goffman, *Stigma: Notes on the Management of Spoiled Identity* (Englewood Cliffs, N.J.: 1963). This letter originally appeared in Nathanael West, *Miss Lonelyhearts* (New Directions, 1962), pp. 14–15. It is fictitious.

21. Goffman does just this in his insightful book *Stigma.*

22. Coles, *Migrants;* Cottle, *Abandoners.*

CHAPTER SIX

Montage

DISCOVERING METHODS

In 1966 a group of social scientists published a book entitled *Unobtrusive Measures,* with which they hoped to "broaden the social scientist's current narrow range of utilized methodologies and to encourage creative and opportunistic exploitation of unique measurement possibilities." The authors went on to write:

> The dominant mass of social science research is based upon interviews and questionnaires. We lament this overdependence upon a single, fallible method.[1]

We must guard against the overdependence cited by these researchers; that is, we must be careful not to be boxed in by a limited repertoire of research approaches.

We have concentrated thus far in this book on two research strategies: participant observation, the mainstay of qualitative methods, and personal documents, less commonly used than participant observation but familiar to most researchers. Moreover, we have adopted a "how to do it" approach with these methods. There is a danger in what we have done, in the limited number of methods we have discussed and in the limited parameters in which we have discussed them. We may have given the impression that there are only two ways to approach subjective understanding and inductive analysis.

With this thought in mind, we shift our focus in this chapter to a discussion of studies based on innovative and "nonstandard" methodologies. If there is anything to be learned from these studies, it is that social scientists must *educate* themselves. We use the word "educate" as opposed to "train" because of an important difference between the two. As Irwin Deutscher notes, one can only be trained in something that already exists.[2] To be educated is to learn to create anew. *We must constantly create new methods and new approaches.* We must take to heart the words written by C. Wright Mills in his conclusion to *The Sociological Imagination:*

> Be a good craftsman: Avoid a rigid set of procedures. Above all seek to develop and to use the sociological imagination. Avoid fetishism of method and technique. Urge the rehabilitation of the unpretentious intellectual craftsman, and try to become a craftsman yourself. Let every man be his own methodologist. . . .[3]

These methodologies are not to be copied, but rather, emulated. They do not determine the range of possibilities: only one's thoughts do.

The studies that follow exemplify the ideal of the social scientist-as-innovator. Some of them have serious weaknesses; we mention them because of their strengths.

We have chosen not to discuss the ethical implications of the following approaches. Ethical issues have been explored in previous chapters. Some of the methods we will discuss kindle the fires of long-standing ethical feuds. As the sex educator does not advocate any particular sexual practice by talking about it, so too we do not advocate any particular research tactic by describing it.

DISRUPTING THE "COMMON SENSE WORLD OF EVERYDAY LIFE": HAROLD GARFINKEL

One hundred and thirty-five people wander into stores and attempt to bargain over the prices of such common items as cigarettes and magazines. Others go out and find unsuspecting partners to play tick-tack-toe: when it is their turn they casually erase their opponents mark and move it to another square before they make their own. One person engages another in conversation and nonchalantly brings his face so close to the other's that their noses are almost touching. After all of these activities, the "tricksters" go home to write detailed notes on their encounters.

Scenes from a Marx Brothers movie? Woody Allen? Candid Camera perhaps? Not quite. All of these are strategies used by Harold Garfinkel and others in their influential studies in ethnomethodology.[4] Garfinkel seems to ask himself: "What can be done to make trouble?" By producing confusion, anxiety, bewilderment, and disorganized interaction, he attempts to discover what is otherwise hidden: the commonsense everyday rules of social interaction.

Let us discuss some of the other strategies Garfinkel has used to accomplish this goal. In one exercise, people are asked to write down on one side of a sheet of paper actual conversations they have had with a friend or relative. On the other side they are asked to write what they understood the other person to have meant by each sentence. The relationships between the two are then examined for what they reveal about what is taken for granted, underlying assumptions, and shared meanings.

In a more provocative exercise, people are told to engage others in conversation and to insist that the others clarify the meanings of commonplace remarks. One person asked one of the experimenters, "How are you?" To this, the experimenter replied, "How am I in regard to what? My health, my finances, my school work, my peace of mind, my . . .?" The partner, red-faced and out of control, shot back, "Look! I was just trying to be polite. Frankly, I don't give a damn how you are."[5]

Another tactic used by Garfinkel is to ask people to look at an ordinary and familiar scene in their own lives from a stranger's perspective. Thus, undergraduate students are instructed to go to their families' homes and to act like boarders. Through this exercise people become aware of things they never notice in their everyday lives, such as table manners, greetings, and other subtle conventions. In a slightly different experiment, the emphasis is placed on the reactions of others to students behaving like boarders in their own homes.

Garfinkel has created a series of strategies allowing him to explore those areas of social interaction in which he is interested. He uses his experimenters to uncover what is seen but usually unnoticed: the commonsense world of everyday life.

THE IMPOSTORS: D. L. ROSENHAN AND OTHERS

A recent article published by D. L. Rosenhan* begins with the following question: "If sanity and insanity exist, how shall we know them?"[6] Rosenhan reflects on that question with the use of data he and his cohorts collected in 12 mental hospitals.

Rosenhan and his co-workers conducted their research as impostors. They were "sane" or "normal" people, who had never been defined by themselves or by others as "mentally ill," and they misrepresented themselves to the staffs of the hospitals under study. These "pseudopatients," three women and five men, included three psychologists, a pediatrician, a psychiatrist, a painter, a homemaker, and a psychology graduate student. The latter, a man in his early twenties, was the youngest of the group.

With the exception of Rosenhan, who forewarned the administrator and chief psychologist of the hospital of his plans, the pseudopatients conducted their experiment without the knowledge of the staffs of the institutions. All of the impostors used pseudonyms. Those who worked in the field of mental health lied about their occupations in order to avoid any special treatment which might be given them. The procedures which the impostors followed are best described in Rosenhan's own words:

> After calling the hospital for an appointment, the pseudopatient arrived at the admissions office complaining that he had been hearing voices. . . .
>
> Beyond alleging the symptoms and falsifying name, vocation, and employment, no further alterations of person, history, or circumstances were made. The significant events of the pseudopatient's life history were presented as they had actually occurred. Relationships with parents and siblings, with spouse and children, with people at work and in school, consistent with the aforementioned exceptions, were described as they were or had been. Frustrations and upsets were described along with joys and satisfactions. . . .
>
> Immediately upon admission to the psychiatric ward, the pseudopatient ceased simulating any symptoms of abnormality. In some cases, there was a brief period of mild nervousness and anxiety, since none of the pseudopatients really believed that they would be admitted so easily. Indeed, their shared fear was that they would be immediately exposed as frauds and

*D. L., Rosenham, "On being sane in insane places," *Science*, 179 (January): 250–258, 1973. Copyright 1973 by the American Association for the Advancement of Science. Used by permission.

greatly embarrassed. Moreover, many of them had never visited a psychiatric ward; even those who had, nevertheless, had some genuine fears about what might happen to them. Their nervousness, then, was quite appropriate to the novelty of the hospital setting, and it abated rapidly.

Apart from that short-lived nervousness, the pseudopatient behaved on the ward as he "normally" behaved. The pseudopatient spoke to patients and staff as he might ordinarily. Because there is uncommonly little to do on a psychiatric ward, he attempted to engage others in conversation. When asked by staff how he was feeling, he indicated that he was fine, that he no longer experienced symptoms. He responded to instructions from attendants, to calls for medication (which was not swallowed), and to dining-hall instructions. Beyond such activities as were available to him on the admission ward, he spent his time writing down his observations about the ward, its patients and the staff. Initially these notes were written "secretly," but as it soon became clear that no one much cared, they were subsequently written on standard tablets of paper in such public places as the dayroom. No secret was made of these activities.

The pseudopatient, very much as a true psychiatric patient, entered a hospital with no foreknowledge of when he would be discharged. Each was told that he would have to get out by his own devices, essentially by convincing the staff that he was sane. . . . They were, therefore motivated not only to behave sanely, but to be paragons of cooperation.

As indicated by Rosenhan, the pseudopatients were all successfully admitted to the hospitals. All but one of the impostors were initially diagnosed as "schizophrenic" and were discharged with a diagnosis of "schizophrenia in remission." The length of hospitalization averaged 19 days with a range from 7 to 52 days.

Rosenhan's work is exciting in a variety of ways. It allowed the impostors to collect data on and, what is most important, to actually experience hospitalization for "mental illness." Rosenhan's pseudopatients were able to examine through first-hand knowledge the process by which people are perceived and categorized as "sane" and "insane." And these researchers had the opportunity to observe the unguarded behavior of the staff.

Although Rosenhan's researchers could have gained many of the same insights through the use of overt participant observation techniques, their impostor status enabled them to live through the experience themselves. They thus developed a subjective understanding that would have been difficult to achieve through other methods.

One does not need to have access to a team of researchers in order to conduct studies similar to Rosenhan's. For example, a number of researchers have conducted covert participant observation studies.[7] And a smaller number have adopted similar, but more innovative, approaches. We know one professor who sends his students on shopping trips feigning a particular disability.[8] He hopes that through this experience they can develop a greater and more personal understanding of people's reactions to the handicapped. Certainly one of the more creative studies of recent years was conducted by the amateur social scientist and author John Howard Griffin.[9] Griffin underwent medical treatments to temporarily change the color of his skin and shaved his head to take on the appearance of a middle-aged Black. He then hitchhiked, walked, and rode buses through the Deep South: Mississippi, Alabama, Louisiana, and Georgia. The journal of his experiences, published in a book entitled *Black Like Me*, makes insightful and interesting reading.

RAP SESSIONS

One method that has been used sparingly in the past but that is particularly relevant to this discussion is the group interview or "rap session." Here the researcher brings together groups of people whom he or she questions using a nondirective approach. These sessions are taped or otherwise recorded and scrutinized in a manner similar to data in participant observation or personal document research. As mentioned earlier, the group interviewer faces special rapport problems that he or she must overcome if the project is to be a success.

Two geographers at Syracuse University, Rowan Rowntree and Barry Gordon, have successfully and creatively employed the group interview approach. During the past year, they have examined how people define geographic space and, more specifically, forests.[10] They initially intended to conduct fieldwork in the place of interest; that is, to go into wooded areas, what they defined as forests, and to place themselves in situations in which they could hear people talk about space and forests. This plan contained a number of problems. In the first place, they were interested in the definitions of people who might never have seen forests as well as those who regularly visited them. In the second place, most people simply do not spend their time talking about forests even if they do happen to be in one.

What the researchers decided to do instead was to assemble groups of people, show them a series of ten slides of forests, and encourage them to talk about what they had seen. Although they have concentrated on college students in the pilot run of the project, they plan to interview groups such as motor cyclists, inner-city children, and people in business. Through their research they hope to capture the different meanings of a forest in both an evaluative and a utilitarian sense among different groups of people.

Other insightful "rap session" studies have been conducted by Thomas Cottle and by a group from the University of Michigan School of Social Work. In the following excerpt, Cottle, well-known for his interviewing, describes the interview on which his excellent paper "The Ghetto Scientists" is based:

It is difficult to say how many of us were speaking that afternoon in the little park near the hospital. So much was going on, like a colossal basketball game and boys darting after girls, or a pretend fight, that our population kept shifting. Still, there were always four or five young people, about ten years old, who joined me on the grass alongside the basketball court, and the conversation tumbled along so that we all could follow it and the newcomers could be cued in easily. The girls and boys were speaking about school, their studies, teachers, parents, and brothers and sisters, although there was an unusual side trip into politics. In times like these I wish I could be totally free to say anything to young people, young black people, in this case. It is not that I am thinking anything particular about them as much as holding back ideas that for one reason or another I feel should remain hidden. Maybe it has to do with the laziness of the day or the fact that none of the young people seem especially eager to latch onto some topic. Maybe it is the way some of us do research; entering poor areas of cities and just speaking with people, letting conversations run on without interpretation or analysis. Maybe too, some of us have a strong desire to know what these people think of us and the work we do.[11]

The Michigan group was concerned with welfare mothers' perspectives on their problems.[12] In this project, mothers in the Aid to Dependent Children program were invited to form discussion groups. Each group focused on one area, such as mothers' employment opportunities, adjustment problems of families with incapacitated fathers, child-rearing difficulties, and school problems, and met weekly for 6 to 12 sessions.

MONTAGE: MICHAEL LESY AND FRIENDS

The word montage is both a verb and a noun. As a verb it refers to the process of making a composition from pictures and words which are closely arranged as in a still picture or presented in short intervals as in a movie; as a noun it refers to the product of such activities. It is not often used to refer to research activities or the products of such enterprises. Yet the word fits very well Michael Lesy's book, *Wisconsin Death Trip*.[13]

Lesy's work is an arrangement of photographs and quotations collected in and around the town of Black River Falls, Wisconsin, and treats the period 1890 to 1910. Using over 30,000 glass plate negatives from the files of the State Historical Society of Wisconsin and quotations and records from the Badger State Banner newspaper, Mendota State Mental Hospital, and other sources, Lesy attempts to capture "the structure of the experience of the people themselves, especially that aspect of the structure that might be regarded as pathological."

Wisconsin Death Trip contains hundreds of quotations and photographs, interspersed with Lesy's own commentary. He uses these materials to look at people as others have not and to implicitly, if not explicitly, challenge our traditional views of the period. In order to give you a flavor of the nature of the work, let us present some of the quotations found in the book:*

> Milo L. Nicholas, sent to the insane hospital a year or two ago after committing arson on Mrs. Nicholas' farm is now at large . . . and was seen near the old place early last week. . . . He has proven himself a revengeful firebug.

*   *   *

> Henry Johnson, an old bachelor of Grand Dyke, cut off the heads of all his hens recently, made a bonfire of his best clothes and killed himself with arsenic.

*   *   *

> The motto of the high school class of 1895 was "Work is the Law of Life."

*   *   *

> John Pabelowski, a 16 year old boy of Stevens Point, was made idiotic by the use of tabacco.

*   *   *

*Michael Lesy, *Wisconsin Death Trip*, copyright 1973, Pantheon Books, a Division of Random House, Inc. Used by permission of the publishers.

George Kanuck, a laborer, is alleged to have sold his 7 year old boy to Italian peddlers who have been working at Manitowoc. The sale is said to have taken place at Kanuck's house during a drunken orgy in which all participated. The Italians, 2 women and a man, left town next day with the boy.

* * *

Billie Neverson's wife was a wierdie. They took over the old Creston place at the other end of the valley. No one knows what really happened. Some say it went back to Billie finding out about her having a kid before they got married. Anyway, she just stayed by herself. Once a year, maybe, someone would see her in town, but she wouldn't even nod her head to say hello. Acting like that nobody ever bothered to visit them either.

* * *

Admitted Nov. 21st, 1899. Town of Franklin, Norwegian. Age 50. Married. Two children, youngest 3 years of age. Farmer in poor circumstances. . . . Has an idea that people are taking what little he has—that they will come to his house even when he is there. Is not homicidal. . . . Poor physical condition . . . January 24th, 1900.: Died today. Exhaustion. . . .

Lesy does not have much to say about his methods. After all, his task was confined to the process of reading through and sorting the materials for presentation to the reader. What is of greater importance than his methodology, moreover, is the perspective and understanding he brings to his data. He reminds us, for example, that none of the pictures he presents were snapshots: since it was necessary to pose to permit the required half-second exposure, people had an opportunity to think about how they wanted to appear. In his introduction, Lesy elaborates on the meaning of the materials he has assembled:

Neither the pictures nor the events were, when they were made or experienced, considered to be unique, extraordinary, or sensational. . . . The people who looked at the pictures once they were taken weren't surprised, and the people who read about the events after they were printed weren't shocked.

And in reference to those who wrote the newspaper he writes:

They didn't question events; they confirmed them. Eventually they may have become particularly sensitive to appearances, but they never doubted their meaning. Charley took hundreds and hundreds of pictures of horses because he was asked to; he took dozens and dozens of pictures of houses and their owners because he'd been offered the job. The Coopers [the editors and writers for the local paper] vilified the Pullman strikers because everyone was Republican; they noted a departure, an arrival, or a visit because everyone always departed, arrived, or visited; they devoted a weekly column to abstinence because it was a Christian duty to remain temperate. Each of them said yes to what he was supposed to and no to what he was supposed to refuse. They were prosaic chroniclers of a conventionalized universe.

Finally, Lesy discusses the process by which he put the book together. He suggests that he was more of an artisan than a technician:

The text was constructed as music is composed. It was meant to obey its own laws of tone, pitch, rhythm, and repetition. Even though now, caught between the two covers of this book, it accompanies the pictures, it was not meant to serve them the way a quartet was intended to disguise the indecorous pauses in eighteenth-century gossip. Rather, it was meant to fill the space of this book with a constantly repeated theme that might recall your attention whenever it drifted from the faces and hands of the people in the pictures.

Lesy is an artist, an historian, and a social scientist *par excellence.* By illuminating a particular town, region, and country at a particular historical period, he illuminates our world now. He enables us to enter the past and to imagine what people in the future will know of us. Historical works like Lesy's lead us to examine our own commonsense understandings of the world from a more detached perspective.

Lesy's work represents just one of the many ways in which different media can further social science understanding. There are some excellent documentary films, such as *Mondo Cane* and *Women's World,* that have reached the commercial market and that are rich in the insights they provide. Available to a more limited audience are the films of Frederick Wiseman: *Titticut Follies, High School,* and *Hospital,* among others.[14] Wiseman takes us through places that we have visited but have never really seen. In the area of photography, the works of Diane Arbus[15] and the photographic essay of institutions for the "mentally retarded" by Blatt and Kaplan are notable for their ability to sensitize us to what we take for granted.[16] Finally, a number of books composed of quotations from newspaper articles have appeared in recent years. One worth noting is *The New York Times* collection of articles arranged in chronological order called *Women: The Changing Roles.*[17]

While none of the works mentioned above was produced by social scientists, there are some indications that the social scientist's traditional reluctance to employ media in research may be yielding to a new trend of flexibility and creativity. Thus, Thomas Scheff, in *Being Mentally Ill,* examines the effects of newspaper comics on societal sterotypes of the "mentally ill."[18] And Ryave and Schenkein report on their use of video-tapes to study, from a sociological perspective, how people "walk."[19]

There is much that the social scientist can learn from the artist. He or she must be willing to free him- or herself from the confining stance of the "empirical scientist" and the resulting confining definition of what data should be.

READING BETWEEN THE LINES: WOMEN ON WORDS AND IMAGES

In a pamphlet entitled *Dick and Jane as Victims,* a group called "Women on Words and Images" examines the way boys and girls are portrayed in children's readers.[20] The authors start with the premise: "The degree to which the treatment of boys and girls differs in Primary School Texts is a good indicator of current social expectations for each sex, and offers some insight into the premises underlying these expectations."

The authors, in a collective effort, studied 134 elementary school readers published by 15 different American companies and that were being used by three suburban New Jersey school systems. After a careful reading of each book, they developed a general classification scheme of the themes contained in these books. As the study progressed, new themes emerged and first impressions yielded to more complex observations. In the final pamphlet, frequency counts of prevalent themes as well as illustrative quotations and pictures were presented.

Since *Dick and Jane as Victims* was published and distributed by small, issue-oriented presses and groups, the authors were able to write it in a style and with a content to meet their own concerns and standards. Such works can provide an important wedge both to diversify materials available in the social sciences and to present strong positions on important social issues.

OFFICIAL RECORDS: POSSIBILITIES
AND PROSPECTS

There is, for all practical purposes, an unlimited number of official records and documents stored away in the files and archives of organizations and available to the qualitative researcher. These range from such materials as court transcripts, *The Congressional Record,* and even the White House Tape Transcripts to more mundane documents such as police records, coroner reports, and institutional records. Of course, the analysis of official records has been one of the mainstays of social science research. There are, for example, countless studies based on police records in the form of crime statistics and coroner records in the form of suicide statistics. When we speak of a qualitative approach to official records, however, we mean something quite different.

The qualitative researcher examines official records not to learn about criminals, delinquents, or suicide victims, but rather to learn about the people who produce and maintain those records.[21] *Like personal documents, official records lend insight into the perspectives, assumptions, and purposes of their authors.* Thus, Harold Garfinkel argues that organizational records are produced for the purpose of documenting the satisfactory performance of that organization's responsibilities towards its clients.[22] In regard to his study of the records of a psychiatric clinic, he writes:

> In our view the contents of clinic folders are assembled with regard for the possibility that the relationship may have to be portrayed as having been in accord with expectations of sanctionable performances by clinicians and patients.[23]

In a slightly different vein, Jack Douglas examined the commonsense understandings and meanings of suicide in coroner records.[24] Finally, Bogdan contrasted Jane Fry's psychiatric records with her own account of her experiences.[25] He revealed the commonsense assumptions that lie behind psychiatric ideologies.

The use of official records and documents in this way opens up many new sources of understanding. Materials that are thought to be useless by those who look for "information" or "facts" are valuable to the qualitative methodologist. For the researcher who is interested in understanding the nature of subjective reality, nothing is too subjective.

*   *   *

In this chapter we have attempted merely to highlight some of the studies which we consider to be innovative in methodology and purpose. Let us conclude Chapter 6 with a quotation from the Nobel Prizewinning scientist P. W. Bridgeman:

There is no scientific method as such. . . . The most vital feature of the scientist's procedure has been merely to do the utmost with his mind, no holds barred. . . .[26]

After the qualitative researcher has collected and analyzed his or her data, he or she must decide how to present his or her findings and understandings to others. The purpose of Part Two is to aid the researcher in that endeavor. Chapter 7 deals with some of the issues involved in writing up findings, while Chapters 8 through 13 contain papers based on data obtained through qualitative methods.

NOTES

1. Eugene J. Webb et al., *Unobstrusive Measures: Nonreactive Research in the Social Sciences* (Chicago: Rand McNally, 1966), p. 1.

2. Irwin Deutscher, *What We Say/What We Do* (Glenview, Ill.: Scott, Foresman, 1973), p. 10.

3. C. Wright Mills, *The Sociological Imagination* (New York: Oxford University Press, 1959), p. 224.

4. The materials found here are drawn from Harold Garfinkel, *Studies in Ethnomethodology* (Englewood Cliffs, N. J.: Prentice Hall, 1967), Chap. II.

5. *Ibid.,* p. 44.

6. D. L. Rosenhan, "On being sane in insane places," *Science,* **CLXXIX,** no. 4070, (Jan.): 250—258, 1973.

7. See, for example, Donald Roy, "Banana time: Job satisfaction and informal interaction," *Human Organization,* **XVIII** (Winter): 158–168, 1959–60, "Efficiency and 'the fix': Informal intergroup relations in a piece work machine shop," *American Journal of Sociology,* **LX** (Nov.): 255–260, 1954, and "Quota restriction and goldbricking in a machine shop," *American Journal of Sociology,* **LVII** (March): 427–442, 1952; M. Dalton, *Men Who Manage* (New York: Wiley, 1961); Laud Humphreys, *Tearoom Trade* (Chicago: Aldine, 1970).

8. William English at Syracuse University.

9. John Howard Griffin, *Black Like Me* (Boston: Houghton Mifflin, 1962).

10. Their ideas were in part precipitated by Kenneth H. Craik, "The comprehension of the everyday physical environment," in Harold M. Proshansky, William H. Ittelson, and Leanne G. Rivlin (Eds.), *Environmental Psychology* (New York: Holt, Rinehart and Winston, 1970), pp. 646–658.

11.   Thomas Cottle, "The ghetto scientists" (Unpublished paper presented at the Annual Meeting of the Society for the Study of Social Problems, 1973).

12.   Paul H. Glasser and L. N. Glasser, *Families in Crisis,* (Evanston: Harper and Row, 1970), p. 57.

13.   Michael Lesy, *Wisconsin Death Trip* (New York: Pantheon Books, a Division of Random House, 1973).

14.   For a brief discussion of Wiseman's work, see "Viewpoint: Shooting the institution," *Time: The Weekly Newsmagazine* (December 9): pp. 95–98, 1974. Wiseman describes his documentaries as "reality fictions: reality, in that the people are real and the events unstaged; fictions, in the sense that I have condensed and ordered those events in a fashion they did not have in real life."

15.   Diane Arbus, *Diane Arbus* (New York: An Aperture Monograph, 1972).

16.   Burton Blatt and Fred Kaplan, *Christmas in Purgatory: A Photographic Essay on Mental Retardation* (Syracuse, N. Y.: Human Policy Press, 1974).

17.   Elizabeth Janeway (Ed.), *Women: The Changing Roles* (New York: The New York Times, 1973).

18.   Thomas Scheff, *Being Mentally Ill* (Chicago: Aldine, 1966).

19.   A. Lincoln Ryave and James N. Schenkein, "Notes on the art of walking," in Roy Turner (Ed.), *Ethnomethodology* (Baltimore, Md.: Penguin, 1974), pp. 265–274.

20.   Women on Words and Images, *Dick and Jane as Victims* (Princeton, N. J.: Women on Words and Images, 1972).

21.   See J. Kitsuse and A. V. Cicourel, "A note on the uses of official statistics," *Social Problems,* 11: 131–139, 1963.

22.   Garfinkel, *Studies in Ethnomethodology,* pp. 186–207.

23.   *Ibid.,* p. 198.

24.   Jack D. Douglas, *American Social Order: Social Rules in a Pluralistic Society* (New York: Free Press, 1971), pp. 106–130. Also see Jack D. Douglas, *The Social Meanings of Suicide* (Princeton, N. J.: Princeton University Press, 1967).

25.   Robert Bogdan, *Being Different: The Autobiography of Jane Fry* (New York: Wiley, 1974), pp. 213–220.

26.   As quoted in Melville Dalton, "Preconceptions and methods in *Men Who Manage,*" in Phillip Hammond (Ed.), *Sociologists at Work* (Garden City, N. Y.: Doubleday, 1964), p. 60.

PART TWO

Writing Up Findings

The Presentation of Findings

The presentation of findings represents the culmination of the research process.[1] After all, *the purpose of research is not only to increase your own understanding but also to share that understanding with others.* It is also when you attempt to write your research report that you clarify your thoughts and tighten the logic of your arguments.

A report, article, or monograph based on qualitative research is not, or should not be, an individual's off-the-cuff view of a situation. Rather, it should be a descriptive and analytic presentation of data that have been laboriously and systematically collected and interpreted. What you report as findings will, of course, depend upon a number of factors. The nature of the data itself, the themes and hypotheses that you have discovered in the analysis stage of your research, will determine what you can and cannot present to your reader. Moreover, your own theoretical perspective will lead you to interpret and, consequently, to present your findings in one way and not in another. Finally, what you report as findings will depend on your own goals. You may, for example, only be interested in certain themes or in certain aspects of the setting. Or you may want to confirm or refute the findings presented by others. In a different vein, you may want to reach a non-social science audience and contribute to social change or reform. Whatever the case, you will probably have more data than you know what to do with. You will therefore, have a wide range of discretion in what to discuss in what you write.

Researchers must also decide the level of description or analysis at which they will present their findings.[2] They may, as illustrated by the papers in Chapters 8 and 9, present their data in an edited, but purely descriptive, form, in which readers are left to interpret the meanings of subjects' words and actions. The essays in Chapters 10, 11, and 12 illustrate another level of description. At this level, researchers present data in terms of one or more themes that they consider central to understanding certain aspects of a setting or a subject's perspective. They thus report their findings in their own words and with their own interpretations. The final level of description at which findings can be presented is exemplified by the essay in Chapter 13. Here Researchers address broad theoretical issues that transcend particular settings or subjects.[3]

In the remainder of this chapter, we offer some suggestions on how to write up findings. We move first to a discussion of some of the things that the researcher should include in his or her research report. In the following section, we offer a note on how to write. Finally, in the concluding section of this chapter, we introduce the papers contained in the chapters that follow, which provide examples of different ways you can report your findings.

WHAT YOU SHOULD TELL YOUR READERS

As a researcher, you owe it to your readers to explain the process by which you collected and interpreted your data. After all, your findings are credible and fully understandable only to the extent that your techniques are open to the scrutiny of readers.[4] One might, for example, interpret the findings of a covert participant observation study differently than one would the findings of an overt study.

We would suggest that you deal with at least some of the following topics when you present your findings. You should probably cover all of these in any major research report or monograph based on your study. For shorter pieces and articles, like those in the subsequent chapters, you probably only need to mention your research techniques, especially if you have used fairly standard methods such as participant observation or open-ended interviewing to conduct your study.

1. *Method.* Your reader should be informed of the methodology on which your findings are based. You should cover both broad topics such as the type of methodology (participant observation, for example) and specific topics such as whether or not the research was covert or overt and whether or not your observations or interviews were taped. You should also describe the techniques you used to solicit data and probe for information.

2. *Time and length of the study.* You should tell your reader how many hours and what period of time you spent in your research. What was your work schedule like?

3. *Nature and number of settings and subjects.* This point should be self-explanatory: let your reader know where and among whom you conducted your research.

4. *How the subject became the subject.* Describe the process by which you found your subjects or your setting. Did you know the subjects beforehand? Had you previously visited the setting? In the case of unsolicited personal documents, discuss how you obtained your data.

5. *The researcher's frame of mine.* You should give your reader a sense of how you defined the project both initially and over a period of time. What was the purpose of your research? What were your working hypotheses, biases, and preconceptions? How did these change, if at all?

6. *Researcher-subject relationship.* You should discuss your rapport with and acceptance by subjects. What was your agreement in the beginning of the project? Did this change over time? How did your subjects react to you? How did this affect your data?

7. *Checks on your data.* Describe any special techniques you used to analyze your data. How did you come to your conclusions? What checks, if any, did you place on your subjects' truthfulness? You should also describe your degree of faith in your various findings.

In short, *the researcher should give readers enough information as to how the research was conducted to enable them to evaluate the findings.* You should always ask yourself whether your techniques have been sufficiently explained to readers.

A NOTE ON WRITING

Some have joked that to be a social scientist is to be a poor writer.[5] We mention this point because the significance of many important works and ideas has been lost or obscured through verboseness and jargonese. In reference to Parsons' *The Social System*, Mills writes:

One could translate the 555 pages of *The Social System* into about 150 pages of straight-forward English. The result would not be very impressive. It would, however, contain the terms in which the key problem of the book, and the solution it offers to this problem are most clearly statable.[6]

Clearly, social scientists have much to learn from journalists, essayists, and other professional writers.

The ability to write clearly and concisely is an important skill. Like many of the other skills discussed in this book, it is learned through discipline, practice, and exposure to exemplary works. Although there are no quick ways to develop a free and easy writing style, we would like to offer a few suggestions which you may find helpful when writing up your findings.[6]

1. *Outline your thoughts on paper before you begin to write.* It is far easier to write with a plan than without one. Moreover, an outline helps you check your ideas for logic and internal consistency. You may find that you need to formulate a new model or to return to your data for clarification. In any case, treat your outline as a flexible working model, something that can be revised as you write.

2. *Inform your readers of your design or purpose early in the paper.* Help your readers along the way by telling them how each subtopic relates to the overall scheme. While repeated statements of purpose can be monotonous, a failure to provide readers with sufficient guidance can be deadly.

3. *Decide what audience you wish to reach and adjust your style and content accordingly.* Put yourself in the role of the reader: "What will he or she take this to mean?" Avoid both condescension and pseudosophistication.

4. *Use short sentences, the active voice, and concise and direct words in your writing.* Social scientists have been accused of using complicated terms when there are simple ones available. Malcolm Cowley brings this point home with the following example:

> A child says 'Do it again,' a teacher says 'Repeat that exercise,' but the sociologist says 'It was determined to replicate the investigation.' Instead of saying two things are alike or similar, as a layman would do, the sociologist describes them as being either isomorphic or homologous. Instead of saying that they are different he calls them allotropic. . . .
>
> . . . A sociologist never cuts anything in half or divides it in two like a layman. Instead he dichotomizes it, bifurcates it, subjects it to a process of binary fission, or restructures it in a dyadic conformation—around a polar foci.[8]

Conciseness adds strength to your writing.

5. *Ground your writing in specific examples.* Qualitative research yields descriptions and quotations that are rich in imagery and that can convey to a reader an understanding of what a situation or person is like. Use these throughout your paper. C. Wright Mills offers sound advice in regard to this aspect: "never write more than three pages without having in mind a solid example."[9]

Illustrative quotations and descriptions also provide evidence that things are the way you report them to be. Thus, representative quotations, if you note that they are representative, make your report so much more credible to the reader. One word of warning: you should resist the temptation to overuse certain colorful materials at the expense of others.[10] There is a tendency, for example, to use the same quote or description repeatedly in the same or in different reports. If you cannot find alternative examples, the point you are trying to make may not be as important as thought originally.

6. Since few writers clearly say what they want to say the first time around, *you should always write more than one draft of a paper.* Let the first draft flow freely. Concentrate on expressing your ideas. After you have completed this draft, leave it for a day or two in order to gain some sense of detachment.

Eliminate all unnecessary words, phrases, sentences, and paragraphs when you write the second draft. You will probably find that your paper can be reduced by as much as one quarter without a loss of content and with a gain in clarity. Remember that verbiage does not make what you have to say any more important, just more verbose.

7. *Have colleagues or friends read and comment on your writing.* Whether or not someone is familiar with your field, he or she can critique your paper in regard to the clarity of your message and the logic of your thought. Of course, people whom you have to ask, "Have you read that paper I gave you a few weeks ago?," are more a hindrance than a help.

How you say it is almost as important as what you have to say. Keep this in mind when you begin to write your findings.

THE PRESENTATION OF FINDINGS: SELECTED STUDIES

The following chapters contain papers written by us and based on studies employing the methodology outlined in this book. We use them here for their pedagogical value: to give you a sense of how you might write up your own findings. We consider these to be good examples of a range of ways to write.

"This is Their Home" is a descriptive piece based on the state institution study cited throughout this work. It was written using edited field notes from three consecutive observation sessions at the state institution. The purpose of "This is Their Home" is simple: to sensitize one to the nature of everyday life on the ward in question. Since the researcher's observations are presented without interpretation, the reader is allowed to draw many of his or her own conclusions. Herein lies the value of this piece. Some will view it as a sensitive portrayal of conditions that should not exist. Others will dismiss it as an unscholarly expose which hints of yellow journalism. Still others will find in it sociological understanding. Whatever the case, "This is Their Home" stands alone. It can be used by the reader for his or her own purposes.

The paper in Chapter 9, "Being Different," is excerpted from the autobiographical study of Jane Fry discussed in Chapter 5. In this paper, Jane gives us a sense of what it is like to be a transsexual. She allows us to put ourselves in her place and to feel what she has felt. In the end, we realize that she is a person like us.

"Being Different," like much of "This is Their Home," is presented in the subject's own words. Her story was pieced together from edited transcripts of taped interviews (see Chapter 5). Although Jane's own story can stand without interpretation, the book in which this paper originally appeared included an introduction and conclusion by the researcher.

Chapters 10, 11, and 12 contain papers organized around certain themes and based on participant observation research. In these papers, the researchers use their subjects' words and behavior to illustrate their points.

"The Chance of a Lifetime," Chapter 10, describes two door-to-door sales training programs. The paper starts with the premise that persuasion is a constant feature of everyday life. It goes on to examine how the strategies of persuasion which most of us take for granted are formalized and taught to trainees in the programs in question. Finally, the paper concludes that trainees are not unlike the clients they are trained to manipulate.

In Chapter 11, we move to a paper with a slightly different focus. "Simplistic Answers to the Problem of Inequality: Teacher Meets Technology" illustrates a study that was based on team research and was conducted for an interested party. Using a symbolic interactionist perspective, the authors of "Teacher Meets Technology" look at the educational use of "instructional technology," or "audiovisual aids," in the context of teachers' perspectives on schools and on their work. They come to the conclusion that "instructional technology" does not live up to the promises of the industry that promotes it.

We return to the state institution study in Chapter 12 with a paper entitled "Doin' a Job." In the symbolic interactionist tradition, the paper juxtaposes attendants' perspectives on and concerns in their work with the institution's ideology. It concludes that attendants regularly subjugate residents' interests in order to further their own and suggests that we should take a closer look at the fronts presented by people who run such institutions.

In the final paper in Part Two, "Working Out Failure," we move away from a description and analysis of a specific setting to a more general discussion of theoretical issues based on the data collected in the previously mentioned participant observation study of a job training program for the "hard core" unemployed. "Working Out Failure" examines some of the ways in which organizations, organizational goals, and measures of success have been traditionally conceptualized and proposes that we begin to conceptualize them from new perspectives.

In short, we have attempted to give you a taste of the kinds of papers that can be written with the use of qualitative data. Treat these papers as examples and not necessarily as models.

NOTES

1. For a critique of styles of reporting qualitative research, see John Lofland, "Styles of reporting qualitative field research," *The American Sociologist* 8 (August): 101–111, 1974. See Fred Davis, "Stories and sociology," *Urban Life and Culture* 3 (October): 310–316, 1974; and Julius A. Roth, "Turning adversity to account," *Urban Life and Culture* 3 (October): 347–361, 1974, for researchers' accounts of how they reported their findings.

2. See Severyn T. Bruyn, *The Human Perspective in Sociology: The Methodology of Participant Observation* (Englewood Cliffs, N.J.: Prentice-Hall, 1966), pp. 237–244.

3. Note that our scheme is similar to Bruyn's, *ibid.*, with the one exception that we combine his second and third levels. These two levels also parallel Barney Glaser and Anselm Strauss's distinction between "substantive" theory and "formal" theory. See their *The Discovery of Grounded Theory: Strategies for Qualitative Research* (Chicago: Aldine, 1967), p. 32.

4. See Irwin Deutscher, *What We Say/What We Do: Sentiments and Acts* (Glenview, Ill.: Scott, Foresman, 1973), pp. 5–6.

5. For one criticism of the way social scientists write, see Malcolm Cowley "Sociological habit patterns in linguistic transmogrification," *The Reporter,* September 20, 170–175, 1956.

6. C. Wright Mills, *The Sociological Imagination* (New York: Oxford University Press, 1959), p. 31.

7. Also see William Strunk, Jr. and E. B. White *The Elements of Style* (New York: Macmillan, 1972, 2nd ed.); Bruyn, *Human Perspective,* pp. 233–254; and H. Taylor Buckner, "Organization of a large-scale field work course," *Urban Life and Culture,* **2,** no. 3 (October): 371–375, 1973.

8. Cowley, "Sociological habit patterns."

9. Mills, *Sociological Imagination,* p. 224.

10. This point comes from Irwin Deutscher in a personal communication. Deutscher guards against this sort of thing by marking "used" across materials in the original field notes after they have been quoted.

CHAPTER EIGHT

This Is Their Home

In this chapter I offer a description of a typical day on a ward for the "severely and profoundly retarded" in a large state institution.[1] While the events depicted here did not all occur on the same day, they do represent actual situations and conditions observed during one year of intensive observation. These particular events have been selected in order to provide a general picture of the ward's routine. I have attempted to neither conceal nor exaggerate the brutality and pathos of ward life.

"You'll find that we are overcrowded on some wards. We do have a lot more residents than we should have, and we could use more money from the state." The Director paused for a moment, and then added, "But we do the best we can with what we have. Nobody's perfect, of course."

With that the Director excused himself, mentioning that he had a budget meeting to attend.

I left the Administration Building and walked toward Building 27 which was located at the rear of a large building complex.

Strange, I thought, was the lonely, but meticulously well-kept, garden in the front of the grounds at Empire State School. Strange, I thought, was the serenity of the institution which contained several thousand people within its walls. Where could all the people be?

It was only as I approached the rear of the complex that I saw a person here, and three more there, and, finally, a group of older men walking double-file and holding hands, with one attendant at the front of the column and another behind. There was no particular destination. They were just walking.

An empty playground stood across the road from Building 27. The sound of childrens' voices was not to be heard here—only lonely cries and screams emanating from Building 27 and Ward 83.

David Dunn, one of the few residents of Ward 83 permitted to roam the halls during the day, stood in the small anteroom (ostensibly intended for visitors, but now in disrepair) inside the front door of Building 27. I waved to Dunn. He looked around cautiously, wondering, perhaps, to whom I could be waving. Not seeing anyone else, he grinned and waved back.

Dunn walked me down the long hallway to the stairs leading to the fourth floor and Ward 83: "You coming up to our ward? I like all the boys up there. They're all good boys."

As I walked up the stairs, David called after me, "I'll talk to you later."

I first noticed the mixed odor of disinfectant and excrement as I climbed the stairs. The smell of disinfectant became progressively weaker and the smell of excrement stronger the closer I came to the fourth floor.

This was a strange "school" indeed: the stairway was enclosed in heavy steel-mesh grating; reinforced wire glass was in the windows.

A large cartoon mural decorated the wall at the top of the stairs. It was matched by several smaller paintings in the dayroom of 83. "Some of these patients here are surprising. See these paintings around here? A patient did them. Yea, a patient. He used to be up here. I can't paint that good. I'll tell ya, some of them have talents you wouldn't believe."*

The hallway of 83 was empty except for Kelly, a frail, 20-year-old resident who was sitting near the dayroom door. Kelly looked up at me as I approached: "Hi, Steve. I missed you. Steve . . . S-T-E-V-E. I can spell dog too . . . D-O-G . . . cat . . . C-A-T." Kelly began to recite the Presidents: "Washington, Adams, Jefferson. . . ." Kelly recited them

---

*Unless otherwise indicated all quotations are taken from the attendants on this ward.

perfectly, and then pleaded, "I'm no dummy. I'm the smartest one here."

An institutional haircut, a shave, standard on this ward, revealed deep scars covering Kelly's head. He explained, "I got hit by a car when I was seven. Brain damage. That's why I'm this way."

Bill, the supervising attendant, and Tresh, a resident, were busy mopping the dayroom floor.[3] As on most warmer days, the majority of the residents had been sent to the porch.

Bill carefully mopped one half of the terrazzo floor until he had come to the 35 or 40 beds, covered with sheets and blankets but no pillows and pushed together at the far end of the room. Tresh mopped the other half of the dayroom as efficiently as Bill if not in as orderly a manner.

"Tresh looks like a little monkey, but he's real sharp. He loves to work. All these kids love to work and it's real good for them. They have nothing else to do so they love to work. Let's face it, it's easier for us too if they do some of the work."

The "dining room boys," so called because they ate their meals in a hall downstairs, slept in this room. The remaining 35 residents, the "dopes" or "low grades," slept in a similar, but smaller dormitory at the other end of the hall. These rooms, along with the bathroom and the porch, formed the setting in which most of life's activities took place for the residents of Ward 83.

Bill finished mopping the floor and walked over to me. Mike, another attendant, opened the porch door and started to let residents into the dayroom. Decidedly annoyed, Bill screamed, "God damn it, Mike, get those bastards back out there. We never let them in till dinner's here at 4:00." Bill turned to me: "We just cleaned this god damn floor. If we let them in now, they'll just get it dirty again."

Bill started for the dayroom door: "Follow me." He led me to a storage closet in the hall. He unlocked the door and pointed to a pile of ripped clothing in the middle of the floor: "This is what they give us to put on them. Now how are we supposed to keep them clothed when this is all they give us? They won't give us no disinfectant either. I have to buy my own. You gotta clean those floors. You gotta have something to pour over the piss and shit. But they won't give us no disinfectant. I got young kids at home. I could take hepatitis or something home from this place and my kids could get it. Maybe the state don't care, but I care."

He shook his head and continued, "I'm too old to get another job. I'm 50 now. Who's gonna hire a guy 50 years old? Besides, somebody gotta do it. Somebody gotta take care of these kids."

It was dinnertime when we returned to the dayroom. Several long tables and benches had been arranged for dinner. The meal had been brought up from the kitchen.

The residents rushed into the room from the porch, pushing and shoving each other out of the way. Half sat down at the tables. The other half, the "dining room boys," sat on the floor behind them. Some of the "working boys" prepared to help the attendants serve dinner.

The attendants, five from this shift and two who would stay until 6:30, unloaded several pans of steaming food from a dining room cart and placed them on a serving table. There were mashed potatoes, stew, corn, bread, cake with blueberries, and coffee.

Food and excrement combined to emit a particularly offensive odor.

One of the residents at the table wore a football helmet. He had a swollen forehead and enlarged lips and cheeks; layers of tissue bulged out from underneath the helmet.

Bill pried the helmet from the resident's head and explained, "We have to keep the helmet on him 'cause he's a biter. He'll bite one of the others and won't let go." The face, shaped by the helmet for so many years, remained the caricature of what it once was.

This was clearly the best time of day. The residents laughed as they impatiently awaited their last food until morning.

The attendants paused to serve themselves and some of the "working boys" cake and blueberries. Mike called over to me, "Want some cake and blueberries? It's good stuff. We'll save you some for later."

A resident at the tables pulled his pants to his knees and urinated. He was ignored by the attendants.

After the attendants had finished their dessert, they dished the food into partitioned trays. Three residents and an attendant served the meal to those at the tables.

The residents ate quickly. Some used the large spoons provided them. Others used their hands. One ate his bread first, stuffing two pieces into his mouth at one time. A more meticulous eater across from him carefully broke his bread into small pieces only to have it stolen by another. "They have atrocious eating habits, don't they? The ones who can eat decently go downstairs."

Flies hovered over the residents and their food.

Not all of the residents could eat by themselves. Four were spoon-fed, two by "working boys" and two by attendants. A "working boy" fed a scoop of mashed potatoes to a resident in two spoonfuls. An attendant poured coffee over a resident's stew and potatoes before shoveling one spoonful after another into his mouth. These residents swallowed quickly without chewing. "They get their food mashed. Can you imagine giving them a turkey leg the way they eat? They'd swallow the whole thing."

Mike "handed out" extra bread and hamburger buns to the residents. He walked back and forth beside the tables, breaking pieces of bread in half and throwing them onto residents' trays.

Dinner was "finished" ten minutes after the first resident had been served. Bill and another attendant pulled slower eaters from the tables and pushed them in the direction of the porch. Partially chewed food covered the shirts of many residents. Many others were still chewing as they left the room. "This is just like the Army. There you don't get any time to eat."

As workers gathered the dinner trays, rinsed them in a large bucket of water, and stacked them on a tray to be taken downstairs, attendants wiped off tables and swept under them. When the residents and attendants finished, they too went out on the porch.

A three-foot wall, topped by a chain-link fence, surrounded the porch. "A while ago one kid jumped off. He only broke his leg though. They don't get hurt like you and me."

The attendants sat in one corner of the room. They joked with each other, commented on this or that resident or supervisor, and occasionally walked around the room.

"All there is here is random activity." A dozen residents walked or stood around. An equal number huddled together on two benches in a corner. The remaining residents sat or lay on the floor.

A look around the room confirmed Bill's earlier remarks on clothing. Most of the residents wore the remnants of heavy green, white, or grey institutional clothing. A few wore outdated, but regular, clothes. And a few others wore nothing.

Two residents were assigned to "the bucket": to clean up the feces and urine of the 20 or so incontinent residents on this ward. One of them was

Mueller. "He's gained 20 pounds. That's why I put him on the bucket. He needs the exercise. He could have a heart attack." The other was Talman. "A guy from the day shift put him on the bucket for a week to punish him. He ate up here one day and then went downstairs with the dining room boys to eat again."

Mueller and Talman remained busy throughout the night. "I'll tell you one thing. I ain't getting down on my hands and knees to clean up shit. I wasn't hired to clean up shit. I won't do it. I don't care what they do. Sure, I'd do it for my own kids, but I won't do it here. They live here. This is their home. Why shouldn't they clean up the shit?"

Mike spotted a resident asleep on the floor and screamed at him to wake up. "We can't let them sleep now or they'll be up all night and the midnight shift will blame us for it. You just can't give them everything they want or you won't be able to control them."

Warner, one of the five residents on this ward with Down's Syndrome, crawled over to Bud, an attendant, and sat down on the floor beside him. Bud put his arm around Warner, who rested his head on Bud's lap. Bud stated affectionately, "Every ward has a pet, and Warner's mine." Warner looked up at Bud and smiled.

Mike walked over to Warner, grabbed his hand, and held it up for me to see. He explained, "See that dry skin? Warner's a mongoloid and mongoloids always have skin problems. You can always tell a mongoloid by his hands. They have a straight line going across. That's the one way you can always tell."

The two attendants from the 6:30 shift and one from the evening shift stood up and started for the door. One yelled, "Get in line." The "dining room boys" ran to the door and followed the attendants out. A crippled resident fell to the floor in his haste to follow the others.

Those two attendants left the porch to have dinner in a dietary kitchen by the stairway. Only Bill and Mike remained.

The porch seemed quiet now. Bill took out a newspaper and distributed sections to Mike and me: "Here, this will help you pass the time."

Bill looked around the room, pointed to a puddle of urine on the floor, and screamed, "Mueller, clean that puddle up." Mueller went over to the puddle, knelt down, and wiped up the urine. He stopped once to wring out his saturated rag with his bare hands. As Mueller stood up, I noticed that feces covered the front of his shirt.

Mike put down his section of the paper, and said, "They're offering this motivation course here. I'd really like to take it. I could do a lot of good for these kids if I had that. I'd really like to do some good for them. I mean, right now we're sitting around reading newspapers, but we usually play with them."

Bill motioned to Mike and pointed to Talman, who was asleep in a corner. Mike quietly left the room and returned a minute later with a bucket of water.

Mike walked slowly toward Talman at first. Bill waved for him to be quiet. Suddenly Mike rushed toward Talman and drenched him with the bucket of water. Talman jumped up, shaken. Mike and Bill broke into laughter. Mike yelled, "That'll teach you to sleep during the day when you're on the bucket, Talman."

Mike continued, "What do you say, Talman?" Talman replied, "Thank you, Mr. Walsh." Mike pressed, "What do you say?" Talman hesitated for a moment and then answered, "Thanks; I needed that." Apparently satisfied, Mike said, "That's right, Talman; you needed that. Now clean that water up."

Mike sat down: "He won't forget that for awhile. You tell me, what's he going to remember more: getting hit or getting a bucket of water thrown on him? Of course, the water. That's what they tell you in training. Give them something they'll remember."

Talman started wiping up the water. Another resident walked past him, slipped on the wet floor, and fell on his back. Undaunted, he stood up again and walked away. Mike shook his head and remarked, "See, they're just like babies. They can fall all day and never get hurt."

Two attendants returned from dinner. Mike and Bill then left.

A resident who was sitting on one of the benches bent over and vomited on the floor. One of the attendants, Roy, queried, "I wonder what made him sick."

Roy looked around the room, and called to Mueller: "Mueller, clean that vomit up." Mueller carried his bucket over to the vomit. He scooped up most of it with his bare hands and spread the rest around on the floor with a rag. Roy called over to Mueller, "Ok, Mueller, go get clean water in your bucket."

Fisher, one of the 15 or so residents who wore shoes, came over to me and proudly pointed to his black leather tie shoes: "I have new shoes."

A resident behind Fisher was not as fortunate. His feet were stained yellow and brown, and his toes were infected with athlete's feet.

The "dining room boys" and an attendant returned from dinner at 6:00.

Mueller walked over to Roy and affectionately placed his hand on Roy's shoulder. Roy jumped up suddenly: "Jesus Christ, Mueller. You're on the bucket. Get the hell outta here." Mueller cringed and hurried away.

There was a crack in the floor where urine gathered. One resident crawled over to it, leaned over, and licked the urine.

Bill returned from dinner.

Mike returned with a tray full of medications. "About half of them have fits of some kind so we give them Phenobarbital and Dilantin. Most of them are on tranquilizers too: Thorazine or Seconol. I heard about one time when they didn't have any medications for two or three days. They couldn't do a thing with them. They just locked the door and got the hell out."

Mike dispensed medications to most of the residents. He approached one resident whose face was still smeared with food from dinner. Mike called to another resident, "Romano, come over here." Mike handed two pills to Romano which Romano placed on the resident's tongue. The resident swallowed without water. "If one of them has food all over his face or if you don't want to put your hand in their mouths, you have Kelly or Romano do it."

Bill noticed feces in the middle of the floor. He stood up: "Talman, Talman!" Bill looked around and, not seeing Talman, yelled, "Kelly, go clean that soil up."

Kelly, his left leg crippled, hopped over to a bucket and dragged it to the feces. He knelt down, carefully picked up the feces with his bare hand, and dropped it into the bucket. He took a rag from the murky bucket and wiped the floor. Kelly hopped back to where he was sitting before and sat down. A minute later Kelly was chewing his fingernails. "Don't ever drink out of something after one of them did. You never know what you might catch. They could be carrying anything."

Franklin, a heavy-set resident in his mid-twenties, had an upset look on his face and was pacing by a far wall. Without warning, he punched one resident and kicked another. The resident he punched crawled away. He was crying as blood poured from his nose.

Bud called Franklin to him and asked, "What's wrong, Franklin?" Bud turned to me: "Franklin's a pretty good kid most of the time." Mike, who was sitting beside me now, joined in, "He's the nicest kid on the ward, but don't get him mad. He'd kill anybody. He'd kill you. Don't worry, though. All these kids respect intelligence. If there's one thing they respect, it's intelligence."

The resident who was wearing the football helmet fell off the chair on which he had been sitting. Another resident helped him back onto his chair, but again he fell, this time hitting his head on the floor. Mike explained, "We have to keep a helmet on him 'cause he falls off all the time. He could go at any time. We always know when they get like that they don't have long to live. Yea, but just wait. He'll die and they'll blame it all on us."

There was a commotion behind us. A naked resident was sitting on a bench and was kicking another resident. "He went blind a while ago. Look how big he is and he's only 15. Can you imagine how hard it would be to handle him in a couple of years if he could see?"

Bill ran over to the resident, screaming. He grabbed him by the shoulder and slapped him twice on the side of the head. The resident, Baer, began to cry.

Mike pointed to Baer: "Don't get the wrong idea. Bill had to hit that kid. I don't go for hitting kids around all the time. Not one bit. But that kid needed it."

Bill dragged Baer to a corner, pushed him, and walked away. Baer crawled to the middle of the room, feeling his way as he went and bumping into other residents. He continued to cry. Mike said, "See how he feels his way around? That's the only way he can tell who anyone is. You have to be careful. Sometimes he can't tell if you're an employee or one of them."

Bill, sitting again, called Talman to him: "Talman, what's 69 and 78?" Talman thought for a second and replied, "69 and 78 is 147." Bill said, "Right, Talman. Now what's 56 and 37?" Talman answered, "56 and 37 is 91." Bill frowned: "No, that's not right, Talman." Talman hesitated, and then said, "93." Bill responded, "That's right, Talman."

Mike leaned over to me and whispered, "Tuesday." He turned then to Talman: "Talman, I was born on March 17, 1942. What day of the week was that?" Talman pondered the question for a moment and replied, "Tuesday." Mike nodded knowingly to me. Mike gave Talman another date, and, again, Talman gave the correct day of the week.

Mike sat back: "That's why this place is so interesting. There's never a dull moment. Like Talman is really something. He was in another ward, but they had to put him up here for his behavior. He jumps up and unscrews light bulbs."

Mike left the room and returned shortly with more medications: tranquilizers. He dispensed them with minor difficulty until he came to one resident who received two medications, one of which was a large "knockout drop." He called to another attendant and to Kelly: "Come hold him for me."

Kelly and the attendant held the resident's arms. Mike grabbed him by the shirt and threw the two pills into his mouth. The resident didn't swallow. Mike slapped him across the face: "You'd better swallow them, boy." Mike slapped him again, and, finally, the resident swallowed.

Mike moved next to Talman: "The doctor says you should take these, Talman. They're for your own good." To Mike's surprise, Talman swallowed the pills without resistance.

Mike finished dispensing the medications and sat down.

A resident standing in the corner removed his pants and threw them toward the middle of the floor. They were covered with feces. He was one of a dozen residents who were now completely naked. "We try to keep them dressed, but they just won't keep their clothes on."

Fisher saw another resident falling and rushed over to him. He caught him and rested him gently on the floor. Mike stood up: "Come on. I want to show you something."

We walked over to the resident. The soles of my shoes stuck to the urine-stained floor as I walked.

The resident was writhing on the floor. He moved his stiff limbs in jerking movements, and his eyelids fluttered. Mike explained, "He's having a seizure. He has one about once a day. He'll be walking around in a couple of minutes." Mike turned around and walked back to his chair.

As I returned to my chair and sat down, Bill called Sherman over and leaned over to me: "You have to see this."

Sherman sat down on the floor in front of Bill. Bill handed him a burning cigarette. Sherman took it and popped it into his mouth. The ash sizzled as it touched Sherman's saliva.

Bill tapped Sherman on the leg: "Swallow it, Sherman. Go ahead. Swallow it." Sherman looked uncomfortable, but swallowed. The attendants laughed at the sight of him swallowing a burning cigarette.

Laughing, Bill remarked, "It doesn't even hurt him. He loves to eat them."

Sherman pointed in the direction of the bathroom. More laughter. Bill said, "Yea, Sherman. You can go get a drink of water." Sherman ran out.

Mike related, "We brought in a cigar for him one day and he ate that too. A little later, he barfed up the cigar and about 20 cigarette butts."

Mike became serious: "Now if you told anybody about this, they'd say we was torturing the kid. But he don't mind. He likes to do it. Now that you've been up here a while, you're beginning to understand this place."

Sam, another attendant, interrupted, "They complain about us up front, but they don't know what it's like here. I say if they don't like the job we're doing, let them do it."

Baer was still crying and crawling around the room. Bill said firmly, "That's it. We're gonna have to give him a shot." Bill and the two other attendants grabbed Baer and dragged him to the sleeping area in the main room. The two attendants held Baer while Bill left the room. Baer cried even harder.

Bill returned shortly with the building supervisor, a nurse. The attendants rolled Baer over onto his stomach and held him tightly as the nurse administered a 100 mg. shot of Thorazine. Baer continued to struggle for a few minutes but finally fell asleep.

Bill came back to the porch and yelled, "Ok, get 'em off." The residents who were still dressed removed their clothes and threw them into the middle of the floor. One resident left the room, returning shortly with a cart and two large laundry bags. He and three other residents gathered the clothes and stuffed them into the bags.

Sam cautiously kicked clothes into a pile: "You have to be careful. You never know when there might be shit or something in them."

Except for the several workers, the residents were all naked. Many of their bodies were bruised and feces-stained.

The "dining room boys" proceeded to the dormitory in the main room; the "dopes" to the smaller dormitory. "We're the only ward in this building that doesn't get pajamas. They won't give us any. The other wards hoard all the clothes."

It was 9:00.

I left the porch with Mike and Roy. We walked to the smaller dormitory, passing the bathroom on the way.

Water and urine saturated the bathroom floor. Smeared feces covered one wall. There were two showers, several sinks, three unflushed toilets, and an open pipe where a fourth toilet used to be. There were no toilet seats, no toilet paper, no soap—none of the conveniences or necessities to which most people are accustomed. One resident sat on a toilet in plain view of any passersby in the hall.

The odor of the feces and urine pervaded the smaller dorm; there were urine stains on the floor and dried feces on bed frames and sheets. "I guess you think this place smells. I don't. I can't smell a thing. You get used to it after a while."

A large barrel of tennis shoes stood in one corner of the room.

Mike turned off the lights and then climbed up on a chair to turn on a television set which was mounted on a wall eight feet above the floor. Kelly and Romano entered the room and sat down on small chairs in front of the television.

Bill came down the hall, looked in the room, and screamed, "Schneider, get to the bathroom." Bill left. Mike explained, "We're trying to toilet train Schneider. It's a real job. We've been working on him for a long time."

One resident sat up in bed and quietly looked around the room. Mike yelled, "Bolin, put your head down and get to sleep."

Kelly looked at the resident: "Go to sleep, Bolin. Get your head down." Mike laughed: "Call him a miserable son-of-a-bitch, Kelly." Kelly yelled at Bolin, "You miserable son-of-a-bitch. You miserable bastard. Get to sleep."

Bill returned to the room: "Romano, Kelly, go get your coffee and bread." Romano and Kelly left. Bill sat down: "We like to give them a reward, a cigarette or coffee, when they work for us. Sometimes they won't work for us and then we don't give them the reward. They think they can get it without doing anything."

Daniels, one of the older residents on the ward, came down the hall and stood by Bill. Bill handed him a cigarette: "Go get your coffee now, Daniels." Daniels replied, "Not yet." Bill said, "Ok, you can stick around for awhile."

Bill turned to me: "Daniels here is a working boy. Aren't you, Daniels?" Daniels answered, "Yea."

Bill spoke to me in a low voice: "You see, Daniels has loose bowels at night. He shits the bed and rubs himself in it. Now they had him over in Building 14 with some of the smarter boys. But, no, it was too much work for them to wake him up every night and trip him to the bathroom. No, they couldn't do that. So instead of tripping him at night, they sent him up here."

Bill left, and then shortly Daniels left also.

The ward was quiet. We were interrupted only by the sound of urine hitting against the terrazzo floor. Roy looked up: "One of them's pissing again."

Daniels returned. "He sleeps in here 'cause he's real bright and can take care of the others."

Daniels went over to a bed in the corner and carefully undressed. He folded his clothes neatly and placed them on a windowsill near his bed. He removed a tobacco pouch and cigarette papers from his shirt pocket and hid them under his bed. Like many of the other residents, Daniels guarded his few possessions by carrying them with him wherever he went.

As Daniels climbed into bed, Mike laughed and called over to him, "Don't play with it tonight, Daniels. It's the property of the state." Daniels put his head down and turned away.

Roy put his head up: "I just heard one vomit. See, after you work here a while, you can hear everything. You have to be alert on this job."

Mike broke in: "This job doesn't require a lot of physical work, but it does take mental work, and, let me tell you, that's harder. You have to use psychology on these kids."

Roy agreed: "Yea, and you gotta be careful with them too. God may have given them no brains, but he gave them superhuman bodies. They're stronger than a regular person."

Mike laughed: "Yea, they have superhuman cocks too." Mike turned to me: "That's just a joke we have around here."

Mike and Roy sat back and watched television for the rest of the evening. They anxiously awaited the midnight shift to relieve them. They were going out for a beer after work. "We go out for a beer every night. We like to leave our troubles at work. Listen, if you don't drink when you start here, you'll be drinking by the time you leave. You gotta drink. It's all the tension you have here."

This shift was relieved at 11:15. I left Ward 83.

"I'd give anything to be able to help these kids, but you can't do it. They're too low-grade.

"You can't ask them to do something. You can't call them by their first name and ask them to please do something. Hell, most of them don't even know their first names. You can't talk to them like you would if it was your own kid, or your cousin, or your nephew, or your neighbor's kid. It just don't work. You have to punch them, kick them, or cuff them on the back of the head. That's all they can understand.

"You gotta feel sorry for them, but you can't let yourself. Well, you can feel sorry for them, but you can't show it. If you start showing it here, you've got big problems. You just can't show it."

NOTES

1.   This "day" consists of the 3:30 P.M. to 11:30 P.M. shift. Ward 83 is officially designated as a ward for "severely and profoundly retarded, aggressive, ambulatory, young adult males." Not all of the residents on this ward are "severely and profoundly retarded" (IQ's range from 6 to 57), not all are aggressive (in actuality, few are), not all are ambulatory (four cannot walk and many others are crippled), and not all are young (ages range from 14 to 44).

2.   For the sake of clarity, attendants will be referred to by their first names, and residents will be referred to by their last names.

CHAPTER NINE

Being Different

Being referred to as a "transsexual" doesn't bother me too much. I would rather be thought of as a "person" first but it doesn't make me angry because that's what I am. A transsexual is a person who wishes to change sexes and is actively going about it. Which is exactly what I am doing.[1]

I have the physical organs of a man but I feel that I am a woman. For a long time I fought those feelings but I don't anymore. I take female hormones and dress and live as a woman and I have for two years. I understand my transsexualism for what it is. Basically it boils down to this: What is a person? Is a person what he is on the inside or what he is on the outside? I know what I am on the inside: a female. There is no doubt there. I could spend 50 years of my life trying to change but I doubt if that would do anything. I know what I am. I like it and I don't want to change. The only thing I want to change is my body so that it matches what I am. A body is like a covering; it's like a shell. What is more important: the body or the person that is inside?

I went for three years of psychotherapy and I couldn't find anything in my childhood to pin this thing down on, nothing that would be differ-

---

This essay was compiled from the transcripts of approximately one hundred hours of open interviewing with Jane Fry (pseudonym). This chapter originally appeared in Robert Bogdan (Ed.), *Being Different: The Autobiography of Jane Fry* (New York: Wiley, 1974).

ent from your background or anybody else's. Sure, if you look hard enough into my childhood you would find things just like if I looked into yours I could find things if I wanted to. You might say that there were psychological reasons for my state if my father was a super drunk or if my mother made me sleep with her or if she wanted a girl so much she dressed me in girls' clothes but there was nothing like that. My father said to me once that there were a few males on his side of the family way back that were fairly feminine. I don't know whether heredity is part of it or not. For sure my father isn't feminine.

I spent three years searching for psychological reasons and other kinds of reasons because I was expected to. I'm not interested in reasons anymore. I don't give a damn what caused it. God could have poked his finger in my bellybutton and said, "You're going to think of yourself as a girl," and that could have caused it. All I want to do is get it fixed. I just want to be myself. But in order to get it fixed you have to convince God knows how many people that you're sane, convince people that you really want the operation, find someone to do it, and come up with the money.

I stopped looking for reasons two years ago. Every doctor you see gives you a different explanation and you just come to the point of knowing that they just don't know what the hell they are talking about. One thing that I did learn in meeting all the doctors is that you have to give a little—pretend a little. Any one of them can kill you physically or emotionally. They can put the dampers on everything. If they decide that I am totally insane because I want to be a female, who knows what they can do. I nod when they tell me their theories now. You have got to learn to give and take which I took some time in learning.

Before I go on and tell you about the operation and transsexualism and the hassle involved in that let me tell you a little about the way I look at life and analyze myself. There is this story I heard once about Freud that pretty much sums it up. He was at a meeting with some colleagues and he lit up this huge stogey. His colleagues around the table started snickering because of the writing about oral complexes and phallic symbols. Freud just looked at it and said, "Yes, gentlemen. I know this is a phallic symbol but it is also a God damned good cigar." That's a good way to look at life. If it's enjoyable, do it as long as it doesn't harm anybody and don't worry about analyzing everything. That is my philosophy. I am the only one responsible for what I do, and as long as I don't harm another human being mentally or physically I'm being a good person. I think that I am a good person because I operate according to my principles. I may break the law but I'm not breaking my law which seems like the sensible one to me. I also think people should help each other, which I try to do. I think people should help me. They shouldn't sit down and try to analyze me or try to figure out why I am the way I am or whether I am eligible for a sex change.

There are two laws that I know of that affect transssexuals—one the police can pick you up for. It's about impersonation; I don't know the actual law but it was put on the books in the 1700s. The reason they had it was farmers were dressing up as Indians in order to avoid paying taxes —some would even dress as women. So they passed this law not allowing people to dress up in public or to paint their faces. That's the law they now arrest transsexuals and transvestites on.

The other law keeps surgeons from doing the operation. That one comes from England. There was a war going on there and the people were trying to get out of the draft by cutting off their fingers or toes and they would have a surgeon do it. So the law states that no surgeon can take away any part of your body that would make you ineligible for the draft. So cutting off my genitals is making me ineligible for the draft. I think the draft board could afford to lose a few, but anyway that's the law that the surgeons are afraid of. I've heard of a couple of times when doctors were ready to perform the operation and were notified by the DA that if they did charges would be pressed.

The doctors usually back off. They don't want to get involved: they don't have the time to get into a test case, and most of the time they don't want that kind of publicity. The hospitals especially don't like that kind of publicity. They don't get donations, I guess, if the public finds out they are doing sexual-change operations. The board of directors and contributors jump down their throats for doing such an atrocious thing and if the word gets out that a hospital is doing the surgery, they get beseiged by transsexuals wanting it performed. Most people don't know the difference between transvestites, homosexuals and transsexuals, so I think I ought to clear up that before I go any further. Most people just lump them all together. I saw one Archie Bunker show on homosexuals that really pointed out how Americans think about people who have different sexual practices. People don't realize how prejudiced they are about homosexuality and transsexuality because they aren't even at a point of knowing that it is something that you can be prejudiced about. They are so sure that the rest of the world is supposed to be the way they are that they don't even think the people who are different have an opinion. They just lump them all together as nuts or perverts. That's the way Archie was on this program.

Well, anyway, a transvestite only wants to dress like a woman. They don't want to go all the way and have an operation and live as a woman. The transsexual wants an operation. It's a difference in the way you think about yourself. The way of thinking of a transsexual is: "I am a female with a birth defect. I am a woman but I have the organs of the other sex. I want to be a whole person again." The term is also used to refer to people who are physiologically women who want to be men.

The way of thinking of a transvestite is: "I am a man but I want to play the role of a female. I know that I am a male but I get kicks out of dressing like a woman." The transvestite gets emotional gratification and psychological good feelings from dressing. A transsexual doesn't. There is an interest in clothing but it's much like a woman's interest. No erotic stimulation or anything like that. Like I am just as happy bumming around in a pair of jeans and a blouse as in some type of fancy low-cut gown with heels.

The difference between a homosexual and a transsexual or a transvestite is that the homosexual knows that he is a man, let's say, but he is sexually attracted to those of the same sex and has sex with them. He says: "I know that I am a man but I want to have sex with a man." Some transvestites are not homosexuals because they don't want to have sex with those who are of the same sex as they are; they want sex with the opposite sex.

I used to be down on homosexuals. Homosexuals and transsexuals usually don't hit it off. I happened to relate well with a group a few years ago and I was able to get over my prejudices and start seeing what we had in common rather than what we differed over. I found it easy to relate to this group because what we had in common was that we were suppressed. We both share some of the dangers of being brutalized because of our beliefs. We can be picked up for impersonation or for vagrancy or anything else they want to pick us up for. We also share being made jokes of or beat up at any time. Like just last week I had a seizure in the middle of the street and someone called an ambulance. The first thing I remember was being in the ambulance strapped to a stretcher. I looked up and there are these two guys laughing and joking. One says to me "Don't worry *dearie*, we've got you figured out." I was so angry I almost couldn't control myself but that is typical of what we have to watch out for.

When you're like me you have always got to be on your guard that you don't get into a position that is going to get you into a jam. Like I went downtown and picketed the recruiting center as part of the anti-war demonstration. I had decided that I was going to perform an act of civil disobedience with a group if they tried to clear us out of the road. But standing around down there, all of a sudden it hit me—if I get busted and get taken to jail, they might throw every charge in the book at me if they found out I was physically a man. I have to be more careful than anybody else that goes on a march like that. I was in the front of the parade in this particular march carrying a banner—but that wasn't smart to do. If people were to ever find out and if it were in the papers, the reporters and the readers would zero in on the fact of what I was and that would have blown the whole issue. Immediately all the hard hats would go back to their favorite sayings: "Look at all those fagot queers with the long hair marching around. They got a real beauty out in front this time." People like me aren't sincere about those issues according to them. We don't count.

It's hard for transsexuals because you don't have many allies. I'm almost totally dependent on white middle-class doctors to give me a fair shake. There are so few doctors that will see me that I have to scrape to get what I want. They are in control. They told me that I have to conform to their standards or I don't get the operation.

I'm probably different from other transsexuals but they probably think the same about themselves. One thing is that it is usually hard for transsexuals to talk about themselves especially after the operation. I'm going to tell you a lot about myself. Talking about it opens up a lot of old wounds. I haven't had the operation so it's a lot easier because the wounds are still in the open and I get new ones every day.

I don't think very many transsexuals have gone through three years of psychotherapy as I have. Most phase it out after 50 sessions or so. I'm different too in that most transsexuals don't go to psychiatric hospitals. Why that is I don't know. Most transsexuals are also very introverted. They want to stay totally under cover outside the public eye. They don't want to upset the apple cart. They have to keep low profiles so as to keep respectable. This is because they don't depend on each other so much as on their physicians.

Your doctor is the most important part of your life. He takes precedence over fathers and mothers in some cases. He is the person who prescribes the hormones and may be able to help you get the operation. You have got to keep him happy. Doctors are like gods to them. Which is why I don't think I get along too well with some doctors because I don't think of them or treat them like God, not anymore anyway—I think they are as fucked up in some respects as me. When you talk to another transsexual the first thing they will talk about is what their doctor is doing for them. I don't think it is healthy or that you can be a person if your whole life is so dependent on someone else who can cut you off any time.

I am talking about the transsexuals I know. I haven't known that many. Maybe I've met a total of 30. There aren't that many in the United States. Dr. Benjamin's book says there are 100,000 or something like that in the United States. Maybe I should just talk for myself.

The vast majority of transsexuals try to make it in the straight world, as the Gay Community calls it. The reason for that is because the operation is not very well advertised. I mean you don't see many articles in popular magazines about it so people don't know about it. People who are transsexuals and don't know about operations are trying to live the role that society says they have to. Like myself, everybody used to say, "You have got to be a little boy." I knew I wasn't but they said I had to. I went into the Navy to try to be. I went into submarine service trying to be. I even got married trying to be. I underwent psychotherapy but that didn't work either. Then I heard about the operation and that's what I have been working toward ever since.

I am presently living in purgatory. A little between heaven and hell. I am working my way upwards, slowly, but when you have to fight the whole damn system single-handed, it's hard. Usually you look for help and people turn their backs on you. I tell them what I want and they say, "*He's* really a sick person." They don't get it through their heads that they are the ones that have made me sick and are keeping me sick. Most transsexuals have had hassles but they don't have the hassles over being a transsexual; they have them over the way society fucks over them. After it fucks over you it asks what can we do to help. So to help they stick you into an institution for the mentally ill that gives you more hassles. It's a cycle. When I went to the VA psychiatric, I was in hell. Now that I am getting hormone shots and living and working as a female it's purgatory. Once I get the operation, although I know it's not going to be perfect, it will kind of be like heaven. I am not going to say that the operation is going to cure everything—I don't consider it a cure-all. I have a lot of hassles to clear up just like most people. It's not going to be a cure-all, but it will sure as hell get rid of many of the pressures and tensions I am under.

The cost of the operation is twice what it would be if it weren't so controversial. The cost in Casablanca is about $8,000 and they go between $3,500 and $5,000 in other places. That is not the cost of the operation; that is just the surgeon's fee. That is not the counting the anesthesiologist, the operating room, the recovery time, medication, etc. Since when does a person get over $3,000 for less than a day's work? What they do is remove parts of the male organ and use part of it to build a vagina. The vagina has the nerve endings from the penis and scrotum so there are sexual feelings.

There are two doctors in the world today who are working toward perfecting the male to female surgery. One is a doctor in Casablanca; the other is in Tijuana. They have their own clinics with operation suites and the whole thing. They are both expensive. You have to deposit the right amount in their Swiss bank account prior to the operation. He gets out of paying the taxes and the hassle of taking that much through customs. These are the men who are doing most of the surgical research.

There are people in the United States doing research but it is mostly statistical or psychological. A couple of places out West did some operations and have decided to wait between 12 and 20 years to find out the results before they do any more. Johns Hopkins did a lot but I don't think they are doing any now either. They were supposed to be doing one every three months or so. There are other places here and there that do them but it's hard to find out for sure who's doing them.

According to Dr. Benjamin who studied over 100 people who had the operation only one was considered unsatisfactory. They had all made a better adjustment to life than before the operation. The one that was unsatisfactory was a medical thing not psychological. So the operation seems pretty foolproof. By the way, psychotherapy has never been known to "cure" a transsexual.

The reason the cost is so high is part of the old supply and demand thing. Transsexuals need one thing, the operation, and there is only a small group of doctors who will do it. If these people stick together in the price they charge, the only thing someone can do is pay their price. You can't very well boycott or picket or stuff like that. There is no recourse but to pay it or not get it done.

People who do the operation have this informal rule that in order to be eligible for it you have to be living as a female for two years. That includes working as a female. You also have to have a recommendation from a psychiatrist you have been seeing for two years. They say that if you can work as a female successfully enough to make the money then you'll make a good adjustment after the operation. It's the kind of a situation where you're so concerned about the operation that it's hard to concentrate on working—if you had the operation, you might settle down. Besides it's almost impossible to get any kind of a job that pays enough for you to save on. The other thing is who is going to write you a recommendation in the first place to get a job and what name are they going to put down, your old one or your new one? Also, what about when they ask you for your social security card and it has a man's name on it? Medicaid won't pay for it and Blue Cross and Blue Shield get upset when you even suggest it. They consider it cosmetic surgery.

The operation is a vicious circle. I want to have the operation so bad that I am under great pressure and strain. The pressure makes it hard to find or keep a good job. The fact that you can't keep a job and that you're uptight is used as evidence that you're not sane. They tell you "If you really wanted it, you could do it." I can see their reasoning but I don't agree with it. I don't know what I can do about it though. They tell you getting the money is part of the therapy. What people don't understand is that transsexuals, myself included, think of this whole operation in the same way you would think of having a wart removed from your nose or having plastic surgery done on your nose. If you think your nose is ugly and you want it fixed, if it's bothering you, instead of worrying about it and while your head is thinking about it the way it is and all that stuff, you go out and get it fixed. That's the way I think of it but most physicians don't. Most people are so uptight about sex in general and about penises and vaginas that they have to find something psychological to worry about. It's funny.

I don't know how you're taking this so far but the majority of people hear about me and they automatically think I have problems—super head problems. Even if I don't have them, they think I'm crazy. You just try to avoid people like that. After I get to know people it works out. If I make them uptight, I leave.

People usually find out that I'm a transsexual not from me but from my "friends." It makes me angry to have to explain it to people because, I don't know, how would you like to have to explain yourself to everyone you met? Explain how you think you're a man or a woman. Why the hell do I have to be explained? I mean to hell with the transsexualism, I'm a human being first and female second and a transsexual third. But people can't respond to it like that. Society doesn't want to know me as a human being. I have to be a transsexual first to do anything. It's almost forget Jane Fry and let's talk about the transsexual. It's almost like when

I went to get my appendix out. They were so much into looking at me as a transsexual that they didn't do anything about my appendix. When I was in the psychiatric hospitals, they concentrated so much on me being a transsexual that they weren't willing to help me with what I needed help with.

I have come to automatically distrust people because of this. I want to be accepted as a human being and people won't do it; they make it so you can't be a human being. This combined with the operation being so hard to achieve that you have to concentrate on being a transsexual 24 hours a day instead of being a person. All your hopes ride on the operation and that's what you keep striving for and that's what you fight for. So you think of it all the time, and people treat you like one all the time, and there you are.

It actually makes it more frustrating for me when people don't know about me before I meet them because you have to jump over a hurdle—I have to explain more or less what I'm about. Sometimes I blow people's minds intentionally. I get a horror or a fear reaction from people who are set in their ways who haven't run across this kind of thing before.

Men get particularly uptight around me. They just don't know how to handle it. Some guys the first time they see me, like all males who see a female, look at me as a female and then all of a sudden they find out and it blows their image of themselves. They say to themselves, "God, I must be queer." A lot of people seem to go through that but I don't know what to do about it. I get along with women a lot better. They don't seem so threatened.

The biggest problem I face is dealing with society in a way that it accepts me and I can accept myself. I have done that to some extent but I feel I'm kind of doing it the easy way by living on the fringes in the freak culture. Most of my friends are either students or hang out in the university section. People are much more open in their thinking; they don't care if you're different or not. It makes life a lot easier than if I was to try to play the role of the super middle-class secretary who lives in the suburbs. The majority of transsexuals do that. They are super straight. Maybe that's easy for them dealing with it that way but I just couldn't make it. By living on the fringe I don't have to face the head hassles they do every day. The majority of transsexuals don't have the time or energy left after fighting the hassles to understand what society is like. They are so busy trying to join in and at the same time fighting it that they don't see what it's all about.

Being a transsexual it seems like you're fighting all society and everybody in it. If you don't have psychological hangups after all that fighting, there is something wrong with you. I've got problems now, quite a few emotional hangups right now. It doesn't mean that I have to be locked up. I recognize them but I also recognize the reason I got them. I spend half my time worrying about what society thinks instead of worrying about me. So you have to end up with problems. Anybody can relate the emotional problems that I have now to my childhood and say that my transsexualism is the reason for it but it's nothing about the transsexualism itself that causes the hangups: it's fighting society.

This doctor told me that my father was a very violent man and in rejecting him I rejected masculinity and violence so I had to be a female. I think that's bullshit. What he didn't stop to think was I probably was a transsexual right from the beginning and I was so worried about the problems that it caused with others I didn't know how to relate to them. You get so wrapped up in your emotions that you can't relate.

I don't think my transsexualism is the direct cause of my emotional problems but I have to let psychiatrists keep saying it is or else they won't treat me. I have got to get back on the road to getting my operation so I have to see one. When I see a psychiatrist now, I just ignore when they start rapping on about my transsexualism. If it gets too bad, I just won't see them anymore.

A lot of people can't even imagine the shit I go through. It's the same thing that they go through except I go through it to a greater extent. They are forced to become one thing or the other; they have to conform to a certain set of standards even though they don't think it fits them. With me it's just more obvious that's all. A normal guy if he likes to cut flowers or wants to be a hairdresser or something like that, his masculinity is questioned and he has pressure on him not to do it. Or a woman who wants to drive a truck: it's the same thing. The male/female thing is just part of it. There are other roles we play too. Masks: that's what I call them. By the time a person is 20 years old you can't see the person from the masks. If someone tries to go against the masks, they are schizophrenic or something else. That's what they are called. That's what is on my medical records.

With the masks, society tries to hide human sexuality. What I mean is that society has taken and stereotyped masculinity and feminity so you don't get a full and real picture of what it is. Everybody is trying to live up to the stereotype image.

It's hard to live away from the stereotype a little, but it is a thousand times harder to go away from it as radically as I have. I am doing what most people can't even think of, going from a man to a woman. My father's first comment when I told him was "Why can't you pick an easier one like being a homosexual?" Which makes a good point. At least if I was a homosexual I would be the same sex, but to do something so obvious like changing dress and everything is something that you can't hide. Women who want to go to work are thought to be crazy. If a normal person wants to change roles, he has to fight a lot; but if he wants to change sex, that's a lot harder.

I guess you can think of transsexualism as more or less a mask too. Or it can be. I'm a transsexual but people try to force me into a stereotype: they try to exaggerate the importance of what I am. It's a part of you, granted, but they make it more a part of you than it really is. I am trying not to make it that way. I'm trying not to fall into the slot but I am forced into it.

NOTES

1. Jane's definition of transsexualism closely parallels the one found in most modern dictionaries and those used by the professional community. Dr. Harry Benjamin, the doctor who first used the term states, "The transsexual male or female is deeply unhappy as a member of the sex (or gender) to which he or she was assigned by the anatomical structure of the body, particularly the genitals. To avoid misunderstanding: this has nothing to do with hermaphroditism. The transsexual is physically normal (although occasionally underdeveloped). . . . True transsexuals feel that they belong to the other sex, they want to be and function as members of the opposite sex. . . ." Harry Benjamin, M. D., *The Transsexual Phenomenon* (New York: The Julian Press, Inc., 1966), p. 13.

CHAPTER TEN

The Chance of a Lifetime

TEACHING AND SELLING AS PERSUASION

According to Goffman, "When an individual appears in the presence of others, there will usually be some reason for him to mobilize his activity so that it will convey an impression which it is in his interest to convey."[1] One can influence the impression others receive by influencing the "definition of the situation the others come to formulate." Thus, the individual, by his or her gestures, dress, posture, tone, words and so on, attempts to induce others to believe something about him- or herself and to act according to his or her plans. Following these thoughts, much of what takes place in interaction might be thought of as persuasion.

In our everyday life, we take for granted what may be termed techniques or strategies of persuasion. We wear nice clothes to a job interview. We speak in a certain way. We try to present outselves as responsible and intelligent individuals. Many of these techniques are so much a part of us that we do not think of "how to do it" or even that we are "doing it." Yet there are certain occupations in which the members

---

This is a significantly revised version of an article that originally appeared as Robert Bogdan, "Learning to sell door to door: Teaching as persuasion," *American Behavioral Scientist*, Sept./Oct., 55–64, 1972. Used by permission.

are consciously involved in persuasion. Certain kinds of salespeople, for example, are trained in the use of strategies on how to persuade a client to buy a certain product.

In this paper, we examine how prospective salespeople are taught to use techniques of persuasion to sell products in a door-to-door sales training program. The data was collected during a participant observation study[2] of two direct sales training programs held in a middle-sized northeastern city. Both one-week courses were sponsored by the sales divisions of national firms with standardized marketing schemes. The observer attended all of the training sessions, accompanied trainees on their first calls, and learned about the courses, as trainees did, by responding to classified ads. One company sold encyclopedias; the other sold vacuum cleaners.

THE SCRIPT

On the first day of class, trainees receive a booklet: "This is the script . . . you'll be expected to commit it to memory." The script, "canned talk," or "spiel," is central to the course. It outlines what the salesperson should say to the client from the moment he or she knocks on the door until the time he or she leaves.

Since the script takes an hour to present, memorizing it seems like an impossible task to many trainees. However, the instructors assure them: "Everybody has trouble doing memory work: all it takes is a lot of practice." Much practice follows. The trainees present the script to the class; they recite it to family and friends; and they hear their instructors repeat it over and over again.

At first, the students' recitals of the script are rather bland and expressionless. With practice and coaching from the instructors, however, their performances become less stiff. The instructors tell them: "smile," "go lean over their shoulders," "use your hands," "sit down," "take a stance of pride," "look him right in the eye," "go through some motions," "emphasize that word."

As the program progresses, the trainees are encouraged to use their own gestures and to make minor modifications in the script: "Change the sentence structure slightly to fit your own personality and your own way of speaking." Thus, they are required to learn only the sequence of topics, the major points, and some of the wording of the script.

The script is both a guide for the trainee and a strategy in itself. Since the salesperson knows precisely what he or she is going to say, she or he has control over and thus an advantage in interactions with clients.

CLIENTS

In general, clients are presented to trainees as people who are either easy to persuade ("nice" or "stupid") or who deserve to be persuaded ("bastards" or "assholes"). Instructors emphasize a positive sales spirit in which everyone can be sold: "You can sell anyone who doesn't have a psychological problem or who isn't God."

In specific instances, however, instructors admit that some people are more difficult to sell than others and that there are even some who are impossible to sell. They tell many stories about salespeople's encounters with clients. Told in great detail, the tales create types. Some people just won't buy what the salesperson is selling:

> One of the boys (a salesman with the company) went out to a house and got test cups and test cups full of dirt. (This is done to show the client that their own vacuum cleaner isn't doing the job.) The people said they didn't care . . . their house was as clean as they wanted it . . . he was a Ph.D. in psychology. . . . They had cats and the house was filthy. . . . They spent their time reading. . . . The dirt of the house didn't concern them. . . . There's nothing you can do about people like that. They didn't have children. . . . People with children are usually more concerned about dirt and health. . . . These people had better things to think about, or at least they thought they did. . . . You can't sell people like that and you're going to run into them.

Others are nothing but "bastards":

> We had this guy in Boston (a salesman). . . . He got in with some real bastard. I mean he really was an S.O.B.. . . . This guy was really loaded too (had money). . . . It was a fifty- or sixty-thousand dollar house. He was giving the demonstration and this S.O.B., that's all I can call him, he says, "You mean all I have to do is give you a list of names and you're going to give me five dollars for each name (the advertising gimmick)." This young man says: "Yeh, that's right."—the bastard, he said: "Can I have that in writing?" This guy (the salesman) didn't know what was up, so he went over to the desk and wrote out "for each name so-and-so gives me he will receive five dollars."—and he signs his name. This bastard writes down the name of 30 people and says: "O.K., when do I get the money?" . . . Now you'll usually run into nice people—you seldom run into a bastard like this. . . .

Clients who know too much make "static" (resist the pitch):

This one man, hell of a nice fella, went out on his first call. He got into this place . . . it was the house of a G.E. engineer. Let me tell you, he really gave the demonstrator a hard time. . . . Asked all questions about the motor. . . .

Finally, some clients are a surprise:

I had the poster open in front of me like this. I was bending down . . . I wasn't too interested in what Mr. and Mrs. Jones were doing. I looked up as I was placing it on the floor (the poster). I looked up and saw them. Hell, they were raising off their chairs like Siamese twins—their eyes glued right to that poster and listening to every word I said. You can't tell—you get those people who yes you up and down: "This is wonderful. This is terrific. What a wonderful plan." And then don't buy. You get the *slow comers*. They're not saying much but they're digesting everything. . . . So don't let up if they don't look enthusiastic, if they're not doing a toe dance around the room for you. Those are the very people that will surprise you.

Trainees are taught to "size up" their potential clients: to look for some of the "types." After all, no salesperson wants to waste his or her time on a client who can't be sold. Moreover, the salesperson's presentation should fit the client from the start. Sizing up enables her or him to withdraw early or to modify her or his presentation.

The vacuum cleaner company checks the credit ratings of potential clients and refers only those in good standing to salespeople. The encyclopedia salespeople are told to go out "cold canvassing" and to rely on their own observations to size up clients. Toys and children on the lawn are positive signs: people buy for their children. Run-down houses suggest low buying power. A modest home assures salespeople that they will not be overmatched educationally or socially.

Trainees in the encyclopedia training program are instructed to engage clients in casual conversation in the preliminary stages of their presentation. This method of sizing up is called small talk. Here a student plays "Mr. Jones" while he is interrogated by an instructor:

INSTRUCTOR.   This is a nice section of town. Fine house you have here, Mr. Jones. Are you the owner?

STUDENT.   No.

INSTRUCTOR.   Oh, I see. You're leasing it then.

STUDENT.   That's right.

INSTRUCTOR.   It certainly is a fine place, Mr. Jones. I have an old friend

	by that name, really a nice fella. He's an engineer. That wouldn't happen to be your line of work, would it?
STUDENT.	No, I'm a salesman.
INSTRUCTOR.	Oh, is that right. With a local firm?
STUDENT.	That's right.
INSTRUCTOR.	Well, that's a demanding line of work. They must keep you pretty busy.
STUDENT.	That's right.
INSTRUCTOR.	I noticed some tricycles on the back lawn. Reminds me of my own place. How many little ones do you have? . . .

After the exercise, the instructor explains the purposes of his remarks. In regards to the phrase "they must keep you pretty busy," he states:

> Now chances are if he's been out of work on illness, or on strike or if he's unemployed, he's going to tell you about it at this time. It's (work) an important part of his life and it's on his mind. He might tell you that he had a hell of a year—that he broke his back and was out of work. Right from the beginning then—you know they're having financial difficulties—you just can't conquer that. You don't have time to waste. There's a door right up the block where the man's been busy all year and a much better prospect.

The trainees also learn how to modify the script for certain types of clients. If a client is wealthy, for example, the salesperson might devote less of his or her presentation to the advertising section of the script since it is directed toward people who can't afford to buy. If a client appears to be educated, certain phrases which might sound "corny" are omitted from the presentation.

LINING UP AND GETTING IN

Instructors and company officials believe that people are leery of door-to-door salespeople. "Lining up" and "getting in" are techniques designed to overcome this resistance.

In the vacuum cleaner training program, trainees learn two methods of lining up: one oblique and the other direct. In the oblique approach, the purpose of the initial contact is misrepresented. A secretary at the company office picks names at random from the local telephone directory. She plays a recording to the people she has selected:

You are one of the lucky persons who have been selected to receive a free gift as part of our new advertising campaign. In order to receive your attractive gift you must call the following number within the next ten minutes. . . .

If the party calls, she says that one of the company representatives will deliver a gift to his or her home. She or he sets up an appointment and the salesperson makes the delivery.

The instructor tells trainees how to get in after the client has been lined up on the telephone:

Go up, knock on the door, smile and say: "Good evening, Mr. Jones. My office called this morning and made an appointment with your wife for seven o'clock. I have a free gift for you out in my car. I'll go get it and be back in a minute." Now Mr. Jones is standing right in the doorway waiting to receive it [the gift]. You go out, get the equipment [for the demonstration], and walk up to the door. There's Mr. Jones holding it open for you. It's right open, ready for you to walk in.

One direct method of lining up is the advertising club. Vacuum cleaner buyers are eligible for membership. They submit the names of friends and relatives; for each of these who accepts a home demonstration, the club member receives five dollars.

Once the vacuum cleaner salesperson is in the door, he or she presents a small gift and says, "In return for this fine gift I am sure you won't mind answering a few questions; if they're not of a personal nature, that is." The question leads to the demonstration. This approach appeals to the client's sense of fairness.

Lining up clients and getting in is more difficult for the encyclopedia salespeople. After knocking on the door, he or she tells the customer that she or he is visiting in the neighborhood to inform people about a new teaching machine. The teaching machine arouses clients' interests, and they allow the salesperson to enter the home as an educator.

In the oblique approach, the salesperson gets in on spurious grounds that do not directly lead to a sale. The salesperson who misrepresents her- or himself must make a transition from the front used in lining up to one more closely related to his or her objective. Handled incorrectly, the client becomes alarmed. To make the transition from educator to book salesperson, trainees memorize a "bridge-phrase": "I represent the manufacturers of the teaching machine. . . . You probably know us better as the publishers of the world-famous Encyclopedia ———." The instructor describes the transition to the trainees:

Now we're going from the teaching machine to being a book salesman. Now this is a tricky transition. It's a touchy part. You think that when you reveal to them that you're associated with a book firm, Mr. Jones is going to hit the ceiling. That's not true. . . . If you told them at the door(that you were with a book firm) they would have been as belligerent as hell. . . . It's an easy transition and tactfully worded. That doesn't mean that he's not going to get somewhat shook. The next sentence takes that into account. Mentioning of the encyclopedia might throw his guard up so the next sentence: "However, I do want to set your mind at ease. I'm not in your home this evening to interest you in the direct purchase of any of our products. That's not my job. I'm here for a much more important reason—to get the use of your name. . . ."

The advertising campaign talk follows.

The trainees are instructed to speak quickly during such transitions in the presentation and to generally put off questions ("How much am I going to have to pay?") that he or she does not want to answer. Once "in," they attempt to stay in control.

THE FALSE FRONT

The instructors teach the trainees to present themselves in a certain way throughout their presentations.[3] The trainees thus learn to maintain a false front or to foster in others false impressions by their posture, speech patterns and content, facial expressions, dress, and the like.

As mentioned earlier, the companies and their training instructors believe that the public imputes foul play to salespeople. The first rule for trainees, then, is that they should not appear to be "peddlers":

You're with the publicity division. Keep that in mind. Stay right within the boundaries of a man in that position. Answer all questions in that frame of mind. Don't step out of it. . . .

In line with this, the trainees are instructed to act indignant if they are asked what they are selling.

The instructors also coach the trainees in how to dress, talk, and gesture in order to present an impression consistent with their false front. The trainee should act like an important person:

You use short sentences. You look at your watch. You are a man in a hurry. You're a man on the go. Your time is important to you. You don't have time to waste. You have to get that feeling across. . . . If your time is important and you present yourself in that way, you've established your own importance.

Similarly, the trainees are told not to wear white socks, sideburns, or moustaches: "They don't go with the image . . . you'll come off as a con man." Finally, the trainee is forbidden to use words such as deal, sale, scheme, buy, cost, and price:

> Don't say deal; people don't like to hear that. They think you're trying to put something over on them. We don't want people to think that we're wheelers and dealers . . . we don't have any deals, remember that, fellars. . . . We have wonderful programs, a terrific machine, but we don't have any deals.

IMMEDIACY AND WITHDRAWAL

Two strategies of persuasion used to close the sale and related to the false front are "immediacy" and "withdrawal." The former strategy refers to the "now or never" nature of the salesperson's presentations. The encyclopedia trainee is told that he or she should impress upon the client that she or he will only be in the area for the day and that if the client doesn't sign for the program now it will be offered to someone else. Thus, one instructor explained:

> [The Front] It's designed to alleviate a problem that has plagued the book salesmen ever since they've been peddling. Sure, encyclopedias are a wonderful idea. Everybody wants them but nobody wants to have them *now*. It's the kind of decision that you can put off making. [By this method] they have to make a decision now . . . they no longer have the opportunity to think about it. They have to make a decision on the spot.

The trainees in the vacuum cleaner sales training program, on the other hand, are instructed that they should tell their clients that three additional attachments will be given free with the machine if the order is placed on that day and that day only.

Underlying this strategy is the belief among salespeople that each presentation is a "do or die" situation. If they allow customers to think the proposition over, they will never make any sales. As the salesperson sees the presentation as a "do or die" situation, so too does he or she make his or her presentation in that way. If the client does not buy immediately, he or she will lose the chance of a lifetime.

The withdrawal technique is taught to trainees to enable them to sell reluctant customers. According to the instructor, the trainee should withdraw her or his offer to sell the product if the client gives any indication of disinterest. He or she should "suggest," first of all, that the client is perhaps unworthy of the offer being made: "I don't think you're the type of people who would think of buying this educational program for your children." At this point, he or she should go through the motions of preparing to leave. The trainees are told that if this technique is successful the advertising representative's front will be substantiated and they will be "home free."

ASSUMING THE SALE

"Assuming the sale" is a technique by which the salesperson treats the client as if he or she will buy the product in order to induce him or her to do so. This technique is implicit throughout the script and the training program. It is based on the belief that the client will be obliged to live up to the salesperson's expectations.

The trainee learns to offer customers a choice between options, neither of which is an alternative to buying. In one instance, for example, an instructor suggested that the trainees ask questions of the following nature:

> The book case comes in either a maple finish as illustrated here or in a blonde finish. Now with the decor of this room, I would suggest the darker wood. What do you think?

*   *   *

Do you want to make it cash or check this evening?

Similarly the trainee is told to ask questions in such a way as to force the client to answer in the affirmative:[4]

Isn't that right, Mrs. Jones?

*   *   *

Now isn't that a wonderful program?

*   *   *

You'll agree that it's a terrific machine.

The trainees are instructed to use "assuming the sale" more and more as they reach the conclusion of their presentations. In the encyclopedia training course, they are advised not to ask the customers whether they would like to buy or whether they would sign the contract. Instead, they are to nonchalantly nod their heads and point to the line on which the client should place his or her name: "Now if you'll put your name right here." As one instructor put it:

> Don't ask them to make out the check or don't wait for them to say something. You assume that they're buying and treat them that way.

INVOLVING THE CLIENT

According to the instructors, the customer should be involved in the salesperson's presentation. The trainee should thus design his or her presentation in such a way as to have the client touch the vacuum cleaner, feel the pages of the encyclopedia, and talk about the positive qualities of the product.

The purpose of "involving the client" is to establish a cooperative relationship between the salesperson and the customer before the end of the presentation. Presumably, this involvement will obligate the customer to be consistent and remain cooperative when the time comes for signing the contract.

A GREAT SAVINGS

It should not be surprising to learn that instructors train students to stress the economical nature of the products they are to sell. In the vacuum cleaner training course, for example, the trainees are instructed to tell the customer that the product can act as a rug shampooer, a hair dryer, a de-moth-er, a painter, and a vaporizer and can consequently save him or her countless money.

The trainees in both of the programs learn how to incorporate "pad talk" into their presentations. Here the salesperson writes down in "black and white" what the customer will save by the purchase. The vacuum cleaner trainee is taught to write down with a magic marker and a large pad the cost of all of the appliances the vacuum cleaner will replace. Without fail, the purchase of the vacuum cleaner represents a savings of two, three, or four times the cost of these appliances.

The encyclopedia salespeople, on the other hand, are instructed to write down the "actual retail price" of all of the items in the educational program. They add these figures and then cross them out with a bold stroke as the client looks on. They explain that the customer can have the entire program for less than half of the "actual retail price": "Which represents a saving to you and a loss to my company of over $600." In point of fact, anyone can purchase the product at the "reduced price."

WORTH AND CREDIBILITY

The trainee learns to establish the worth of his or her product and the credibility of her or his company in order to persuade the customer to buy the product. The purchase of the product is described as a "noble act" befitting of a person who is intelligent, achievement-oriented, and happy.

The instructors suggest various methods by which the trainees can demonstrate the quality of the product and the reputation of the company. These include written and verbal testimonials from famous and typical Americans; repeated associations with famous products ("The Cadillac of the Industry"), with large companies, and with prestigious institutions; and statements of pride ("Our company is too proud to have its products sold in bargain basements or in wholesale houses").

OTHER TECHNIQUES

We have discussed only a few of the techniques of persuasion used by salespeople and taught in sales training programs. There are others. In some instances, trainees are advised to "divide and conquer" when they are faced with one member of a family in favor of the purchase and the other against. In others, they are instructed on how to create an intimate atmosphere with their customers. And in still others, they are taught to give the impression that their own concern is to help the client. While these strategies are mentioned less frequently than the others discussed in this paper, they are nevertheless included in the prospective salesperson's repertoire of techniques of persuasion.

CONCLUSION

In the beginning of this paper, we mentioned that everyone uses techniques of persuasion in his or her everyday life. Everyone has false fronts; everyone uses strategies to deal with others' resistance; everyone threatens to withdraw in the hope that he or she will be asked to stay. There can be no doubt that persuasion is a constant feature in human interaction.

This paper has focused on strategies that sales trainees learn in order to persuade their clients to buy certain products. As the observer conducted his research on these two training programs, he realized that the instructors and company officials use the same techniques on trainees that trainees are taught to use on customers. Ads run in the local newspaper line up trainees. Both companies misrepresent the job, not mentioning selling or the companies' names. The encyclopedia company's ad speaks of learning to demonstrate teaching machines, while the ad for the vacuum cleaner company reads: "five neat appearing men with cars to deliver free advertising gifts. . . ."

It is only when the prospective trainee arrives for the class that he or she learns that it is a course in sales techniques and that she or he has been recruited as a salesperson. The company representative gives a presentation to those he has assembled. He persuades them to come to the next day's session. He establishes the credibility of the company. He promotes selling by an appeal to the noble:

Hell, if this isn't your cup of tea what is your cup of tea? If you don't have what's demanded here [in selling]; if you can't discipline yourself and push yourself, then you are not going to make it anywhere. Life is a sacrifice and you are going to have to believe that. I'm working behind that desk 16 hours a day. . . . Why am I there? Because I'm the kind of guy who wants to give my wife and children the kinds of things they deserve. I can't stand to see them in need. If you think that this job is going to be a hayride and you are going to smile through each day and enjoy everything you are doing, you're sadly mistaken. If you haven't come to the point in your life when you say, "Hell, I'm not the only person." If you haven't lost this selfishness and don't have the concern of your family at heart, I don't think you're much of a man. There are certain things that are distasteful to us but there are some things that are more important than our own tastes. No, I imagine for some people, this isn't their cup of tea. They don't have the drive, the qualities, and the motivation it takes to do this. . . .

Assuming the sale is also used. The instructor does not ask potential trainees whether or not they will attend the course; he offers them a choice of one or two alternative times. The effectiveness of the script is an important selling point, driven home by forcing the trainees to say "yes, yes, yes." In time, trainees begin to remark: "You get that down and you can't miss . . . the script is real good." Instructors describe their own successful selling years, introduce company salespeople who have "made it big," and display company sales records. Each trainee goes out with the sale manager, an expert who often "connects." Sale or not, the trainee returns with tales of how the sales manager had the client eating out of his hand.

Full of confidence, the trainee, with his or her equipment in his or her car and the training sessions behind her or him, drives away from the company office to knock on the first door. According to a regional sales representative, most of the trainees will drop out after the first month. Some of these, like their customers, probably feel "taken" by the sales pitch. Many others blame their own lack of talent as they see others "making it." Successful or not, the trainee is exposed to a perspective on life to which he or she may not have been exposed before. In the encyclopedia sales course, the instructor shares with the trainees his view of the world: "It's a dog-eat-dog world and you have to bite to survive." Some trainees adopt this view of the world and learn to bite. Others fall victims and are bitten.

NOTES

1. This first paragraph is drawn from the Introduction of Erving Goffman's *The Presentation of Self in Everyday Life*. (New York: Doubleday Anchor Books, 1959). Many of the ideas in this paper stem from this book.

2. See Robert Bogdan, *Participant Observation in Organizational Settings* (Syracuse, N. Y.: Syracuse University Press, 1972).

3. Goffman, *Presentation of Self*, p. 22.

4. See Dale Carnegie, *How to Win Friends and Influence People* (New York: Simon and Schuster, 1937), Chap. V.

CHAPTER ELEVEN

Simplistic Answers to the Problems of Inequality

TEACHER MEETS TECHNOLOGY

Following World War II, educators in the United States began to nurture a serious courtship, which they hoped would lead to marriage, between pedagogy and technology. Phrases such as audiovisual aids, overhead projector, filmstrips, educational television, educational radio, teaching machine, and language laboratory became part of everyone's vocabulary, layperson and educator alike. Recently, the vocabulary has grown, as has the financial outlay in educational hardware and software. One has only to pick up a periodical directed toward teachers and scan the advertisements to find support of that statement. The newest vocabulary includes such terms as computer assisted instruction, echo reading, multimedia packages, cassette learning programs, recorded social vocabulary training programs, listening centers, resource laboratories, multipurpose auditory training programs, and concept filmstrips.

In the earlier days of instructional technology (the days of audiovisual

We would like to thank Martin Dodge for his contributions to this paper. Our thanks also go the Nancy Brogan and Richard Lewis who were fieldworkers in this study.

aids), media development was directed almost exclusively toward the brighter, collegebound student. It is now oriented more toward children who are defined as having learning difficulties (the "disadvantaged" urban school pupil and children with "learning disabilities"). In the past, instructional technology was associated with helping with the cold war and the race to the moon; increasingly it is associated with solving the problems of inequality in schools. The present promise of instructional technology is illustrated in advertisements in teacher magazines:

Musical Multiplication Records are the ideal answer

*   *   *

Blank Filmstrips make English Come Alive

*   *   *

Blank Company Instructional System makes learning happen for Every Child

*   *   *

created by a distinguished team of psychologists and educators specifically to help you develop readiness skills in pre-readers, slow learners and children with learning disabilities.

Research in the field of instructional technology has been concerned chiefly with the relationship between specific variables such as children's attention spans and audio volume in controlled laboratory environments.[1] While technology appears to be a standard part of every school, little has been written and no research has been conducted that examines the use of media in the school and how the hard- and software are defined and used by teachers.[2]

In this paper we report data collected by a team of four participant observers[3] in 12 urban elementary classrooms, 8 of which were designated by the school system as classes for children with "learning disabilities." These researchers spent a full academic year in the classroom concentrating on teachers' uses and definitions of media. The team worked independently but under the auspices of a school agency that was attempting to encourage these teachers to use more media in their classrooms and to use it more effectively.

THE WORLD OF THE TEACHER

In order to comprehend the use of instructional materials by the teacher, we must understand what the daily life in the classroom is like. In this paper we organize our discussion around the key themes in the teachers' classroom lives, the themes with the most direct and strongest bearing on how mechanical media is viewed and used by them: 1) discipline and control; 2) time; 3) scheduling; 4) teacher knows best. (These themes emerged from our data.)

Discipline and Control

Although the classrooms varied in terms of the definitions of acceptable and unacceptable student behavior, the control of disruptive behavior was a pervasive concern among all of the teachers we observed. One teacher explained, "You can't think about doing anything in the class until you have order." The teachers spent a significant part of their day devising behavior charts, threatening children, giving punishment, providing rewards, and using other techniques and devices aimed at reducing and (hope of hopes) eliminating disruptive behavior.

It is hardly surprising that one important criterion of the teacher's evaluation of media (or any other input from outside the classroom) is: How does it affect the control that has been established in the classroom? Any object, machine or human, that is perceived as having even the potential for distraction or disruption is regarded by the teachers as one more thing in the class to worry about. Many forms of media fit this description.

Teachers express the view, foreign to the outsider, that children will, given the opportunity, use instructional materials for their own purposes. That is, the presence of an item such as a motion picture projector has a meaning for the child, and that meaning is not necessarily what the designer of that machine or the teacher has for it. The child can do something with that object that the teacher may disapprove of, and this possibility lessens the control over the child and may even encourage disruptive behavior.

There are many examples in our field notes of children using resources for their own amusement and pleasure or as weapons against the teacher in a struggle for control. It was common for children to stick their hands in front of movie projectors to make shadow pictures on the screen, to record four-letter words onto the cards that are fed into Language Masters, and to attempt to play with the control knobs on an overhead projector. Even a "benign" item like a filmstrip projector can become a potent "weapon" in the hands of a child.

Teachers define equipment as expensive and express an obligation to keep it intact. Most teachers, for example, had rules against touching the equipment, and enforcing these rules was one more element of control with which the teachers had to contend:

> Calvin, put that projector down! If you break it, you'll have to pay for it!

> *   *   *

> Didn't I tell you not to touch that?! No, you can't play with the overhead projector. It's not a toy, Donald.

One teacher took an extreme view in this regard: "if you put equipment into the room and don't watch it, the kids will destroy it."

A point we will discuss more fully later refers to the use of media, to a limited extent, by teachers to help them control disruptive behavior. They use films as bribes and rewards to keep order. "If you're not quiet I won't show the film." "If you're good we have a film to show." Even used in this way it is questionable to some teachers whether the equipment adds more than it detracts. For all teachers, but especially for those who define themselves as having problems in maintaining law and order, equipment inputs are something to watch in addition to watching the children.

Time

All teachers observed felt that they didn't have sufficient time for proper planning and preparation of their classes. Teachers spent a good deal of time outside their classes in school-related activities: arriving early to prepare for their classes, staying late to catch up on paperwork, and attending a variety of functions and meetings. They felt that they had too many time demands for what they considered to be worthwhile activities and were unwilling to invest their time in activities with highly uncertain payoffs for them and their students. Chasing down instructional equipment, for example, took time, so equipment and materials that were not readily available were not considered for use. Similarly, materials and pieces of equipment that required the teacher to spend hours in preparation were unlikely to be used.

The teachers in this study also shared the perspective that there were serious time constraints on them during the hours that classes were in session. They often complained that they didn't have enough time to accomplish what they wanted. A number of teachers in the study felt that using new resources without preparing for their use ahead of time (because there isn't time outside class hours for such preparation) was useless and that the materials would amount to nothing more than distractors. This opinion was held particularly by those who placed a heavy emphasis in their classes on traditional academics (the three R's). These teachers have certain things that must be taught, and using an "unproven" or "untested" peice of equipment was seen as running a risk of missing the essentials.

When media was used it was in ways that demanded the least amount of preparation: ways that were once euphemistically called "enrichment." That is, they were used as instructional frills: add-ons to break up the routine of the day, "baby sitting" devices, modes of entertainment, methods of providing rest breaks for the teachers, or, at best, something to provide a common experience for the children, giving them something to talk about, as a field trip or a walk through the neighborhood might.

While teachers are favorably disposed to devices and programs that individualize instruction, that is, devices that are used by the children one at a time these demand almost constant teacher supervision for proper use. And many of the teachers feel that they don't have enough time to add this supervision chore to those they already have. As one teacher put it:

> They come up with some neat devices, but the trouble is you need someone to supervise them, and who has the time to do that?

We did observe instances in which machines designed to individualize instruction were used to entertain potentially disruptive children. In these cases, the machine turned out to be an involving toy.

While the primary resources on which teachers have depended for many years (that is, books) may not be all he or she would wish them to be, at least he or she is comfortable in using them and feels they have some effect. Newer resources, on the other hand, are untried, untested, and perhaps uncomfortable for him or her. There is some risk involved in depending on new gimmicks that are unproven or on old gimmicks that are disruptive. From the point of view of the teacher, the use of these is gambling with his or her time.

Schedules and Routines

Not only do teachers follow the schedules and routines endemic to the schools in which they work, they also create their own routines and schedules. And abiding by these system-imposed and self-imposed schedules is a dominant theme in teachers' classroom lives. Schedules, after all, comprise an obvious way for the teacher to manage his or her time problems.

The teachers we observed are not favorably disposed toward altering their rather rigid schedules. They often must, however, because of forces they can't control, such as school buses late in delivering children, an approaching PTA event, children not learning the materials on schedule, children being absent, or the teacher being sick. There are also a variety of forces which we might term "red tape" that get in the way of teachers' schedules: immediate needs not responded to by superiors, supplies not arriving on time, extra forms to fill out and so on. As one teacher said regarding supplies:

> We have to order the materials we want in the fall for delivery the following school year. Then we're never sure of what we'll need and whether we're even going to get what we ordered.

Another teacher complained: "I still don't have the books I need," and, regarding requests for special help for children, another said:

> You call in a request for a psychologist to come down, and it's three months before one comes around to administer a test on a kid.

An important factor in determining if the teacher will attempt to use a resource is whether or not he or she feels that it will arrive in her or his class when it's supposed to and whether or not it will work as it's supposed to. Our field notes are loaded with teachers' references to various times when equipment didn't work, broke down during operation, or functioned poorly.

Whether being used for the whole class or for an individual student, broken equipment or resources that don't arrive on time place a great strain on a teacher who is concerned with staying on schedule. He or she believes that he or she already contends with enough annoyances and disruptions without having the added annoyances created by inefficient delivery and improper functioning of resource inputs:

"I just have no confidence in the listening center," said one teacher. "Some days it works, other days it doesn't. The earphones are always breaking down."

*   *   *

Another teacher made reference to a machine which she said had repeated-ly broken last year and which she had a difficult time getting serviced. "That's why I'd never build a program around it," she said. "It would break, then it would take about three weeks to get it fixed. I'd never use it for teaching concepts. You just can't rely on it."

*   *   *

"Half the equipment they have doesn't work like it should," said another teacher. "You'd think they would have someone around full-time who could repair it."

Teachers who use media attempt to combat red-tape problems with what one audio visual specialist called being "squirrel-ey." They would, according to the specialists, check out equipment then hide it in their rooms so that no one else could gain access to it. They would then have it ready when needed.

The statement "I like to have things in my room so they will be right here when I want to use them" was communicated to us, with slight variations, by a number of teachers. It reflects their experience with the media specialists' poor logistics record. Too often, with the failure of ma-terials to arrive on time or with devices being out for repairs for long periods, things simply are not there when teachers perceive a need for them. When these things are in the classroom, teachers naturally want to keep them there even if they never come to a point where they perceive a need for them.

Almost every class observed had as part of its regular routine at least one "free time" period during the day when the children may "play." All children in a class generally have such a period just before or just after lunch break. In addition, individuals are granted free time when they have completed their work. During this time there is little or no teacher supervision of student activities (unless pupils get very raucous). Pupils may talk with each other, play "house," play cards, put jigsaw puzzles together, play board games, and the like. That individualized media resources find their most frequently use during these periods may tell us something about how the teacher defines his or her use of time and what this form of instructional technology means to him or her.

The Teacher Knows Best

During our observations we saw and heard evidence that strongly suggests that the teachers define themselves as knowing what's best in relation to their children and as viewing outsiders as not really knowing what it's like in the classroom. We are not saying that the teachers define themselves as the only experts in the field or that they believe that they couldn't be helped by outside experts. We are simply saying that they think that they are the best ones to know their own particular situations. An extension of this belief is the fact that we found teachers looking to other teachers for help and guidance. If one teacher recommended a piece of instructional material to another, there was a high likelihood that the second teacher would try it. Again, it's not that teachers won't try "outsiders' " recommendations; it's just that these sources don't have the credibility of the teacher next door. The media specialists involved with the schools we observed were defined by teachers as outsiders who "really didn't know what it was like" and as being more concerned with fancy equipment than with what the teachers "really needed." In short, teachers didn't define the instructional technologists as having credibility.

There seemed to be a general view among teachers that mass-produced media products could not meet their specific needs. Things were too advanced for their students, too simple for them, too abstract, too divorced from their world experience and the like. Teachers took the view that mass-produced media resources produced by "outsiders" could not be tailored to their needs or the needs of their students. What may be needed is an exploration of definitions held by teachers (and the general public) of "manufactured goods." It is indeed possible that definitions of mass-produced goods and of "individualized instruction" and "relevant educational materials" may be contradictory.

CONCLUSIONS

Our observations have led us to conclude that, at least in the "learning disability," "inner-city" classrooms we have observed, teachers do not significantly integrate instructional equipment into their curricula. Given the demands of the situation, teachers' definitions of instructional technologists and technology, and the nature of the material itself, it is highly unlikely that teachers will use it, or that it can be used, as some in the field of instructional technology say it can: that is, as a way of solving the problems of educational inequality. We now see selling media in this way as, at best, evidence that certain segments of the education profession and manufacturers of educational equipment embrace a rather simplistic answer to the problems of inequality. More critically we see it as a cruel hoax: a method of selling manufactured goods and advancing the status of the field of Instructional Technology.

Teachers we have studied use what Instructional Technology has to offer largely to fill gaps in schedules and as entertainment and diversions for pupils. We see this use as legitimate and as performing an important function in schools. The problem appears to be that this use is not enough to legitimate the instructional technologist to the field of education nor to justify the large expenditures that are made to support and equip the field.

We realize that our concluding remarks are strong and sweeping, given the data we have. What amazes us and, we believe, justifies our alarm is that other than the research reported here we know of no study that has looked at the actual use of instructional technology in the schools. In Instructional Technology Centers across the country old films are being tested in experimental laboratory situations to measure their cognitive teaching potential for children. This research is being funded with millions of dollars of federal funds and is typical of the research thrust in the field. Our research suggests that teachers do not choose films on the basis of their cognitive teaching potential but on the basis of their entertainment value. Teachers don't show *old* films. All of this would be humorous if it were not for the needs of the children and their teachers.

NOTES

1.   Martin Dodge, *Selling Technology: A Participant Observation Study of the School Media Specialist* (University Micro-films, dissertation, 1973).

2.   Seymour Sarason, *The Culture of the School and the Problem of Change* (Boston: Allyn and Bacon, 1971), makes the point that we know very little about "the culture of the school and the problem of change." See his book for a refreshing contribution in this regard.

3.   Robert Bogdan, *Participant Observation in Organizational Settings* (Syracuse: Syracuse University Press, 1972).

CHAPTER TWELVE

Doin' a Job

ATTENDANTS AND THEIR WORK AT A STATE INSTITUTION

Empire State School,[1] responsible for the care and treatment of the mentally retarded, is one of several State Schools in the Department of Mental Hygiene of [State]. . . . Some of the aims of the school are: (1) to care for those residents who are unable to help themselves; (2) to help those who are able to be accepted back into the community as useful citizens; and (3) to teach each resident to be as self-sufficient as possible.

This statement, set forth in an attendants' training bulletin at Empire State School, reflects the ideology of the institution in which it is used.[2] Thus, it reinforces the image of the institution as a goal-oriented organization, the purpose of which is to serve the needs of the "retarded."

The purpose of this paper is to examine the relationship between this ideology and the perspectives and concerns of lower-level personnel, or attendants, on one ward in this institution. Our analysis begins with a look at attendants' perspectives on their jobs and on work.[3] We proceed

This is a revised version of a paper presented as Steven J. Taylor, "Doin' a job: Attendants and their work at a state institution." Annual Meeting of the Eastern Sociological Society, Philadelphia, April, 1974.

to relate these perspectives to attendants' concerns in their everyday work. But first, a word on the methodology and the setting.

THE METHODOLOGY AND THE SETTING

This paper is based on a participant observation study[4] of a ward at a large (over 3,000 population) state institution for the "mentally retarded." It was conducted over a period of one year and included over 110 hours of actual observation. Detailed field notes were recorded after each observation session.

Although the attendants on this ward were aware that the observer was a student in sociology, they were aware of neither the observer's specific interests in visiting the ward nor the rigor with which the field notes were recorded. They assumed, without encouragement from the observer, that he was there to study the "mentally retarded."

The nature of attendants' reactions to the observer changed over time. While they were initially guarded in much of their behavior, they came to accept the observer as a natural participant in the setting as the study progressed. For example, the attendants freely committed acts in the presence of the observer that they hid in the presence of superiors and attendants from other wards and shifts, and some attendants related personal experiences and feelings to the observer that they guarded from their fellow workers.

The ward on which this study was conducted is officially designated as a ward for "severely and profoundly retarded, aggressive, ambulatory, young adult males." In actuality, the residents on this ward fit no single "type" or "category." Many of the 70 residents have IQs over 35,[5] few are aggressive, by any standard, four are completely nonambulatory, and many are over 30 years of age (age range: 14 to 44).

Although this ward is not typical of all wards at all state mental hygiene facilities, it does parallel other "back wards" at large institutions for the "retarded." Blatt, who served as Director of the Division of Mental Retardation for the State of Massachusetts, offers the following descriptions of wards which he observed and which are similar to this ward:

In toilets, I frequently saw urinals ripped out, sinks broken, and toilet bowls backed up. . . . Beds are so arranged—side by side and head to head—that it

is actually impossible, in some dormitories, to cross parts of the room without actually walking over beds.[6]

*   *   *

In each of the dormitories for severely retarded residents, there is what is
called, euphemistically, the day room or recreation room. The odor in each
of these rooms is overpowering. . . . Most day rooms have a series of
bleacher-like benches on which sit denuded residents, jammed together
without purposeful activity or communication or any other kind of
interaction.[7]

While the observer had occasion to meet over 30 male attendants and
to observe the ward during all shifts, the actual study concentrated on 12
attendants who worked on the evening shift at one time or another.[8]
The observer also had the opportunity to spend time with some of the
attendants outside of the setting.

A JOB IS A JOB: PERSPECTIVES ON WORK

There are many reasons why an individual may choose to work at an
institution for the "mentally retarded." For some, the institution represents a place in which to practice special skills learned through years of
training or to act out an ideology of dedication to the "retarded." As one
physical therapist at Empire State School put it: "We've only just begun,
and I know we can help these people." For others, the institution provides a stepping stone from which they can advance professionally.
Many physicians at Empire, for example, work there only until they can
pass their state certification requirements.

Unlike these professionals, the typical attendant possesses neither special skills, nor ideologies, nor plans for the future. He comes to the
institution not for the intrinsic benefits to be gained through his work,
but rather for the extrinsic benefits his job provides. He defines himself
as a worker and his job as a job: nothing more and nothing less.

None of the attendants on this ward had had prior experience, training, or interest in the fields of mental health or mental retardation. Most
applied for employment at the institution for reasons unrelated to the
nature of the work. Several, in fact, initially hoped to find jobs at Empire
that would not entail ward work. One originally applied for a carpenter's
helper position. Another worked in the laundry before he became an

attendant. A third drove a truck before he was assigned to the ward. He later transferred to the motor pool.

For the attendant, given his range of options, Empire offers an available and attractive job. Many, over half on the evening shift, came to the institution immediately after being discharged from the armed services or being unable to find other employment. In the following quotation the evening "ward charge," or supervising attendant, gives his account:

> See, I was on unemployment and I had to be lookin' for a job. I knew they wasn't hirin' anybody here, but I applied anyway. . . . I just applied to this place cause they was on my back about always lookin' for a job at the same places. Well, two days after I came here I got a call from them and they asked me to come back down again. So I came back and had an interview and everything, and I got the job.

Other attendants found physical labor, and especially construction work, too demanding or too sporadic. Institutional work, on the other hand, offered the promise of good benefits and security:

> You can't beat the benefits here. Nobody's got better benefits than the state. (Is that why you work here?) Yes, security.

> *   *   *

> (Why did you want to work here in the first place?) Good benefits. The state gives great benefits. We get a day off when we want it. And the pay's pretty good too.

Finally, many attendants were drawn to the institution because they could receive higher wages there than they could anywhere else:

> Where else would a guy without a college education, or even one with one, get a job that pays like this? I've got friends with college degrees who don't even have jobs.[9]

> *   *   *

> Everybody is here for one reason, and one reason only—money. That's right, they're all here for the money. That's why they took this job. That's why I took this job.

And, as illustrated by the following excerpt, many would undoubtedly leave if a better paying job came along:

Well, I was hired four years ago, but then I went into the Service so I didn't start workin' here til I got out. I came back here in April, but the hirin' freeze was still on. They said I could be an attendant's assistant, but I didn't want that. I mean, I already passed the test so I could be an attendant whenever they started hirin' them again. But I didn't wanna be an attendant's assistant; so I took a job at the mill. I mean, why work as an attendant's assistant for 5,000 when I can work at the mill for 7,000?

What the attendant's job means to him, then, is a place to earn a day's wages for a day's work. It is nothing more than one of a series of short-term, semiskilled jobs that helps pay the bills.

ATTENDANTS' CONCERNS

As we have seen, attendants come to the institution with a certain perspective on work. A job is a job, nothing more and nothing less. As such, they want from their jobs at Empire the same things they would want from any other jobs: pleasant working conditions; enough things to pass the time, but not too much or too difficult work; congenial relationships with fellow workers; and good relations with superiors upon whom they depend for promotion and, in some cases, continuation of employment. In short, they concern themselves not with the nature of the work, but rather, with the circumstances of the work.

It follows that, while the attendants may sometimes sympathize with or help residents, they orient their everyday work to practical aspects related to their own concerns. In the remainder of this section, we focus on three broad concerns that dominate attendant's conversations and behavior and that arise in the context of conditions on the "back ward": cleanliness and order, avoiding work, and passing time. We shall see how attendants can subjugate the residents' interests in order to further their own.

Cleanliness and Order

The 70 residents on the back ward, some of whom are severely handicapped, receive neither programming nor training in basic skills at the institution. Most spend their days and their lives in ennui. Some sit hour after hour in front of a blaring television. Others, some of whom are blind or deaf, sit idly on the floor or on old wooden benches. In the face of boredom and deprivation, almost one-third of the residents are incontinent; several abuse themselves or others; several others will, given the opportunity, smear feces or urine over their bodies.

At the same time, attendants are judged by the criteria most visible to their supervisors, who visit the ward on each shift once or twice daily. They act busy whenever superiors appear on the ward. They maintain careful records of ward events in order to "cover their asses." They place a resident, a so-called watchdog, in a strategic position to forewarn them of the approach of any unexpected visitors to assure that they are not caught in embarrassing situations.[10] Most important for them is creating the appearance of cleanliness and order for they are responsible for the general condition of the ward and the residents:

> I've gotta protect myself. I'm responsible for anything that happens up here, and if one of 'em died, I'm to blame.

*   *   *

> You see, they knew I was clean. They knew I'd keep this place clean. That's why they wanted me up here. This place was the dirtiest place in the world.

Attendants, then, strive to maintain a proper front for supervisors.[11] And to maintain a proper front is to prevent or at least conceal feces and urine- stained floors, bruised residents, and residents covered with feces.

The attendants must also deal with those from other shifts. On several occasions, for example, the members of one shift registered a formal complaint about another shift that had left them a filthy ward. On another occasion in an attempt to protect itself, one shift reported to supervisors that a resident had sustained injuries during another shift.

Finally, attendants have their own reasons for keeping the ward clean and orderly, for, as they state, they have to work there every day. Thus, one attendant who buys his own disinfectant for the ward explained:

> Sure, I get discouraged. They don't give us enough disinfectant or anything. The state don't care what we take home to our kids. Well I care. I'm not takin' home hepatitis or somethin' to my kids. I'm gonna keep this place clean. I just can't stand filth.

The attendants have at their disposal a number of means to maintain cleanliness and order on the ward. Some of these, of course, are sanctioned by the institution. For example, most residents regularly receive large dosages of tranquilizers as prescribed by institutional physicians, and others are straitjacketed when "disorderly" with the approval of supervisors. At times, however, attendants take matters into their own hands. In some situations, attendants give "difficult" residents the sedatives prescribed for others. In other situations, taking care not to leave marks, they covertly tie or straitjacket residents who pick at themselves or who won't stay in bed. Or they may use physical means to control residents:

> Now sometimes you gotta hit 'em. If you let one go and then another, pretty soon they'll be runnin' this place. You won't be able to control 'em. So you gotta cuff 'em on the back of their head to let 'em know what's right.

Attendants also maintain close supervision over the activities of residents. The bathroom door is sometimes locked during the day to prevent residents from clogging the toilets with rags or from soiling the floor. Moreover, residents are often forced to sit still throughout the day, presumably in the belief that they cannot cause trouble if they do not wander around.

Residents themselves, finally, are used as workers and ward disciplinarians, without pay or regard to institutional rules. At least two residents are "assigned" to "the bucket" on each shift. These residents clean the floor of feces and urine with a bucket, a rag, and their bare hands. Other residents clean floors, make beds, collect laundry, and control their fellow residents. One resident takes care of another who rubs feces over his body: holding onto him during the day and sleeping beside him at night.

Avoiding Work

Although the attendants on this ward strive to maintain order and cleanliness, they also avoid too much work and specific jobs they consider distasteful. As illustrated above, for example, they assign residents to certain tasks such as "the bucket."

The attendant cares less about the needs of the residents than about his own concerns and the tasks for which he is directly accountable. Thus, he defines his work in severely circumscribed terms:

> We're supposed to feed 'em and keep and eye on 'em and make sure they're o.k. They have people in recreation—psychologists, sociologists. They're the ones who are supposed to train 'em and work with 'em—not us.

*   *   *

> I'll tell ya one thing. I ain't gettin' down on my hands and knees to clean up
> shit. I wasn't hired to clean up shit. I won't do it. I'd do it for my own flesh
> and blood. But I won't do it here. They live here. This is their home. Why
> shouldn't they clean up the shit?

He found it incomprehensible that other attendants at the institution
will clean excrement, for this contradicted his perspective on work; that
is, a job is a job:

> Can you believe that right there at the institution there's some women who
> will clean up shit? Yea, over on the other side. Man, are they dumb. I don't
> know why in hell they do it.

Even when attendants accept responsiblity for certain tasks, they view
and perform those tasks in terms of work, trouble, and inconvenience,
rather than in terms of the residents' interests. As such, they dispense
with them as quickly as possible. Meals provide a case in point. At approximately ten minutes after the first resident has been served his meal,
the attendants begin to send the residents away from the dinner tables.
Slow eaters are pulled from their seats. They then wipe the tables and
sweep under them as some of the so-called working boys gather the
dinner trays, rinse them, and stack them on a cart to be taken downstairs. The entire process takes no more than one half hour. Despite this
haste, there is no work for the attendants to do in the next hour.

Passing Time

"Work time,"[12] time spent or wasted working, is something to be avoided
or, if necessary, reluctantly accepted:

> I like it here . . . here, you don't have that much work. You can sit around all
> day. The only real work we have to do is clean the floors at night.

Yet those who choose to avoid work must find some other way to pass the
time during the long hours on the ward. Thus, the attendants on the
back ward expresses a common concern over boredom although they do
not always agree on whether work on this particular ward is boring:

Like it here? I love it here. I really do. You can play with the kids up here,
and there's enough to do so you don't get bored.

*   *   *

I don't know. There are worse wards than this one. It gets boring here
though. Like I'd like to be able to go out and play baseball or somethin' with
'em.

Attendants pass the time by engaging in a variety of activities, both on
and off the ward. They may "spell" each other on the ward: one or two
will stay with the residents while the others withdraw to the ward office
or a back room to drink beer or coffee, read, or "bullshit." Or they may
all stay with the residents in the dayroom or dorm or on the porch and
watch television, read the newspaper, talk, pitch nickels, or banter
among themselves.[13]

On most days, the residents are drawn into the attendants' bantering or
conversations in one way or the other. One resident gives the attendants
the days of the week for specific past or future dates. Another repeats
the attendants' obscenities and other sayings.

The "entertainment" is not always so benign. Certain residents are
encouraged to masturbate or to perform fellatio on one another. Others
are chased around the room with brooms: all a joke, of course, but the
residents don't know it. And one particular resident is forced to swallow
burning cigarettes.

CONCLUSION

In his everyday work, the attendant orients himself not to the residents'
best interests, but rather, to his own. To view him in terms of serving the
needs of the "retarded," then, is not viewing him in terms of his primary
goal. He is not out to care, to help, to teach. He is out to "get by" in the
easiest way he knows how.

Other researchers have argued that aides, or attendants, at institutions
similar to Empire "genuinely wish to help their patients."[14] If this is so
with the attendants in this study, we have not seen it. All that these
attendants have to offer are reasons why the residents cannot be helped.
There are no attempts.

One would be wrong, however, to place the responsibility for what Empire is on the shoulders of the attendants. After all, there is not much they could do to improve the *general* quality of life at Empire even if they wanted to. The wards are overcrowded; they are understaffed; they are barren.

We must begin to question the intentions of those who tell us that the aims of Empire are to care, to help, and to teach. We must examine their ideology. In the end, we might find that it is all a front.

NOTES

1.   This, as are all names associated with the institution in this paper, is a pseudonym. It is misleading to think of this institution as a "school." Less than one-half of the school-age population (which composes less than one-half of the total population) receive any schooling and less than one-twelfth receive the amount provided children in public school.

2.   See Thomas Szasz, *Ideology and Insanity: Essays on the Psychiatric Dehumanization of Man* (Garden City, N. Y.: Doubleday, 1970); and Anselm Strauss et al., *Psychiatric Ideologies and Institutions* (New York: Free Press, 1964).

3.   For a related discussion, see Robert Bogdan et al., "Let them eat programs: Attendants' perspectives and programming on wards in state schools," *Journal of Health and Social Behavior,* **15** (June): 142–151, 1974.

4.   See Robert Bogdan, *Participant Observation in Organizational Settings* (Syracuse: Syracuse University Press, 1972).

5.   See Rick Heber, *A Manual on Terminology and Classification in Mental Retardation* (Washington: The American Association on Mental Deficiency, 1961).

6.   Burton Blatt, *Exodus from Pandemonium* (Boston: Allyn and Bacon, 1970), p. 13.

7.   *Ibid.,* p. 16.

8.   There are actually seven attendants assigned to this shift. There are seldom this many working, however. It is not uncommon to find only two attendants on the ward on weekends.

9.   I have met only one attendant with a college degree (in psychology) and he works on another ward.

10.   Willoughby, as quoted in Erving Goffman, *The Presentation of Self in Everyday Life* (Garden City, N. Y.: Doubleday, 1959), p. 110, observed similar behavior among attendants at a state mental hospital. Also see Erving Goffman, *Asylums: Essays on the Social Situation of Mental Patients and Other Inmates* (Garden City, N. Y.: Doubleday, 1961).

11.   Goffman, *Presentation of Self.*

12.   I have borrowed this term from Barney Glaser and Anselm Strauss, *Time for Dying* (Chicago: Aldine, 1968), pp. 66–68.

13.   This is similar to what Donald Roy, "Quota restriction and goldbricking in a machine shop," *American Journal of Sociology,* **LVII** (March): 427–442, 1952, observed among factory workers. These attendants resemble factory workers in many ways.

14.   See Strauss et al., *Psychiatric Ideologies,* pp. 122–124.

CHAPTER THIRTEEN

Working out Failure

In the past few years social scientists have said much and put a good deal of effort into the topic of evaluation research.[1] In particular, there has been concern with how one goes about measuring success and how effective certain social service programs and services agencies have been (for example, schools, Head Start, welfare programs, job training, and hospitals). In this paper we discuss the evaluation of the success of one program and then raise some larger questions about evaluation research in general. Our course of action is to see how various evaluation procedures were used in this particular program and what commonsense assumptions lay behind these procedures. We also question the commonsense assumptions of social scientists about organizations and organizational goals.

CIVIC PROGRAM FOR THE "HARD-CORE UNEMPLOYED"

The data comes from a study of a local program for the "Training and

A modified version of this paper was presented by Robert Bogdan at the 23rd Annual National Meeting of *The Society for the Study of Social Problems* in New York City on August 26, 1973.

Employment of Hard-Core Unemployed Citizens" (Civic Program). The agency that administered it was a large, private, influential, civic-businessman's organization. It operated from funds received through a grant from the State Department of Labor. It consisted of aggressive recruitment of "hard-core" unemployed, pre-job training and counseling for those recruited, and job placement.

The training phase was operated by a division of a large, international industrial firm located in "Civic City." The "Civic Organization" had subcontracted with "Big Company" to do this. New training classes started every four weeks and lasted four weeks. Approximately twelve trainees were in each cycle. Upon completion of training, they were to be placed in jobs in Civic Organization member companies and to be retrained in these positions as full-time workers.

In collecting the data, I went through training cycles as a participant observer and conducted unstructured interviews with trainees some months after they had completed the training. I also informally interviewed personnel managers of various companies, various officials related to the Civic Program as well as officials from similar programs.

Civic Program's Goals

In short, the goal of the Civic Program was to change the employment status of unemployed and underemployed "disadvantaged persons."

Evaluation of the Program's Success

In the evaluation of any organization there seems to be an almost inevitable tendency in our society to quantify. The Civic Program was no exception. At first it would seem simple and revealing for officials to engage in a quantitative evaluation of the program. It had a relatively unambiguous goal that should have led to a simple scheme for measuring effectiveness. This was not the case.

Table 1 represents an attempt to quantify the program at various stages in its progression. It represents a composite of the eight training cycles which were observed. In addition to the information presented in Table 1, some additional material is needed to understand the following discussion.

Table 1   Stages of the training program, the number of trainees engaged at each stage, and the number of 'leavers' who find employment on their own

A	B	C	D
a = 7	b = 6	c = 4	d = 3
97	79	63	57

E	F	G	H
e = 3	f = 4	g = 1	
38	28	18	12

A = *The First Day Training*   97 individuals appeared for at least one day of training.

B = *Start of the Second Week*   79 trainees were still enrolled at the start of the second week of their cycle.

C = *Start of the Third Week*   63 trainees were still enrolled at the start of the third week.

D = *Last Day of the Training Program*   57 trainees completed the training phase of the program. Some people did not complete the full four weeks of training but were placed on jobs by the staff before completion. This figure includes these trainees also.

E = *First Day on the Job*   38 People completed the training phase of the program, were offered jobs by the program, accepted them and appeared at least the first day at work.

F = *Beginning of the Second Week of Employment*   28 trainees were placed on jobs by the program and were still employed on the same job at the beginning of the second week.

G = *Beginning of the Second Month*   similar to F only for a different time period.

H = *Three Months after Completion*   12 trainees were employed at the same job that the program placed them in at the end of a three month period.

a, b, c, d, = the number of trainees who dropped out of the program between the stages as indicated and who found jobs on their own and were employed three months after they left the program.

e, f, g = the number of trainees who left the jobs they had got through the program and then got jobs on their own and were employed for a period of three months.

I was able to obtain employment background information on 79 of the original 97 trainees. While one might assume that all trainees had been unemployed for a long period of time prior to training, this was not the case. At least 35 of the trainees had been unemployed less than three months prior to the program. At least 5 of the trainees had left jobs to enter the program. While some of the positions that trainees had held prior to training were undesirable from the trainees' perspectives, many of the jobs in which trainees were placed were comparable to those they had held before training. These were unskilled factory jobs with starting salaries around the minimum wage.

During my research many of the officials who were related to the training program and others working with similar programs (officers of the State Department of Labor, Civic Association Employees, and Big Company officials) spoke of the program's success in terms of "success rate," "retention rate," "completer rates," and "slot drop rate." These phrases were often accompanied by percentage figures and represented an attempt to compare the number of trainees at one stage of the program with the number in another stage. For example, an official might look at the ratio between the 97 trainees who started the program (see Table 1) and the number of trainees placed by the program who were still working at the same jobs at the end of three months (12/97) and speak of a success rate of 12.3 percent. This particular method of calculation, however, was not common.

Assuming that the training program had something to do with motivating trainees toward employment one could compare the total number who were holding jobs (obtained on their own or through the program) at the three month period (40) (that is; $a + b + c + d + e + f + g + h$) with those who started (97) and come up with a success rate of 41 percent.

If we assumed that the training program's effect could not be felt unless the trainee had completed training and that the goal of the program was only to place trainees, the success rate might be calculated by comparing those who completed the training program (57) with the number who accepted a job and appeared at least once (38). This comparison would give us 38/57 or 66.5 percent. There are a great number of ways, many much more complicated than those presented, to calculate various percentages and use them as program officials do to indicate success. As illustrated, one can vary one's "success rate" at least from 12.3 percent to 66.5 percent, depending on one's disposition and the assumptions one uses in the calculation.

Using percentage figures to present the success of the program was most common when program officials were speaking to outsiders. When percentages were used, little reference was made to how the figures were calculated, and when officials were asked, their explanations tended to be unclear at best.

People engaged in the training phase of the program and people who had prolonged contact with trainees seldom made reference to success rates while lower-level civil servants and upper-level officials used them more frequently. Although lower-level state officials to some extent treated measures as significant and meaningful, Civic Officials seemed to see the arbitrary nature of the measures of success. In spite of this overt recognition they used them as the quotation below illustrates:

> How do you judge success or failure? These statistics they don't tell you much . . . you can make anything you want out of them. . . . The purpose of the program is to get people jobs, get people off the welfare rolls, people who are dependent, people who aren't making it on their own, getting them out into industry and getting them jobs. Well, to some extent we've done that, but the 52 percent who didn't make it . . . can we call that failure? (Civic Program Official)

Changing one's success rate, of course, can be accomplished by changing one's method of calculating success. One government official spoke of the success rate of the program as increasing 25 percent after they stopped calculating trainee placement on the basis of people who were working only in specific jobs they had been trained for and began counting any employment as a placement. The fellow seemed to judge the change as real, rather than a product of the change in counting procedures.

This arbitrary calculation of "success rates" made them meaningless in an absolute sense, but one could suggest that they could have meaning in a comparative sense. Officials compared their success with that of other programs: a meaningful approach should programs follow the same calculating procedures. In point of fact, various programs used different calculation and data-compiling methods. Government officials collected data from various programs that were supposed to be comparable, but the looseness of the definitions associated with the data collection gave the people who were counting much leeway for interpretation and made comparing figures from different programs pointless. In programs that are government-funded but subcontracted to private agencies, many aspects of the counting are carried out by the agencies and sent to the other government counters.

The following quotation provides an illustration of the importance of official "counters" in the quality of the data collected. They decide whom to count on the basis of their own assumptions.

I said, "Is the program evaluation standardized?" He said, "To a certain extent it is. We fill out this form that everyone has on the trainees and evaluations are done on the basis of these." I said, "Is there a manual that describes the procedure?" He said, "Not exactly, I don't have a manual as such." I said, "What kind of information are you concerned with? What do you count?" He said, "For one thing the number of completers." I said, "What is the definition of a completer?" He said, "It's anyone who goes through a given program and is ready for work." I said, "Who makes the judgment or how do you judge whether he is ready for work?" He said, "His teacher or the people in charge of a specific program." I said, "Then is the completer really anyone who finishes the program and is placed on a job?" He said, "Not completely . . ." I said, "Well, how do you handle drop-outs who go out and get jobs on their own? People who start the program and stay a few weeks and then quit and go out and find a job on their own? Are they completers?" He said, "It all depends on what we know about him. Generally, in a case like that I would see it as: the program fulfilled something that the trainee was lacking—I don't know what it might be— something—or a push that he needed—that made the difference between being employed or not."
(Civil Servant involved in Evaluation)

Counters vary from the official procedure as specifically outlined if it is unrealistic or burdensome but present the material as having resulted from following the standarized procedure:

> Another civil servant in the same office said: "Are you interested in fol-low-up?" I said, "Yes, how do you handle follow-up?" She said, "Well, we send out form XXXX to all the completers at three months and then at six months. They are asked to send them back." I said, "What kind of a return rate do you get?" She said, "About 20 percent. Those that don't return the form, we try to contact on the telephone. If we can't talk to them we try to talk to a relative or someone who knows what they are doing." I said, "What percent of the completers do you find?" She said, "They say 70 to 80 percent. That's what they say anyway." I said, "Is the rate different from that?" She said, "Remember what I am telling you is the official procedure."

Many of the variations in the procedure can be understood from a sociological perspective. Often the counters are supervised by intermediary personnel who are more interested in getting the job done than in how it is done. Counters have a tendency to please their closest supervisors. Standards on the quality of the data and counting procedures followed are often established in the work group as they are in the factory.[2] The "fudge factor" replaces "goldbricking."

Even if all programs were all evaluated using the same procedures and we could control the reliability of the data, they would be difficult to compare because they vary in ways that make comparison impossible (for example, in who is recruited into the program).

While all trainees have to meet certain criteria to be eligible for any state or federally funded program, the programs do not necessarily serve the same "quality" of trainee. Some programs handpick trainees; others take anyone. Program officials usually deny that they are "creaming",[3] or accepting only trainees with a high potential for success.

Of course, the more "employment prone" a recruitee is, the more likely he or she is to be successful in finding employment and the better the program will appear statistically. It is ironic that the more programs serve the least disadvantaged the better they appear statistically.

Programs also vary in many other ways that are difficult to measure such as the quality of the jobs in which trainees are placed; the nature of the labor market varies making comparisons of programs that operated in different time periods difficult.

Among themselves, most program officials did not speak of the Civic Program as a success, but they were also reluctant to deem it a failure. Even if the statistics presented might be considered unfavorable, they presented the program in a more favorable light than might other methods of calculation. For example, in the calculations of the figures officials used, the disposition of the trainees before the training program was never mentioned. Calculations seemed to assume that trainees were totally incompetent and nonjob prone upon entering the program and that any employment extrainees were engaged in was a product or a result of the training.

There were staff members and others who were critical of the program and deemed it a failure, but no matter how strongly one felt no one was prone to deem it a complete failure. A justification for the program was always presented.

The quotations below will relate some of the cliches used by program officials in justifying the program's existence:

> I said, "So you think you have been fairly successful." He said, "Hell, we're not solving the problem—it's too big for that, but we're making a dent. Giving a few people a new lease on life. A chance to get a new identity. You've got to try—that's all. If you don't fail, you're not trying in this business."

*   *   *

The only thing I can say is it's the type of program where you learn from your mistakes.

                              *   *   *

Success is a funny thing in this kind of program. The day before yesterday they had a success right in the back of this building. The trainees were assembling radios. They finished the first radio and they got some sound— the trainees started yelling and calling Ted down (program official). That was success and the kind that most people overlook. Here men had the experience of building something from start to finish and had developed an interest and a feeling of accomplishment from having participated in the project. Those kinds of experiences are an important measure of success.

These justifications appear to be standard in certain service organizations and might be thought of as the pilot or "learn from experience" justification, the "if you have lit one candle" justification, and the "you can't measure your true impact" justification.

SO WHAT

The foregoing discussion was not intended as a reflection on the integrity, honesty or straightforwardness of the people in the Civic Program. The purpose was to provide some data on the nature of official statistics and counting procedures in evaluating the success of organizations with intangible and difficult products to count. We are not suggesting that these organizations purposely attempt to misrepresent themselves. We don't see the Civic Program as an example of incompetence or corruption. There is a distinction between intentionally manipulating statistics in order to look good and just having them happen that way. Program officials recognize this distinction as the following quotation from a state official illustrates:

> Our figures [of one group of programs] may not be entirely meaningful but they are honest. We don't try to present a false impression. . . .

Again, what we have suggested so far was not meant to be an indictment of the particular methods of evaluation used by these programs or of those who compile the figures. What we have tried to illustrate is that success measures lose significance when looked at carefully. It is not that the figures have no meaning, but rather that they are different from what is commonly understood. Because of the nature of some organizations, any measure that officials, or any social scientists for that matter, come up with, using the yardstick of the stated goals, would be of dubious value. In short, there is no way of measuring success that does not involve so many judgments that the resulting figures become totally subjective.

The meaning and significance of goal-attainment measures in organizations with intangible, hard-to-measure products and goals do not lie in their expressed function of being numerical measures of effectiveness on the yardstick of stated goals. Rather, they have a meaning and function whose viability is a result of people's commonsense belief in the significance of numbers; that is, the desire of people to have measures of achievement.

ONE VIEW OF ORGANIZATIONAL GOALS AND MEASURING SUCCESS

The idea of organizations as goal-directed instruments has also been the basis for much of social scientists' thinking about formal organizations.[4] Most definitions of formal or complex organizations found in the literature have as their major component the idea that organizations are instrumental and directed at specific goals. For example, Blau and Scott[5] define an organization as a number of men who have formed a social unit for the explicit purpose of achieving certain goals.

Amitai Etzioni states:

> Organizations are social units oriented toward the pursuit of specific goals. In this sense they can be conceived as tools which gain their meaning and direction from their function.[6]

Many studies looking at specific organizations focus on how well the organization does in reaching its stated goals. Studies concentrating on informal organization often look at its affect on the organization's ability to approach its stated purpose. Studies focusing on the problematic nature of goals have done so by starting with the original goals and exploring how these became bastardized. Goal displacement is a key concept here.[7] Other studies have examined the conditions under which and the methods by which organizations change their goals; the key concept here is goal succession.[8] In most studies, the goal is seen as the executive presents it: as the star that guides the ship. While at times the sea is rough and survival takes precedence over direction, a star is still present and is a major point of reference.

From this view an organization's output is thought to be closely related to its goals. It follows that output is the measuring stick of organizational effectiveness. The extent to which output approaches the goal is the mark of organizational success or effectiveness. Output versus goals has been the measuring stick of organizations by organization officials, the public, and, to some extent, social scientists. In the beginning of his chapter on organizational effectiveness, Theodore Caplow states:

> As we have seen, organizations are devices for accomplishing definite purposes. The concept of success or failure follows inevitably from this view of the organization. . . .[9]

Etzioni states:

> Organizations are constructed to be the most effective and efficient social units. The actual effectiveness of a specific organization is determined by the degree to which it realizes its goals.[10]

The concept of organizational goals as the star to guide the ship and as the yardstick for measuring effectiveness does not apply to the setting of the Civic Program as we have described it.

LOOKING AT STATED GOALS AND MEASURES OF SUCCESS FROM A DIFFERENT PERSPECTIVE

If interpretations of goals vary so greatly and the measures of success have no "objective" significance, what is the meaning of stated goals and success rates in organizations such as the Civic Program? The following discussion is meant to suggest other ways of looking at stated goals and measures of success. These thoughts come from and are congruent with our data from the Civic Program.

Goals and Success Measures as an Expression of our Commonsense Assumptions

We have suggested that defining organizations as a group of people brought together for a specific goal and attempting to measure the organization in terms of how well it lived up to the goal is similar to the lay approach to organizations. This definition reflects a commonsense assumption that formally organized individuals should do something purposeful and does not necessarily describe what they actually do. It is only natural that we think of organizations as having a goal. To have one is to have a pragmatic, rational justification for existence which legitimates them. The measures of success give further support for the value of the organization and legitimate it by reinforcing the rationality of our commonsense assumptions. The measures make the organizations appear to be guided by rational principles, and they support myths and beliefs hidden in the organization's goals.

While internally it might not have been apparent what the goal of the Civic Program was or even that there was one, the stated goal supplied a legitimation for the organization's existence: something that people could point to to find reason in a situation that at times seemed unreasonable. No matter how spurious the measure was, nor how bad it appeared, it was interpreted as proof that in fact the organization was achieving. Measuring success becomes synonymous with and can replace achieving success.

Goals as an Excuse to Get Together

People in our society find it difficult to get together without a stated purpose. Or, at least, having stated purposes makes it easier or legitimates getting together. Conventions are perhaps the best-known and most confessed example of this phenomenon.

One might see the goals of the Civic Organization in this light. The stated goal grew out of a desire or a need on the part of various segments of the community that were in conflict to function and communicate with each other. Each segment had its own intentions or goals which could be facilitated in a coalition under the umbrella of the stated organizational goal. Getting together and deciding on a goal may have been the result of this desire to get together, with the goal as a symbol of this desire rather than as an agreement of purpose.

Measures of success, then, may be seen as similar to a convention program: something concrete but in many ways irrelevant to what occurs.

Like stated goals measurements of success can function to bring parties closer together or to separate them.

Goals as the Arena in which Organizational Activity is Fought

Goals in service organizations are often stated so generally that they provide a good deal of room for interpretation and for individual emphasis as to what activities are vital for the organization to perform. The goal might be thought of as the most general statement that organizational members could agree upon or one under which all their various concerns and goals would fit. This general statement shows the area for possible conflict. The goal of the Civic Organization was broad enough to bring people with divergent views and interests together. Once together, they fought out what was to be the concern of the organization, and what they accomplished was in part a function of power relations.

Goals and Success Measures as Organizational Protection from its Larger Environment

Goals can be purposeful misrepresentations of an organization's intent; they may be means of arriving at purposes other than those stated. Organizational goals can be a "front"[11] to protect the organization from assault or to hide its true purposes. Here we see the goals as tools for survival in struggles with the outside. Presenting an acceptable image legitimates the organization to the public and allows it to operate freely. This procedure, of course, is popular in the underworld as well as in the business world. Businesses attempt to cash in on the good name and trust of service organizations by presenting something intangible as their most important product.

To some extent the goals of the Civic Program were used in this way. The organization's goals were stated in an altruistic way, with the emphasis always on service. In fact, the companies involved and the Civic Organization needed the program in order to establish decent community relations and to hire a sufficient number of the "hard core" to satisfy government nondiscrimination regulations. The goals of those who were involved from the business sector clearly focused on these self-interests. (It was smart business to be in the poverty business.)

The goal here represents the shield or weapons one side of the power relationship can use to set a tone of consensus. Perhaps the delicate relationship of goals as symbols of consensus and instruments of power directs us to an area of organizational theory that needs more exploration: relationship between conflict and functionalist models.

Goals as Prerequisites for Funding

In order to become operative, organizations must have funds. If organizational founders have only a sketchy idea of what they want their organization to accomplish or don't know what is possible to accomplish because they don't have enough funds to explore the possibilities, they often are forced to fabricate specific goals and procedures that are unrealistic and untenable in order to obtain funds. Foundations or individuals who provide money like to know what it's for. Stated goals, then, are tools by which organizations get funded and may represent the desire of the organizational founders to get started rather than the organization's specific intentions.

Informal knowledge as to how goals are to be written up in proposals and how certain intentions should be presented is handed around in various organization sets. In many service organizations (as well as in research organizations), writing proposals, outlining goals, and the like are often exercises in fantasy. As one officer in the Civic Program stated:

> You know what they do with a proposal after (a training program) gets started? They turn it face down on the desk and never look at it. . . . Just as long as you write a nice neat package, just as long as it looks like its going to work all right. They just assume it works that way. Write how many hours the trainees are going to do this, how much they are going to do that. Just a lot of bullshit. But they can pay people to write these things up. . . .

Measures of success as organizational accomplishments can be used to obtain more money and more funders. The Civic Organization was able to become involved as main contractor for an even larger program because of its success and experience with the Civic Program.

Goals and Measures of Success are Good for Morale

Finally, organizational goals, paricularly in service organizations, are often based on high ideals and are stated in abstract ways touching on benevolence and self-sacrifice, honored motives in our society. In this sense, goals provide abstract slogans that motivate organizational members and generally allow people to feel good about the work they are doing. They provide an interpretation of behavior that is complimentary to those involved. Abstract goals can make work rewarding. Measures of success provide a similar moral boost.

CLOSING REMARKS

In conclusion I want to suggest that the way organizational goals and measures of success have commonly been conceptualized in the social science literature may not be useful and may be misleading in understanding organizations such as the Civic Program. While the Civic Program might not be the prototype of modern organizations, it may be an example of a whole class of organizations that do not readily fit the theoretical model that suggests we should view organizations as rationally coordinated instruments for attaining goals. Our conceptualizations of organizations may be more the wishful thinking of social scientists and administrators living in an achievement-oriented society than they are an objective statement concerning the character and nature of the social phenomena we commonly refer to as "organizations."

While we know that prisons don't reform, mental hospitals don't cure, and urban schools don't teach, we continue to measure them as if they were structured to do these things and to treat them conceptually as ineffective or deviant types. Organizational goals, measures of success, and organizations in general must be viewed from new perspectives. I have suggested a few in this paper. In general, it might be useful to think of a large number of organizational types as expressive rather than instrumental; they allow societies to act out their beliefs. Measures of success may serve the myth of the instrumental nature of organizations as well as myths societies hold in regard to the nature of certain problems.

NOTES

1. Regional and national meetings now have sessions devoted to the subject and journals have come out specifically dealing with it.

2. Donald Roy, "Quota restriction and goldbricking in a machine shop," *American Journal of Sociology,* **LVII** (March): 427–442, 1952, and F. J. Roethlisberger and W. J. Dickson, *Management and the Worker* (Cambridge: Harvard University Press, 1939).

3. For a discussion of creaming in poverty organizations, see S. M. Miller et al., "Creaming the poor," *Trans-Action,* **VIII,** no. 8 (June): 39–45, 1970. Creaming refers to poverty programs only serving the poor who are at the top and who perhaps need the least help.

4. I am not only referring to discussions based on goal models but also to system models in which goal attainment is only one of a number of aspects of the organization that has to be satisfied. These have been referred to as effectiveness system models; see Amitai Et-

zioni, *A Comparative Analysis of Complex Organizations* (New York: Free Press, 1961), p. 78; and Amaitai Etzioni, "Two approaches to organizational analysis: A critique and suggestion," *Administrative Science Quarterly*, V, no. 5: 257–278, 1960. Also, see James L. Price, "A review of the goal approach and the system resource approach to the study of organizational effectiveness" (Paper prepared for presentation at the 65th Annual Meeting of the American Sociological Association, August 31–September 3, 1970).

5.   Peter Blau and W. Richard Scott, *Formal Organizations* (San Francisco: Chandler Publishing Co., 1961), p. 1.

6.   Amitai Etzioni, *Complex Organizations* (New York: Holt, Rinehart and Winston, 1962) and Amitai Etzioni, *Modern Organizations* (Englewood Cliffs, N.J.: Prentice-Hall, 1962), p. 143.

7.   Robert Merton, *Social Theory and Social Structure* (London: Free Press, 1957); Robert Michels, *Political Parties* (New York: Dover, 1959); Burton Clark, "Organizational adaptation and precarious values," *American Sociological Review*, **XXI**: 327–336, 1956.

8.   Peter Blau, *Bureaucracy in Modern Society* (New York: Random House, 1956), pp. 91–100; David L. Sills, *The Volunteers* (Glencoe, Ill.: Free Press, 1957); and James Thompson and William McEwen, "Organizational goals and environment," *American Sociological Review*, **XXIII**: 23–31, 1958.

9.   Theodore Caplow, *Principles of Organization* (New York: Harcourt, Brace, 1964), p. 119.

10.   Etzioni, *Complex* p. 8.

11.   *Ibid.*, p. 71.

CHAPTER FOURTEEN

A Closing Remark

Our purpose has been to introduce qualitative research as an approach to phenomenological understanding. Any book can only take you so far; it is up to the reader to carry on. Not everyone can excel in the research approach we have described. Who makes the best fieldworkers? The outgoing? The quiet steady type? Early practitioners suggested that the marginal person, the one caught between two cultures, has the greatest potential to become a good fieldworker since he or she possesses the detachment that this kind of research demands. Who knows? From our experience, a number of different people from varied backgrounds have become successful qualitative researchers. Yet all who do well have had an ability to relate to others on their own terms and in their own situations. They have also shared a passion about what they do. It excites them to be out in the world and to develop understanding of different settings and people. For some, research becomes part of life, part of living.

But research methods can be dull and unexciting, especially if they are learned in a classroom or studied behind a desk. Qualitative research is a craft that can only be learned and truly appreciated through experience. It requires skills and a devotion that must be developed and nurtured in the field. We would therefore advise readers, and especially novices, to read this book in conjunction with their own fieldwork.

In Part One, we merely presented the techniques, logic, and procedures that we have used and that are consistent with our notions of ethics and the goals of social science research. All researchers will develop their own ways to conduct fieldwork. In some instances, they will find our suggestions essential. In others, they will reject our advice for techniques better suited to their own particular styles and interests. Some researchers may conclude that we have overstated certain points: for example, that participant observers should spend no more than an hour in the field during the early stages of the research project. We have intentionally stated our preferences on such matters clearly and strongly. By doing so we hoped to sensitize the readers to issues and dilemmas in fieldwork. Whether or not all fieldworkers accept our positions, they will be conscious of the issues at stake.

The essays that appear in Part Two of this book serve as examples of ways in which to report qualitative research findings. We have tried to demonstrate that people who adopt qualitative research methods can use their skills in a variety of ways and can report findings in styles that serve a variety of purposes. Although social science studies can provide human understanding to all people, articles and books written by social scientists for popular audiences are held in disdain by some in the academic community. We believe that articles that transmit knowledge about social processes and situations to the general public should be encouraged. Qualitative research can be used to address organizational and other problems. Journals in the applied professions present another important place to report qualitative findings. These represent real and meaningful alternatives for the qualitative researcher.

Many, if not most, people who are attracted to the social sciences are not lured to them by the kind of work that appears in professional social science journals and publications. Although the culture of the university makes it difficult to admit it, many come with a desire to understand their world and to make it better. These "do-gooders," along with the "journalist types," are intimidated by the academic world and the culture of the social sciences. This attitude must change if social science is to take an important role in the university or in society. Hopefully, this book, in addition to supporting the social science tradition, will provide some alternative definitions of what research can be.

While qualitative studies have been conducted throughout the history of the social sciences, those who have practiced qualitative research have been few. This is an exciting time for those dedicated to qualitative research methods, for interest in the products of such methods is increasing. We have reached a point where a great many researchers are needed to go to the people. There is much to be learned and many are needed to carry out the work.

Field Notes

This appendix contains a set of field notes from the state institution study discussed in the text. They are intended to provide an example of what participant observation field notes should look like in terms of form and content.

A brief note of explanation: Since these field notes were recorded during the observer's ninth visit to the setting, they do not describe the setting and the subjects as thoroughly as they were described in earlier notes. Participant observers must describe their setting and subjects in detail only once. As their studies progress, they can omit many of the details already covered.

OBSERVATIONS AT STATE INSTITUTION

Field Notes #9
Friday, October 20, 1972
6:50 p.m. til 7:55 p.m.

Diagram:

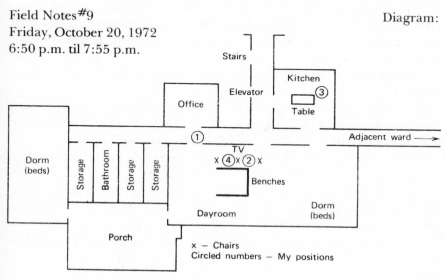

225

I drive onto the grounds of the state school and proceed to the rear of the institution. The grounds are almost empty at this time of the evening, with the exception of a few people I see sitting in front of the buildings on the way in. After I park, I see a double line of people (at least 100) walking in the direction of the school building from the women's side of the institution. Although the people are too far away for me to see them clearly, I can hear women's voices.

I walk to Building 27. The small anteroom is empty and dark. To the left of the door are several rows of benches, arranged in such a way that people could look out the windows of the room.

The hallway inside the building is also empty, and relatively dark—a few ceiling lights are on. I walk past the various offices off of the hallway —speech and hearing, X-ray, and some others. They are all empty. I proceed to the stairway which is about three quarters of the way down the hall.

As I reach the stairway, I begin to hear some muffled voices coming from the upper floors. (O. C. There are no wards on the first floor.) The smell that I first noticed when I entered the building becomes slightly stronger as I reach the stairs. (O. C. It is not as strong as it sometimes is. Perhaps this has to do with the cooler weather.) It is a funny smell— perhaps feces and urine, steamed food, and disinfectant.

I walk up the stairs which are encased in a yellow steel mesh grating. The pastel green walls are worn—paint chipped, stained. My footsteps echo as I walk the stairs. Some of the voices become louder now, especially as I go past the doors which lead to the wards on the various floors. Several windows are open on the stairway—some fresh air blows in as I pass them.

I hear a loud scream as I near the fourth floor. It echoes through the stairway.

I get to the fourth, and top, floor. The door is open. A large cartoon wall painting is in the hall as I get to the top floor. It's about five feet long and three high. Blue, orange, and yellow dominate the mural.

I turn right and walk to the central hallway, past the attendants' kitchen and the elevator.

I look down to the left as I reach the hallway. I can see an attendant at the dayroom door of the ward adjacent to Ward 83. (O. C. There are only two wards on this floor.)

The woman attendant, who is heavy-set, wears a pink nurse's aid type dress and white shoes, has blonde hair and glasses, and is about 50, ignores me as I walk out into the hall. (O. C. The women on this ward neither know me nor want to know me for some reason. They appear content as long as I don't go down to visit their ward. It just occurred to me that many of the women attendants at the institution wear some kind of uniforms—pink, white, or blue, whereas only two of the male attendants on "my" ward, out of about the 30 who are assigned to it throughout the day, wear white uniforms. Perhaps this has something to do with how they see their jobs, or maybe it has something to do with sex-role differences. I'll have to try to question some of the attendants about this.)

I can also see a couple residents in the dayroom of the adjacent ward. Both are boys around 14. One is naked and appears to be just walking around the room. The other is wearing some kind of gray clothes and is sitting in a chair and rocking.

As I turn right down the hall to get to Ward 83, I can hear the loud noise of the TV coming from the dayroom. The hall of 83 is empty now, as well as one of the dorms at the end of the hall. The doors to the dayroom are closed except for one half-way down the hall.

I can see Bill Kelly, a resident in his early twenties, sitting by the dayroom, half in the dayroom and half in the hall. (O. C. According to the attendants, Kelly serves as the "watchdog." From his position, he can see anyone coming down the hall. He warns the attendants when a supervisor is coming.)

Kelly waves to me as I approach. He is smiling. Kelly is wearing gray pants made from some kind of heavy material standard on this ward, a white t-shirt, and black tennis shoes without socks. His hair appears to have been cut recently. The scars on his head stick out. (O. C. Kelly's hair, like the other residents', is never long. The residents' hair seems to be cut every few weeks. Presumably, this is to prevent parasites which would spread rapidly on this ward.)

As I get to the dayroom door, I see that all of the residents are in the room. I can only see two attendants: Vince and another younger man. (O. C. It's interesting how I automatically assume that this other man is an attendant as opposed to a resident. Several hints: long hair, moustache and glasses; cotton shirt and jeans, brown leather boots. He's also smoking a cigarette, and a resident, Bobby Bart, is buffing his shoes with a rag. Thus, this attendant's dress and appearance differ from that of the residents.) Vince, who is 21, is wearing jeans, brown leather boots, and a jersey that has "LOVE" printed on it. He has long hair, sideburns, and a moustache.

I wave to Vince. He half-heartedly waves back. (O. C. I don't think that Vince has quite gotten use to me coming.) The other attendant doesn't pay any attention to me.

Several residents wave or call to me. I wave back.

Kelly is smiling at me. (O. C. He's obviously happy to see me.) I say to Kelly, "Hi, Bill, how are you?" He says, "Hi, Steve. How's school?" (O. C. Kelly knows that I'm a university student from before.) I say, "OK." He says, "School's a pain in the ass. I missed you." (O. C. According to the attendants, Kelly attended school at the institution several years ago.) I say, "I missed you too." (O. C. Kelly's considered one of the brightest residents on the ward by the attendants. He seems so friendly, and so willing to talk to anyone.)

I walk over to Vince and the other attendant. I sit down on a hard plastic rocker between Vince and the other atten., but slightly behind them. (O. C. The other atten. still doesn't pay attention to me. Vince doesn't introduce me to him.)

The smell of feces and urine is quite noticeable to me, but not as pungent as usual.

I, along with the attendants and perhaps five or six residents, am sitting in front of the TV, which is attached to the wall about eight feet off the floor and out of the residents' reach.

Many of the 70 or so residents are sitting on the wooden benches which are in a U-shape in the middle of the dayroom floor. A few are rocking. A couple of others are holding onto each other. In particular, Deier is holding onto the resident the attendants call "Bunny Rabbit." (O. C. Deier is assigned to "Bunny Rabbit"—to keep a hold of him to stop him from smearing feces over himself.)

A lot of residents are sitting on the floor of the room—some of these are leaning against the wall. A few others—maybe ten—just seem to be wandering around the room.

Maybe three or four residents are completely naked. I make a quick count and see that five are wearing any kind of shoes. Most of the residents are wearing their usual clothes—heavy institutional clothes or remnants of regular clothes.

Apparently, Miller and Poller are "on the bucket." Miller is sitting on one of the beds in the dormitory half of the room. His metal bucket is by his feet. Poller is sitting on the floor with his bucket not far from me.

Tresh comes over to greet me. He grins, waves, and mumbles something that I can't understand. (O. C. Tresh tries to talk, but he is not understandable.) Tresh has a ball of rags which he throws up into the air about five feet and catches. (O. C. There are no other things that the residents can use to throw or play with on this ward. It seems so sad that one must play with rags to have something to do.)

Bobby Bart is still buffing the attendant's shoes. The attendant lights up a cigarette. He says to me and to Vince, "All I need is for the supervisor to come up and catch me smoking in here and letting him shine my shoes. They're not supposed to shine shoes." He says this sort of whimsically. He then goes back to watching TV. The atten. have positioned their chairs so that they can see the whole room but still watch TV.

I ask the atten., "Where are all the other guys tonight? Are a lot of them off?" (O. C. There are usually three or four attendants working on a Friday night, if not more.) Vince answers, "No, they're just out to lunch. They'll be back in a little while." (O. C. It's interesting how men who work the evening shift refer to their evening meal as lunch.)

I ask, "When's Mike coming back?" (O. C. Mike has been working on a ward downstairs for the past month since that ward is short-staffed.) Vince says, "He should be back pretty soon—maybe next week. He was up here for a little while tonight."

Vince says something about the number of residents on this ward. I can't exactly catch what he says. I ask, "Weren't they supposed to transfer some of them?" Vince says, "Yea, but I don't know how many now. They came up here for some, but Bill (O. C. The supervising atten.) wasn't here so they didn't take them."

David Dunn, a resident of about 35–40 years of age, comes over. David is shy, but friendly. He is wearing an orange jersey, jeans—no belt, and tennis shoes. His hair is short and prematurely gray. (O. C. The residents who are better dressed and wear shoes are also those who are considered more intelligent by the atten. Of course, they also tend to be the ward workers. I wonder if the clothes they receive stems from the fact that they work or that they care more about clothing than the others.)

I say to David, "Hi, David, how are you?" He says, "Just fine." Vince interrupts, "David Dunn's not going to Building 48 after all. They're

going to keep him here to take care of Igor." (O. C. "Igor" is the attendants' nickname for a tall resident with hard features. They have nick-
names for many of the residents. Many of these I consider
dehumanizing. Somehow the atten. do not see the residents as true
human beings. I noticed here how Vince talked about David in front of
him but not to him. This is common. The atten. act as though the
residents do not matter at times. Vince's comment reveals something
very interesting—placement policies are based not on the welfare of the
resident, but on his usefulness on the ward. Atten. hate to lose good
workers. David takes care of another resident on a 24-hour basis.)

Bobby Bart finishes shining the attendant's shoes. The atten. says to
Bobby, "I don't have any pennies now, Bobby. I'll pay you later." (O. C.
Pennies for a shoeshine?!?!)

Bill, the atten. in charge, enters the room with a cup of coffee. Jim and
Nick, two other atten., follow him. They all wave to me. I wave back. (O.
C. I get along quite well with Bill and Jim especially.)

Bill comes right over to me and says, "Hi, Steve. Want some coffee? Go
get yourself some if you want some." I say, "Not right now, thanks, Bill.
Mayber later."

Bill and the other atten. are all wearing dark pants, cotton shirts—
various colors, and black tie shoes. All have relatively short haircuts and
are older than the two atten. in this room. Bill's about 50 and the other
two are about 30. Bill is wearing a "key caddy" from his belt. He also has
a name plate on his shirt with his name on it. He is the only one on the
ward to have a name plate. (O. C. It seems strange for Bill to have this
name plate. The ward gets almost no visitors, and he knows all of the
atten. and residents on the ward. A sign of status? It's also interesting
that the older atten. seem to stick together.)

As Nick and Jim walk toward me, I see Nick try to whisper something
to Jim. Jim doesn't seem to hear him, for he doesn't look at him or
acknowledge him. (O. C. I wouldn't be surprised if Nick said something
about me being here, like "Oh, no, he's here again.")

Nick comes over to me and gives me a friendly, "Hi, Steve."

Nick and Jim leave the room again.

I notice a resident behind me and to my right who has his pants pulled
down and is masturbating. He doesn't seem to be paying attention to
anyone else in the room.

Miller gets up and goes over to a puddle of urine to my left. He kneels
down, wipes the floor with a wet rag, wrings out the rag, and then throws

it back into the bucket. He goes by me as he walks back to his chair. The smell is overpowering. Feces are floating in the water. (O. C. Miller, unlike other residents, automatically cleans up feces or urine on the floor. Many of the others wait for feces or urine to be pointed out to them.)

Miller frequently cleans up feces and urine throughout the time I am on the ward.

Bill, who has been standing near me, pulls a chair over and sits down beside Vince. (O. C. There are five plastic chairs in the room. These are used by the atten. The residents seldom try to sit in any of them. When they do, they are castigated by the atten.)

A resident named Jim is sitting on the floor in front of all of us. Jim is in his late teens, is wearing gray pants and shoes, but nothing else. The new atten. says, "Hello Jim, hello, Jim. O.K. O.K." (O. C. He says it in a mocking tone.) Jim repeats him, "Hello, Gem. O.K. O.K." The atten. says, "O.K., Gem, O.K. O.K." Jim repeats him again. The atten. then says, "Fuck you, Gem. Fuck you." Jim waves his arms around, swatting the air. The atten. all laugh. Bill, laughing, looks over at me. (O. C. As though to share the laughter.) I smile. (O. C. Situations like this are always difficult. I feel guilty smiling, but somehow feel that I don't want to seem like I'm putting the atten. down.)

The new atten. turns around to Bobby Bart. He says, "Fuck you, Bobby," and sticks his middle finger up vigorously. Bobby returns the gesture, laughing. (O. C. Bobby cannot hear, according to the atten., but is quite intelligent.)

This same atten. begins to sing (O. C. He seems to be joking around.): "It's beginning to look a lot like Christmas. . . ." Bill says, "You're a little early, aren't you?" He says, "Na, it'll be Christmas any time now."

Romano, about 21, comes running over to me. He has cerebral palsy and is crippled on the left side of his body. (O. C. He always runs although it is difficult for him to do so.) Romano says to me, "Hi, Steve." I say, "Hi, Vito, how are you?" He smiles.

Vito walks over behind Bill and starts to rub his back. Bill screams at him, "Get the hell outta here, Vito. I don't want my back rubbed."

Bill points to the new atten. and says, "Go rub his back, Vito." The atten. says, "He won't rub my back 'cause of what I did to him that one night. Remember?" (O. C. The atten. says it in such a way that I don't think I should pursue the matter—too sensitive at this time. I don't want to seem like a snooper.)

The atten. then says to Vito, "What's the matter Vito? Don't you want to rub my back? Don't you like me?" (O. C. He says this mockingly.) Vito is behind me so I can't see his face, but the atten. says, "Why not, Vito? Come on, rub my back." Vito goes over to him and begins to rub his back.

Vince asks me, "Has Vito ever rubbed your back?" Then he says to Vito, "Come rub Steve's back." I say, "Yea, he's rubbed my back." Vince says to Vito, "That's O.K., Vito. Never mind," and then to me, "Oh, then you know what he's like. He really rubs hard."

One of the residents wanders over to the dayroom door. Bill yells at him, "   , get away from that door."

The new atten. points to Tresh's ball of rags and says, "Give that to me." Tresh gives it to him. He throws the rags at the resident by the door and hits him in the back. The resident runs away from the door.

Miller is behind me and is wiping up a puddle of urine. A resident near us pulls his pants to his knees and crouches on the floor. Vince yells to Miller, "Miller, get up. Hurry! Take him to the bathroom. Hurry up before he goes on the floor!" Miller grabs the resident's hand and leads him out of the room.

Vito is still rubbing the new attendant's back. This atten. asks Vince, "Should I pay him for the backrub?" Vince says, "I usually give him a nickel if he does a good job. He doesn't deserve it if he rubs too hard."

Bill says something about the trouble he's having trying to keep residents from "pissing and shitting on the floor." He then says something to the effect, "These patients here are low grades."

Bill continues, "I'd love to be able to train them. I really would. But you can't do it. Not here you can't." Bill points to a resident who is a couple of feet away from us and says, "This isn't bad. You can teach him something." He points to Vito and says, "This one isn't bad either. You can teach them something. I mean, you can teach them so much. There's a limit. They have a borderline. You can do so much with 'em, but that's all. They have a borderline and you can't go beyond on them. They can talk so you can tell 'em what to do. If they can talk you can do somethin' with 'em. They can comprehend."

Bill continues, "See, if they can talk, you can do something with 'em. You can tell them to do something, and they'll do it. Most of these here you can't talk to. They only listen to two things." Bill pauses, makes a fist, and says, "This." He makes a slapping motion and says, "Or this."

Bill stands up and asks me, "You want some coffee, Steve? Come on."

Bill starts for the door. I stand up and follow him. We walk out of the room and down the hall to the kitchen.

Both of us take a cup and get coffee from a perculator in the room. Bill walks over to a refrigerator in the room and takes out a large carton of milk. He pours some into his coffee and then hands it to me. We sit down at a table in the kitchen. There are five loaves of bread and a box of green bananas on a table by the refrigerator.

Bill lights a cigarette, sits back, and says, "The supervisor just told us that we have to start taking the low grades to a special dance just for low grades. So this Tuesday we have to take them. What we have to do is dress them all up in their own clothes and then one employee has to take them over to the dance and stay with them the whole night. How are we going to do that? We don't have enough employees. We'll get them all dressed up and start taking them over and then one will shit his pants and we'll have to bring them all back."

I ask Bill, "Well, why are they having this special dance?" He says, "I'll tell ya why. It's because they get federal grants for having so many patients in a program. That's why they have so many programs around here. (O. C. From Bill's perspective there are too many programs. Yet very few residents actually receive programming.) See, they get state grants, county grants, and federal grants. They may have the program anyway, but the government gives them more money if they have more patients in it. They had record hops before. They had one employee to run the hi-fi. What they did was add more patients to get the federal grant. Where's the money going? There's still that one employee running the hi-fi. The money ain't goin' to the patients and it ain't goin' to the employees so where's it goin'? Well, I know where it's goin' and I think you know too—it's goin' to graft. The people runnin' this place are gettin' rich on graft. The people above them know it, but they don't care."

Bill goes on, "I'll tell ya, I know there's graft around here. Every year around January they start cuttin' down on food. See, the year starts in April so January's the end of the year for money. So they start scrimpin'."

I say, "Well, it's not even January and you don't have enough stuff here." Bill says, "That's right. They don't give us enough disinfectant. That's why I have to buy it myself—with my own money. Hell, in 29— the medical building—they have all they need. That's cause they get all the visitors there. Nobody comes here, but these are the buildings that need it the most."

I ask Bill, "Where were you before you came up here?" He says, "I was downstairs before. I was second in charge. The charge down there didn't care about nothin'. He never cleaned the place. He said if the place was dirty he wouldn't get any visitors and I guess he was right. I was second charge and every time the charge was off I cleaned the whole place. Then the supervisor told me he wanted me to be charge up here."

Bill goes on, "You see, they knew I was clean. They knew I'd keep this place clean. That's why they wanted me up here. This place was the dirtiest place in the world. The charge up here didn't care. He just put his watchdogs at the door and played cards. I got this place clean too. I just can't stand filth. So now that I'm up here they won't give me the things I need to keep this place clean."

I say, "You must get discouraged." Bill says, "Sure I get discouraged. They won't give us any disinfectant or anything. The state don't care what we take home to our kids. Well, I care. I'm not takin' home hepatitis or somethin' to my kids. I'm gonna keep this place clean. I just can't stand filth."

Bill stands up quickly and says, "If I don't take a leak now, I'm gonna piss my pants. I'll be back in a second. Go ahead, have another cup of coffee." Bill hurries out of the room.

(O. C. Bill has given me important insights into how he defines his supervisors and his job. I'll have to follow up on this graft and this cleanliness thing.)

I pour myself another cup of coffee and sit alone for a couple minutes.

Bill returns and immediately begins to speak, "Everybody is here for one reason and one reason only—money. That's right. They're all here for money. That's why they took this job. That's why I took this job. I'm 50 years old now and when I came here I was 40. Who's gonna hire you at 40? Nobody wants a guy who's 40 years old."

I ask Bill, "Do you have a problem keeping good men? I mean, is there a lot of turnover?" He answers, "No, I have good employees now. They'll do what I say. They're clean like I am."

Bill continues, "My wife's a supervisor, but she lets people take advantage of her." I ask, "Where does she work—over on the other side?" He answers, "Yea, over in 18." I ask, "Isn't 18 the children's building?" He says, "Yea, my wife has them until 12 to 16—whenever they mensurate [sic]. When they mensurate [sic] they put them in another ward. There are only three employees on my wife's ward, and on weekends they only have two. My wife's supervisor was makin' them work 8½ hours without lunch on weekends. Can you believe that?" (O. C. I am amazed at how many atten. have relatives working at the institution. The institution almost makes this a company town.)

Jim comes into the room with a box and different slips of paper. These are for a lottery on the World Series. Bill fills out a slip and gives Jim one dollar. Jim leaves after some small talk about baseball.

Bill stands up, goes over to the sink, and washes out his coffee cup. I do the same. We walk back to the dayroom. We had spent about 25 minutes in the kitchen.

Jim and Nick are in the dayroom now and are sitting in front of the TV. Vince and the other atten. are in the dayroom too. Bill walks around the room. I sit down beside Vince.

A resident walks up behind me and stands there. Vince looks at him and screams, "Harris, get out of there. Leave him alone." Vince says to me, "Don't ever let them behind you. You don't know what they might do. They could choke you. One time, Bobby Bart got a kid in a choke hold and wouldn't let go. Nobody could get him off either." (O. C. I've never seen a resident attack or strike an atten. Neither have I ever seen Bobby Bart hurt anyone.)

Bill leaves the room.

Nick and Jim talk about snowmobiles and watch TV.

Vince asks me, "Have you ever seen Frankie tie shoes?" I answer, "No," and he says, "You should see him. He really does it different." Vince looks around the room and calls, "Hey Frankie, come here." Frankie ignores Vince. Instead, he kicks a resident who is sitting on the floor. The resident doesn't do anything. Vince calls to Frankie again. Frankie comes over this time. Frankie is a heavy-set man in his early twenties. He is not wearing shoes but has on institutional clothing.

Vince says to Frankie, "Tie Steve's shoes, Frankie." Frankie unties my shoes and then methodically ties them again without even looking at them.

Vince says to Frankie, "Tie my shoes, Frankie." Vince is wearing boots which do not have shoelaces. Frankie doesn't respond to Vince.

The new atten. says, "Hey Frankie," makes a fist, and points to a young Black resident who is sitting against the wall and near the TV. Frankie walks over to the resident and punches him in the head. The resident cringes and runs away toward the dormitory part of the room. Frankie wanders away also. The atten. don't pay attention to what Frankie did. (O. C. There are three Black residents on the ward. The atten. all seem to be racist by their behavior toward these residents and by how they refer to them.)

Vince points a puddle of urine out to Miller. Miller goes over to it and wipes it up.

I ask Vince, "What did Miller do to get on the bucket?" He answers, "He didn't do anything. He doesn't mind being on the bucket. He knows that if he's on the bucket, he'll get extra food. We give extra food to whoever is on the bucket. Miller knows that so he doesn't mind. Some of the other ones aren't that smart, but Miller is."

Vince starts to talk to the new atten. about baseball.

I decide to leave. I say to Vince, "Well, I think I'd better get home now. I'll be seeing you." He says, "O.K., I'll see you later." I wave good-bye to the other atten. and to some of the residents. I leave the room. I walk past the office in the hall.

Bill is sitting at the desk in the office. He is filling out some kind of chart. I say, "I'm leaving now, Bill." He says, "O.K., Steve, take it easy. Stop up any time." I leave the ward and the building.

As I walk to my car, a man comes up to me. (O. C. I assume that he is a resident by his clothes—old and baggy, his hair, and the way he speaks.) He says, "I don't have a day off until Sunday. I work all the time." He walks with me. He points to a tree and says, "My brother cut a branch off that tree. He works here. I have another brother who works here too. One at home too."

We get to the parking lot. He asks, "Which one is your car?" I point to it and say, "That one." He says, "I see it. You need someone to wash it? I'll wash it for you some time. It'll only cost you a quarter. I do a good job." I say, "O.K., I'll be seeing you." He walks away. I walk to my car. The man comes back over to me, and says, "I work over in Building 22. Come get me if you want your car washed—inside and out." I say, "O.K.," and leave the institution. (O. C. It was important to this man for me to believe that he was an employee and not a resident here. This probably has something to do with the stigma of being "retarded.")

Bibliography

Adams, R. N., & Preiss, J. J. (Eds.). *Human Organization Research*. Homewood, Ill.: Dorsey Press, 1960.

Allport, F. H. *Systematic Questionnaire for the Study of Personality*. Chicago: Stoelting, 1924.

Allport, G. *The Use of Personal Documents in Psychological Science*. New York: Social Science Research Council, 1942.

Allport, G., Bruner, J. S., & Jandorf, E. M. "Personality under social catastrophe: An analysis of 90 German refugee life histories." *Character and Personality*, 5(10): 1–22, 1941.

American Sociologist Staff. "Toward a code of ethics for sociologists." *American Sociologist*, 3 (November): 316–318, 1968.

Anderson, N. *The Hobo*. Chicago: University of Chicago Press, 1923.

Angell, R. "A critical review of the development of the personal document method in sociology 1920–1940." In L. Gottschalk, C. Kluckhohn, & R. Angell, *The Use of Personal Documents in History, Anthropology, and Sociology*. New York: Social Science Research Council, 1945.

Angell, R. *The Family Encounters the Depression*. New York: Scribner, 1936.

Angell, R. D., & Freedman, R. "The use of documents, records, census materials, and indices." In L. Festinger and D. Katz (Eds.), *Research Methods in the Behavioral Sciences*. New York: Holt, pp. 300–326, 1953.

Angell, R. D., & Turner, R. H. "Comment and reply on discussions of the analytic induction method." *American Sociological Review*, 19: 476–478, 1954.

Arbus, D. *Diane Arbus*. New York: An Aperture Monograph, 1972.

Arensberg, C. M. "The community-study method." *American Journal of Sociology*, 60: 109–124, 1954.

Argyris, C. "Diagnosing defenses against the outsider." *Journal of Social Issues*, 8(3): 24–34, 1952.

Arrington, R. "Time sampling in studies of social behavior." *Psychological Bulletin*, 40: 81–124, 1943.

Babchuck, N. "The role of the researcher as participant observer and participant-as-observer in the field situation." *Human Organization*, 21(3): 225–228, 1962.

Back, K. W. "The well-informed informant." *Human Organization*, 14(4): 30–33, 1956.

Bader, C. "Standardized field practice." *International Journal of Opinion and Attitude Research*, 2: 243-244, 1948.

Bain, R. "The impersonal confession and social research." *Journal of Applied Sociology,* **9:** 356–361, 1925.

Bain, R. K. "The researcher's role: A case study." *Human Organization,* **9**(1): 23–28, 1950.

Baldamus, W. "Incentives and work analysis." *University of Birmingham Studies in Economics and Sociology,* No. Al., 1951.

Baldwin, A. L. "The statistical analysis of the structure of a single personality." *Psychological Bulletin,* **5**(37): 518–519, 1940.

Ball, D. "An abortion clinic ethnography." *Social Problems,* **5**(14): 293–301, 1966–1967.

Banaka, W. H. *Training in Depth Interviewing.* New York: Harper & Row, 1971.

Barber, B. "Research on human subjects: Problems of access to a powerful profession." *Social Problems,* **21** (Summer): 103–112, 1973.

Barker, R. G. (Ed.). *The Stream of Behavior.* New York: Appleton-Century-Crofts, 1963.

Barns, J. A. "Some ethical problems in modern field work." *British Journal of Sociology,* **14** (June): 118–134, 1963.

Bartlett, F. C. "Psychological methods and anthropological problems." *Africa,* **10:** 401–420, 1937.

Bartlett, F. C., Lindgren, E. J., Ginsberg, M., & Thouless, R. H. (Eds.), *The Study of Society.* London: Kegan Paul, 1939.

Barton, A. H., & Lazarsfeld, P. F. "Some functions of qualitative analysis in social research." *Frankfurter Beiträge zur Soziologie,* **1:** 321–361, 1955.

Bateson, G. "Experiments in thinking about observed ethnological materials." *Philosophy of Science,* **8:** 53–68, 1941.

Beals, R. L. "Native terms and anthropological methods." *American Anthropologist,* **59:** 716–717, 1957.

Beals, R. L. *Politics of Social Research.* Chicago: Aldine, 1968.

Becker, H. S. "The career of the Chicago public school teacher." *American Journal of Sociology,* **57** (March): 470–477, 1952.

Becker, H. S. "Interviewing medical students." *American Journal of Sociology,* **62:** 199–201, 1956.

Becker, H. S. "A note on interviewing tactics." *Human Organization,* **12**(4): 31–32, 1954.

Becker, H. S. "Notes on the concept of commitment." *American Journal of Sociology,* **66** (July): 32–40, 1960.

Becker, H. S. (Ed.). *The Other Side.* New York: Free Press, 1967.

Becker, H. S. *Outsiders: Studies in the Sociology of Deviance.* New York: Free Press, 1963.

Becker, H. S. "Problems in the publication of field studies." In A. J. Vidich, J. Bensman, & M. R. Stein (Eds.), *Reflections on Community Studies.* New York: Wiley, pp. 267–284, 1964.

Becker, H. S. "Problems of inference and proof in participant observation." *American Sociological Review,* **23:** 652–660, 1958.

Becker, H. S. *Sociological Work: Method and Substance.* Chicago: Aldine, 1970.

Becker, H. S. "The teacher in the authority system of the public school." *Journal of Educational Sociology,* **27** (November): 128–141, 1953.

Becker, H. S. "Whose side are we on?" *Social Problems,* **14** (Winter): 239–247, 1966–1967.

Becker, H. S., & Carper, J. W. "The development of identification with an occupation." *American Journal of Sociology,* **61** (January): 289–298, 1956.

Becker, H. S., & Carper, J. W. "The elements of identification with an occupation." *American Sociological Review,* **21** (June): 341–348, 1956.

Becker, H. S., & Friedson, E. "Against the code of ethics." *American Sociological Review,* **29:** 409–410, 1964.

Becker, H. S., & Geer, B. "The fate of idealism in medical school." *American Sociological Review,* **23** (February): 50–56, 1958.

Becker, H. S., & Geer, B. "Latent culture: A note on the theory of latent social roles." *Administrative Science Quarterly,* **5** (September): 304–313, 1960.

Becker, H. S., & Geer, B. "Participant observation and interviewing: A comparison." *Human Organization,* **16**(3): 28–32, 1957.

Becker, H. S., & Geer, B. " 'Participant observation and interviewing': A rejoinder." *Human Organization,* **17**(2): 39–40, 1958.

Becker, H. S., & Geer, B. "Participant observation: The analysis of qualitative field data." In R. N. Adams & J. J. Preiss (Eds.), *Human Organization Research.* Homewood, Ill.: Dorsey Press, pp. 267–289, 1960.

Becker, H. S., Geer, B. & Hughes, E. *Making the Grade.* New York: Wiley, 1968.

Becker, H. S., Geer, B., Hughes, E. C., & Strauss, A. L. *Boys in White: Student Culture in Medical School.* Chicago: University of Chicago Press, 1961.

Becker, H. S., & Horowitz, I. L. "Radical politics and sociological research: Observations on methodology and ideology." *American Journal of Sociology,* **78** (July): 48–66, 1972.

Becker, H. S., & Strauss, A. L. "Careers, personality and adult socialization." *American Journal of Sociology,* **62** (November): 253–263, 1956.

Becker, H. S. et al. (Eds.). *Institutions and the Person: Essays Presented to Everett C. Hughes.* Chicago: Aldine, 1968.

Beecher, H. K. *Research and the Individual: Human Studies.* Boston: Little, Brown, 1970.

Beezer, R. H. "Research on methods of interviewing foreign informants." George Washington University Human Resources Research Office Technical Report, No. 30, 1956.

Bendix, R. "Concepts and generalizations in comparative sociological studies." *American Sociological Review,* **28:** 532–539, 1963.

Benjamin, H. *The Transsexual Phenomenon.* New York: Julian, 1966.

Bennett, J. W. "The study of cultures: A survey of technique and methodology in field work." *American Sociological Review,* **13:** 672–689, 1948.

Bensman, J., & Vidich, A. "Social theory in field research." *American Journal of Sociology,* **65:** 577–584, 1960.

Berger, P. "On existential phenomenology and sociology (II)." *American Sociological Review,* **31** (April): 259–260, 1966.

Berger, P. L., & Luckmann, T. *The Social Construction of Reality.* Garden City, N. Y.: Doubleday, 1967.

Berk, R. A., & Adams, R. A. "Establishing rapport with deviant groups." *Social Problems,* **18** (Summer): 102–117, 1970.

Bernard, J. "Observation and generalization in cultural anthropology." *American Journal of Sociology,* **50:** 284–291, 1945.

Bevis, J. C. "Interviewing with tape recorders." *Public Opinion Quarterly,* **13:** 629–634, 1950.

Bickman, L., & Henchy, T. (Eds.). *Beyond the Laboratory: Field Research in Social Psychology.* New York: McGraw-Hill, 1972.

Bierstedt, R. "A critique of empiricism in sociology." *American Sociological Review,* **24:** 584–592, 1949.

Biklen, D. (Ed.). *Human Report 1: Observations in Mental Health, Mental Retardation Facilities.* In collaboration with the Workshop on Human Abuse Protection and Public Policy, Syracuse University, 1970.

Blalock, H. M., Jr. *Social Statistics.* New York: McGraw-Hill, 1960.

Blatt, B. *Exodus From Pandemonium.* Boston: Allyn & Bacon, 1970.

Blatt, B., Biklen, D. & Bogdan, R. (Eds.). *The Monolith and the Promise: Surplus Children in the Land of Opportunity.* Forthcoming.

Blatt, B. & Kaplan F. *Christmas in Purgatory.* Syracuse, N. Y.: Human Policy Press, 1974.

Blau, P. M. *Bureaucracy in Modern Society.* New York: Random House, 1956.

Blau, P. M. *The Dynamics of Bureaucracy.* Chicago: University of Chicago Press, 1955.

Blau, P. M. *Exchange and Power in Social Life.* New York: Wiley, 1964.

Blau, P. M. "Orientation toward clients in a public welfare agency." *Administrative Science Quarterly,* **5**(3): 341–361, 1960.

Blau, P. M., & Scott, W. R. *Formal organization.* San Francisco: Chandler, 1962.

Blum, F. H. "Getting individuals to give information to the outsider." *Journal of Social Issues,* **8**(3): 35–42, 1952.

Blumer, H. *An Appraisal of Thomas and Znaniecki's 'The Polish Peasant in Europe and America.'* New York: Social Science Research Council, 1939.

Blumer, H. "Society as symbolic interaction." In J. Manis & B. Meltzer (Eds.), *Symbolic Interaction.* Boston: Allyn and Bacon, 1967.

Blumer, H. "Sociological analysis of the 'variable.' " *American Sociological Review,* **21** (December): 683–690, 1956.

Blumer, H. "Sociological implications of the thought of George Herbert Mead." *American Journal of Sociology,* **71** (March): 535–544, 1966.

Blumer, H. *Symbolic Interactionism: Perspective and Method.* Englewood Cliffs, N. J.: Prentice-Hall, 1969.

Blauner, R. & Wellman, D. "Toward the decolonization of social research." In J. Ladner (Ed.), *The Death of White Sociology.* New York: Vintage Books, 1973.

Bogdan, R. "Autobiographies." In B. Blatt, D. Biklen, & R. Bogdan (Eds.), *The Monolith and the Promise: Surplus Children in the Land of Opportunity.* In press.

Bogdan, R. *Being Different: The Autobiography of Jane Fry.* New York: Wiley, 1974.

Bogdan, R. "Learning to sell door to door." *The American Behavioral Scientist,* September/October, 55–64, 1972.

Bogdan, R. *Observing in Institutions,* Syracuse: Human Policy Press, 1972.

Bogdan, R. *Participant Observation in Organization Settings.* Syracuse, N. Y.: Syracuse University Division of Special Education and Rehabilitation, 1972.

Bogdan, R., Taylor, S., DeGrandpre, B., & Haynes, S. "Let them eat programs: Attendants' perspectives and programming on wards in state schools." *Journal of Health and Social Behavior,* **15** (June): 142–151, 1974.

Bonacich, P. "Deceiving subjects: The pollution of our environment." *American Sociologist,* **5** (February): 45, 1970.

Bonaparte, M. A. "A defense of biography." *International Journal of Psycho-Analysis,* **5**(20): 231–240, 1939.

Bowers, R. V. "Research methodology in sociology: The first half-century." In R. F. Spencer (Ed.), *Method and Perspective in Anthropology*. Minneapolis: University of Minnesota Press, pp. 251–270, 1954.

Brookover, L. A., & Back, K. W. "Time sampling as a field technique." *Human Organization*, **25:** 64–70, 1966.

Brown, C. *Manchild in the Promised Land*. New York: New American Library, 1965.

Bruyn, S. T. *The Human Perspective in Sociology: The Methodology of Participant Observation*. Englewood Cliffs, N. J.: Prentice-Hall, 1966.

Brymer, R. A., & Faris, B. "Ethical and political dilemmas in the investigation of deviance: A study of juvenile delinquency." In G. Sjoberg (Ed.), *Ethics, Politics and Social Research*. Cambridge, Mass.: Schenkman, pp. 297–318, 1967.

Buckner, H. T. "Organization of a large scale field work course." *Urban Life and Culture*, **2**(3) (October): 361–379, 1973.

Burchard, W. W. "Lawyers, political scientists, sociologists—and concealed microphones." *American Sociological Review*, **23:** 686–691, 1958.

Burgess, E. W. "Research methods in sociology." In G. Gurvitch & W. Moore (Eds.), *Twentieth Century Sociology*. New York: Philosophical Library, pp. 20–41, 1945.

Burgess, E. W. "Sociological research methods." *American Journal of Sociology*, **50:** 474–482, 1945.

Burgess, E. W. "Statistics and case studies as methods of sociological research." *Social Forces,* **12:** 103–120, 1927.

Burgess, E. W. "What social case records should contain to be useful for sociological interpretation." *Social Forces,* **6:** 524–532, 1925.

Burr, A. R. *The Autobiography: A Critical and Comparative Study*. New York: Houghton Mifflin, 1909.

Campbell, D. T. "Factors relevant to the validity of experiments in social settings." *Psychological Bulletin,* **54:** 297–312, 1957.

Campbell, D. T. "The informant in qualatative research." *American Journal of Sociology,* **60:** 339–342, 1955.

Campbell, D. T. "Systematic error on the part of human links in communication systems." *Information and Control,* **1:** 334–369, 1959.

Campbell, D. T. "The informant in qualitative research." *American Journal of Sociology,* Chicago: Rand McNally, 1966.

Cannell, C. F., & Axelrod, M. "The respondent reports on the interview." *American Journal of Sociology,* **62:** 177–181, 1956.

Caplow, T. "The dynamics of information interviewing." *American Journal of Sociology,* **62:** 165–171, 1956.

Caplow, T. *Principles of Organization*. New York: Harcourt, Brace, 1964.

Caplow, T., & McGee, R. *The Academic Marketplace*. New York: Science Editions, 1961.

Carey, A. "The Hawthorne studies: A radical criticism." *American Sociological Review,* **32**(3): 403–416, 1967.

Carnegie, D. *How to Win Friends and Influence People*. New York: Simon & Schuster, 1937.

Cartwright, D., & French, J. R. P., Jr. "The reliability of life history studies." *Character and Personality,* **8:** 110–119, 1939.

Caudill, W. *The Psychiatric Hospital as a Small Society*. Cambridge, Mass.: Harvard University Press, 1958.

Cavan, R. S. "Interviewing for life-history material." *The American Journal of Sociology,* **35:** 100–115, 1929–1930.

Cavan, S. *Liquor License: An Ethnography of Bar Behavior.* Chicago: Aldine, 1966.

Cavan, S. "Seeing social structure in a rural setting." *Urban Life and Culture,* **3** (October): 329–346, 1974.

Chapin, F. S. *Field Work and Social Research.* New York: Century, 1920.

Chein, I. "An introduction to sampling." In C. Selltiz, M. Jahoda, M. Deutsch, & S. W. Cook, *Research Methods in Social Relations.* Revised edition. New York: Holt, pp. 509–545, 1959.

Chesler, M., & Schmuck, R. "Participant observation in a superpatriot discussion group." *Journal of Social Issues,* **19**(2): 18–30, 1963.

Chinoy, E. *Automobile Workers and the American Dream.* Garden City, N. Y.: Doubleday, 1955.

Church, J. *Three Babies.* New York: Random House, 1966.

Cicourel, A. *Cognitive Sociology.* Baltimore: Penguin, 1973.

Cicourel, A. *Method and Measurement in Sociology.* New York: Free Press, 1964.

Cicourel, A. *The Social Organization of Juvenile Justice.* New York: Wiley, 1968.

Cicourel, A., & Kitsuse, J. *The Educational Decision-makers.* Indianapolis: Bobbs-Merrill, 1963.

Clark, B. *The Open Door College.* New York: McGraw-Hill, 1960.

Clark, B. "Organizational adaptation and precarious values." *American Sociological Review,* **21**(3): 327–336, 1956.

Clark, K. *Dark Ghetto.* New York: Harper Torchbooks, 1967.

Coles, R. "Part I Method." *Children of Crisis.* Boston: Little, Brown, 1964.

Coles, R. *Migrants, Sharecroppers, Mountaineers.* Boston: Little, Brown, 1971.

Cole, S. *The Sociological Method.* Chicago: Markham, 1972.

Coleman, J. S. "Relational analysis: The study of social organizations with survey methods." *Human Organization,* **17**(4): 28–36, 1958.

Colfax, D. J. "Pressure toward distortion and involvement in studying a civil rights organization." *Human Organization,* **XXV** (Summer): 140–149, 1966.

Collier, J., Jr. *Visual Anthropology: Photography as a Research Method.* New York: Holt, 1967.

Colvard, R. "Interaction and identification in reporting field research: A critical reconsideration of protective procedures." In G. Sjoberg (Ed.), *Ethics, Politics, and Social Research.* Cambridge, Mass.: Schenkman, pp. 319–358, 1967.

Comte, A. *The Positive Philosophy.* Translated by Harriet Martineau. London: George Bell & Sons, 1896.

Cook, P. H. "Methods of field research." *Australian Journal of Psychology,* **3**(2): 84–98, 1951.

Cooley, C. H. *Human Nature and the Social Order.* New York: Scribner, 1902.

Cooper, K. J. "Rural-urban differences in responses to field techniques." *Human Organization,* **18**(3): 135–139, 1959.

Coser, L. A., Roth, J. A., Sullivan, M. A., Jr., & Queen, S. A. "Participant observation and the military: An exchange." *American Sociological Review,* **24:** 397–400, 1959.

Cottle, T. J. *The Abandoners: Portraits of Loss, Separation, and Neglect.* Boston: Little, Brown, 1972.

Cottle, T. J. "The ghetto scientists," unpublished paper.

Cottle, T. J. "The life study: On mutual recognition and the subjective inquiry." *Urban Life and Culture,* **2**(3) (October): 344–360, 1973.

Cottle, T. J. *The Voices of School: Educational Images Through Personal Accounts.* Boston: Little, Brown, 1973.

Cowley, M. "Sociological habit patterns in linguistic transmogrification." *The Reporter,* September 20, 170–175, 1956.

Craig, K. H. "The comprehension of the everyday physical environment." In H. M. Proshansky, W. H. Ittelson & L. E. Rivlin. *Environmental Psychology.* New York: Holt, Rinehart & Winston, 1970.

Cressey, D. "Limitations on organization of treatment in the modern prison." In R. Quinney (Ed.), *Crime and Justice in Society.* Boston: Little, Brown, 1969.

Cressey, P. G. *The Taxi-Dance Hall.* Chicago: University of Chicago Press, 1932.

Dalton, M. *Men Who Manage.* New York: Wiley, 1961.

Dalton, M. "Preconceptions and methods in *Men Who Manage.*" In P. E. Hammond (Ed.), *Sociologists at Work.* New York: Basic Books, pp. 50–95, 1964.

Daniels, A. K. "The low-caste stranger in social research." In G. Sjoberg (Ed.), *Ethics, Politics, and Social Research.* Cambridge, Mass.: Schenkman, pp. 267–296, 1967.

Davis, A. J. "Sexual assaults in the Philadelphia prison system and sheriff's vans." *Trans-Action,* **6** (December): 8–16, 1968.

Davis, F. "The cabdriver and his fare." *American Journal of Sociology,* **63**(2): 158–165, 1959.

Davis, F. "Comment on initial interaction of newcomers in Alcoholics Anonymous." *Social Problems,* **8**(4): 364–365, 1961.

Davis, F. "Definitions of time and recovery in paralytic polio convalescence." *American Journal of Sociology,* **61** (May): 582–587, 1956.

Davis, F. "Deviance disavowel: The management of strained interaction by the visibly handicapped." In H. S. Becker (Ed.), *The Other Side.* New York: Free Press, 1964.

Davis, F. "The martian and the convert: Ontological polarities in social research." *Urban Life and Culture,* **(2)**(3) (October): 333–343, 1973.

Davis, F. *Passage Through Crisis.* Indianapolis: Bobbs-Merrill, 1963.

Davis, F. "Stories and Sociology." *Urban Life and Culture,* **3** (October): 310–316, 1974.

Davis, F. "Uncertainty in medical prognosis." *American Journal of Sociology,* **66** (July): 41–47, 1960.

Dean, J. P. "Participant observation and interviewing." In J. T. Doby (Ed.), *An Introduction to Social Research.* Harrisburg, Pa.: Stackpole, pp. 225–252, 1954.

Dean, J. P., Eichhorn, R. L., & Dean, L. R. "Observation and interviewing." In J. T. Doby (Ed.), *An Introduction to Social Research.* 2nd edition. New York: Appleton-Century-Crofts, pp. 274–304, 1967.

Dean, J. P., & Whyte, W. F. "How do you know if the informant is telling the truth?" *Human Organization* **17**(2): 34–38, 1958.

Dean, L. R. "Interaction, reported and observed: The case of one local union." *Human Organization,* **17**(3): 36–44, 1958.

DeLaguna, F. "Some problems of objectivity in ethnology." *Man,* **57:** 179–182, 1957.

Denzin, N. *The Research Act: A Theoretic Introduction to Sociological Methods.* Chicago: Aldine, 1970.

Denzin, N. (Ed.). *Sociological Methods: A Sourcebook.* Chicago: Aldine, 1970.

Deutscher, I. "The bureaucratic gatekeeper in public housing." In I. Deutscher & E.

Thompson (Eds.), *Among the People: Encounters with the Poor.* New York: Basic Books, 1968.

Deutscher, I. "Looking backward: Case studies on the progress of methodology in sociological research." *The American Sociologist,* **4** (February): 34–42, 1969.

Deutscher, I. "Notes on language and human conduct." The Maxwell Graduate School of Social Sciences and the Youth Development Center, Syracuse University, 1967.

Deutscher, I. *What We Say/What We Do: Sentiments and Acts.* Glenview, Ill.: Scott, Foresman, 1973.

Deutscher, I. "Words and deeds: Social science and social policy." *Social Problems,* **13** (Winter): 233–254, 1966.

Deutscher, I., & Thompson, E. *Among the People: Encounters with the Poor.* New York: Basic Books, 1968.

Dewey, J. *Human Nature and Conduct.* New York: Modern Library, 1930.

Dexter, L. A. "The good will of important people: More on the jeopardy of the interview." *Public Opinion Quarterly,* **28**: 556–563, 1964.

Dexter, L. A. *Elite and Specialized Interviewing.* Evanston: Northwestern University Press, 1970.

Dexter, L. A. "On the politics and sociology of stupidity in our society." In H. S. Becker (Ed.), *The Other Side.* New York: Free Press, 1967.

Dexter, L. A. "Role relationships and conceptions of neutrality in interviewing." *American Journal of Sociology,* **62**: 153–157, 1956.

Diesing, P. *Patterns of Discovery in the Social Sciences.* Chicago: Aldine-Atherton, 1971.

Dodge, M. *Selling Technology: A Participant Observation Study of the School Media Specialist.* Unpublished Ph.D. Dissertation, University Microfilms, 1973.

Dollard, J. *Caste and Class in a Southern Town.* 2nd edition. New York: Harper, 1949.

Dollard, J. *Criteria for the Life History.* New York: Social Science Research Council, 1935.

Donovan, F. R. *The Woman Who Waits.* Boston: Badger Press, 1920.

Dorn, D. S., & Long, G. L. "Brief remarks on the Association's code of ethics." *American Sociologist,* **9** (February): 31–35, 1974.

Dornbusch, S. M. "The military as an assimilating institution." *Social Forces,* **33**(4): 316–321, 1955.

Douglas, J. D. *American Social Order: Social Rules in a Pluralistic Society.* New York: Free Press, 1971.

Douglas, J. D. (Ed.). *Deviance and Respectability: The Social Construction of Moral Meanings.* New York: Basic Books, 1970.

Douglas, J. D. *Observations of Deviance.* New York: Random House, 1970.

Douglas, J. D. (Ed.). *Research on Deviance.* New York: Random House, 1972.

Douglas, J. D. *The Social Meanings of Suicide.* Princeton, N. J.: Princeton University Press, 1967.

Douglas, J. D. (Ed.). *Understanding Everyday Life: Toward the Reconstruction of Sociological Knowledge.* Chicago: Aldine, 1970.

Driscoll, J. "Transsexuals." *Trans-Action,* 8(5–6), 28–38, 1971.

Driver, H. E. "Introduction to statistics for comparative research." In F. W. Moore (Ed.), *Readings in Crosscultural Methodology.* New Haven: Human Area Relations Files, pp. 303–331, 1961.

DuBois, C. "Some psychological objectives and techniques in ethnography." *Journal of Social Psychology,* 285–301, 1937.

Durkheim, E. *The Elementary Forms of Religious Life.* New York: Free Press, 1915.

Durkheim, E. *The Rules of Sociological Method.* New York: Free Press, 1938.

Durkheim, E. *Suicide: A Study in Sociology.* Translated and edited by George Simpson. New York: Free Press, 1951.

Earle, W. *The Autobiographical Consciousness: A Philosophical Inquiry into Existence.* Chicago: Quadrangle, 1972.

Eaton, J. W., & Weil, R. J. "Social processes of professional teamwork." *American Sociological Review,* **16:** 707–713, 1951.

Eggan, F. "Social anthropology and the method of controlled comparison." *American Anthropologist,* **56:** 743–763, 1954.

Elsner, H. (Ed.). *Robert E. Park: The Crowd and the Public, and Other Essays.* Chicago: University of Chicago Press, 1972.

Emerson, R. *Judging Delinquents: Context and Process in Juvenile Court.* Chicago: Aldine, 1969.

Epstein, A. L. (Ed.). *The Craft of Social Anthropology.* New York: Barnes & Noble, 1967.

Erikson, K. T. "A comment on disguised observation in sociology." *Social Problems,* **14:** 366–373, 1967.

Etzioni, A. *A Comparative Analysis of Complex Organizations.* New York: Free Press, 1961.

Etzioni, A. (Ed.). *Complex Organizations.* New York: Holt, Rinehart & Winston, 1962.

Etzioni, A. *Modern Organizations.* Englewood Cliffs, N. J.: Prentice-Hall, 1962.

Etzioni, A. "Two approaches to organizational analysis: A critique and suggestion." *Administrative Science Quarterly,* **5:** 257–278, 1960.

Faulkner, R. *Hollywood Studio Musicians.* Chicago: Aldine, 1971.

Festinger, L. & Katz, D. (Eds.). *Research Methods in the Behavioral Sciences.* New York: Holt, 1953.

Festinger, L., Riecken, H., & Schacter, S. *When Prophecy Fails.* Minneapolis: University of Minnesota Press, 1956.

Fichter, J. H., & Kolb, W. L. "Ethical limitations on sociological reporting." *American Sociological Review,* **18:** 544–550, 1953.

Filstead, W. (Ed.). *Qualitative Methodology: Firsthand Involvement with the Social World.* Chicago: Markham, 1970.

Forcese, D. P., & Richer, S. *Social Research Methods.* Englewood Cliffs, N. J.: Prentice-Hall, 1973.

Form, W. H. "The sociology of social research." In R. T. O'Toole (Ed.), *The Organization, Management, and Tactics of Social Research.* Cambridge, Mass.: Schenkman, 1971.

Francis, R. G. *The Rhetoric of Science.* Minneapolis: University of Minnesota Press, 1961.

Frank, A. *The Diary of a Young Girl.* New York: Doubleday, 1952.

French, J. R. P., Jr. "Experiments in field settings." In L. Festinger & D. Katz (Eds.), *Research Methods in the Behavioral Sciences.* New York: Holt, pp. 98–135, 1953.

French, K. S. "Research interviewers in a medical setting: Roles and social systems." *Human Organization,* **21**(3): 219–224, 1962.

Frenkel-Brunswik, E. "Mechanisms of self-deception." *Journal of Social Psychology,* **5**(10): 409–420, 1939.

Friedman, N. *The Social Nature of Psychological Research: The Psychological Experiment as a Social Interaction.* New York: Basic Books, 1967.

Gallaher, A., Jr. "Plainville: The twice studied town." In Arthur J. Vidich, Joseph Bensman, & Maurice R. Stein (Eds.). *Reflections on Community Studies.* New York: Wiley, pp. 285–303, 1964.

Galliher, J. F. "The protection of human subjects: A reexamination of the professional code of ethics." *The American Sociologist,* **8** (August): 93–100, 1973.

Gans, H. *The Levittowners.* New York: Random House, 1969.

Gans, H. *The Urban Villagers.* New York: Free Press, 1962.

Gardner, B. B., & Whyte, W. F. "Methods for the study of human relations in industry." *American Sociological Review,* **11:** 506–512, 1946.

Garfinkel, H. "Conditions of successful degradation ceremonies." *American Journal of Sociology,* **59** (March): 420–424, 1956.

Garfinkel H. *Studies in Ethnomethodology.* Englewood Cliffs: Prentice-Hall, 1967.

Geer, B. "First days in the field." In P. E. Hammond (Ed.), *Sociologist at Work.* New York: Basic Books, pp. 322–344, 1964.

Geer, B., Haas, J., Vivona, C., Miller, S., Woods, C., & Becker, H. S. "Learning the ropes: Situational learning in four occupational training programs." In I. Deutscher & E. Thompson (Eds.). *Among the People.* New York: Basic Books, 1966.

Giallombardo, R. *Society of Women: A Study of a Woman's Prison.* New York: Wiley, 1966.

Glaser, Barney G. "The constant comparative method of qualitative analysis." *Social Problems,* **12:** 436–445, 1965.

Glaser, B. (Ed.). *Organizational Careers.* Chicago: Aldine, 1968.

Glaser, B., & Strauss, A. *Awareness of Dying.* Chicago: Aldine, 1965.

Glaser, B., & Strauss, A. *The Discovery of Grounded Theory: Strategies for Qualitative Research.* Chicago: Aldine, 1967.

Glaser, B., & Strauss, A. *A Status Passage: A Formal Theory.* Chicago: Aldine, 1971.

Glaser, B. G., & Strauss, A. L. *Time for Dying.* Chicago: Aldine, 1968.

Glasser, P. H., & Navarre, E. L. "The problems of families in the A. F. D. C. program." In P. H. Glasser & L. N. Glasser (Eds.), *Families in Crisis.* New York: Harper & Row, 1970.

Glazer, M. *The Research Adventure: Promise and Problems of Field Work.* New York: Random House, 1972.

Goffman, E. *Asylums: Essays on the Social Situation of Mental Patients and Other Inmates.* Garden City, N. Y.: Doubleday, Anchor Books, 1961.

Goffman, E. *Behavior in Public Places: Notes on the Social Organization of Gatherings.* New York: Free Press, 1963.

Goffman, E. *Encounters.* Indianapolis: Bobbs-Merrill, 1961.

Goffman, E. *Interaction Ritual.* Garden City, N. Y.: Doubleday, 1967.

Goffman, E. *The Presentation of Self in Everyday Life.* Garden City, N. Y.: Doubleday, 1959.

Goffman, E. *Relations in Public.* New York: Harper & Row, 1971.

Gold, D. "Comment on 'A critique of tests of significance.'" *American Sociological Review,* **24:** 328–338, 1959.

Gold, R. "Janitors versus tenants: A status-income dilemma." *American Journal of Sociology,* **57** (March): 486–493, 1952.

Gold, R. L. "Roles in sociological field observations." *Social Forces,* **36:** 217–223, 1958.

Goldner, F. H. "Role emergence and the ethics of ambiguity." In Gideon Sjoberg (Ed.), *Ethics, Politics, and Social Research.* Cambridge, Mass.: Schenkman, pp. 245–266, 1967.

Goode, W. "Community within a community: The professions." *American Sociological Review,* **22** (April): 194–200, 1957.

Goode, W. "Encroachment, charlatanism, and the emerging professions: Psychology, sociology, and medicine." *American Sociological Review,* **25** (December): 903, 1960.

Goode, W. J., & Hatt, P. K. *Methods in Social Research.* New York: McGraw-Hill, 1952.

Gorden, R. L. "Dimensions of the depth interview." *American Journal of Sociology,* **62:** 158–164, 1956.

Gottschalk, L., Kluckhohn, C., & Angell, R. D. *The Use of Personal Documents in History, Anthropology and Sociology.* New York: Social Science Research Council, 1945.

Gouldner, A. *The Coming Crisis of Western Sociology.* New York: Basic Books, 1970.

Gouldner, A. "Cosmopolitans and locals: Toward an analysis of latent social roles." Part I and Part II. *Administrative Science Quarterly,* **2** (December): 281–306, 1957, and **3** (March): 444–480, 1958.

Gouldner, A. *Patterns of Industrial Bureaucracy.* New York: Free Press, 1954.

Gouldner, A. "The sociologist as partisan: Sociology and the welfare state." *The American Sociologist,* **3** (May): 103–116, 1968.

Gouldner, A. *Wildcat Strike.* New York: Harper & Row Torchbook, 1965.

Griffin, J. H. *Black Like Me.* Boston: Houghton, Mifflin, 1962.

Gross, N., & Mason, W. "Some methodological problems of eight hour interviews." *American Journal of Sociology,* **59** (November): 197–204, 1953.

Gullahorn, J., & Strauss, G. "The field worker in union research." *Human Organization,* **13**(3): 28–32, 1954.

Gusfield, J. G. "Field work reciprocities in studying a social movement." *Human Organization,* **14**(3): 29–34, 1955.

Haas, J. *From Punk to Scale: A Study of High Steel Ironworkers.* University Microfilm, 1970.

Habenstein, R. *Pathways to Data: Field Methods for Studying Ongoing Organizations.* Chicago: Aldine, 1970.

Hader, J. J., & Lindeman, E. C. *Dynamic Social Research.* London: Kegan Paul, 1933.

Haley, A. (Ed.). *The Autobiography of Malcolm X.* New York: Grove Press, 1964.

Haley, A. "Epilogue." In Malcolm X, *The Autobiography of Malcom X.* New York: Grove Press, 1966.

Hall, O. "The informal organization of the medical profession." *Canadian Journal of Economics and Political Science,* **12:** 30–44, 1946.

Hall, O. "The stages of a medical career." *American Journal of Sociology,* **53** (March): 327, 1948.

Hall, O. "Types of medical careers." *American Journal of Sociology,* **55** (November): 248, 1949.

Hammond, P. E. (Ed.). *Sociologist at Work: The Craft of Social Research.* New York: Basic Books, 1964.

Hannerz, U. *Soulside: Inquiries into Ghetto Culture and Community.* New York: Columbia University Press, 1969.

Haring, D. G. "Comment on field techniques in ethnography, illustrated by a survey in the Ryuke Islands." *Southwestern Journal of Anthropology,* **10:** 255–267, 1954.

Harper, D., & Emmert, F. "Work behavior in a service industry." *Social Forces,* **42** (December): 216–225, 1963.

Harvey, S. M. "A preliminary investigation of the interview." *British Journal of Psychology,* **28:** 263–287, 1938.

Heap, J. L., & Roth, P. A. "On phenomenological sociology." *American Sociological Review,* **38** (June): 354–367, 1973.

Heber, R. *A Manual on Terminology and Classification in Mental Retardation.* Washington: The American Association on Mental Deficiency, 1961.

Henry, F., & Saberwal, S. (Eds.). *Stress and Response in Field Work.* New York: Holt, Rinehart & Winston, 1969.

Henry, J., & Spiro, M. "Psychological techniques in projective tests in field work." In Alfred Kroeber (Ed.), *Anthropology Today.* Chicago: University of Chicago Press, pp. 417–429, 1953.

Herskovits, M. J. "The hypothetical situation: A technique of field research." *Southwestern Journal of Anthropology,* **6:** 32–40, 1950.

Herskovits, M. J. *Man and His Works.* New York: Knopf, 1948.

Herskovits, M. J. "Problems of method in ethnography." In R. F. Skinner (Ed.), *Method and Perspective in Anthropology.* Minneapolis: University of Minnesota Press, 1954.

Horowitz, I. L. (Ed.). *The Rise and Fall of Project Camelot.* Cambridge: M.I.T. Press, 1967.

Heyns, R. W., & Lippitt, R. "Systematic observational techniques." In G. Lindzey (Ed.), *Handbook of Social Psychology,* Vol. I. Cambridge, Mass.: Addison-Wesley, pp. 370–404, 1954.

Hinkle, R. D., Jr., & Hinkle, G. J. *The Development of Modern Sociology.* New York: Random House, 1954.

Hoffman, N., Horowitz, I. L., & Rainwater, L. "Sociological snoopers and journalistic moralizers: Comment—An exchange." *Trans-Action,* **7**(7): 4–10, 1970.

Homans, G. C. "Contemporary theory in sociology." In R. E. L. Foris (Ed.), *Handbook of Modern Sociology.* Chicago: Rand McNally, pp. 951–977, 1964.

Homans, G. C. *Social Behavior: Its Elementary Forms.* New York: Harcourt Brace, 1961.

Horton, J. "Time cool people." *Trans-Action,* **4**(5): 5–12, 1967.

Huber, J. "Symbolic interaction as a pragmatic perspective: The bias of emergent theory." *American Sociological Review,* **38** (April): 274–284, 1973.

Hughes, E. C. "Institutions and the person." In A. L. McClung (Ed.), *Principles of Sociology.* New York: Barnes & Noble, 1951.

Hughes, E. C. "Institutional offices and the person." *American Journal of Sociology,* **43** (November): 404–413, 1934.

Hughes, E. C. *Men and Their Work.* New York: Free Press, 1958.

Hughes, E. C. "A study of a secular institution: The Chicago Real Estate Board." Unpublished dissertation, Department of Sociology, University of Chicago, 1928.

Humphreys, L. *Tearoom Trade.* Chicago: Aldine, 1970.

Humphreys, L. "Tearoom trade: Impersonal sex in public places." *Trans-Action,* **7**(3): 10–25, 1970.

Hyman, H. H. "Do they tell the truth?" *Public Opinion Quarterly,* **8:** 557–559, 1944.

Hyman, H. H. *Survey Design and Analysis.* New York: Free Press, 1955.

Hyman, H. H., Cobbs, W. J., Feldman, J. J., Hart, C. W., & Stember, C. H. *Interviewing in Social Research.* Chicago: University of Chicago Press, 1954.

Jacobs, G. (Ed.). *The Participant Observer.* New York: Braziller, 1970.

Jacobs, J. (Ed.). *Deviance: Field Studies and Self Disclosures.* Palto Alto, Calif.: National Press, 1974.

Jacobs, J. *Getting By: Illustrations of Marginal Living.* Boston: Little, Brown, 1972.

Jacobs, J. "A phenomenological study of suicide notes." *Social Problems,* **15** (Summer): 60–72, 1967.

Janes, R. W. "A note on phases of the community role of the participant observer." *American Sociological Review,* **26:** 446–450, 1961.

Janeway, E. (Ed.). *Women: The Changing Roles.* New York: The New York Times, 1973.

Junker, B. H. *Field Work: An Introduction to the Social Sciences.* Chicago: University of Chicago Press, 1960.

Kahn, R. L., & Cannell, C. F. *The Dynamics of Interviewing.* New York: Wiley, 1957.

Kahn, R. L., & Mann, F. "Developing research partnerships." *Journal of Social Issues,* **8**(3): 4–10, 1952.

Katz, D. "Psychological barriers to communication." *Annals of the American Academy of Political and Social Science,* **250:** 17–25, 1947.

Kelman, H. C. "Human use of human subjects: The problem of deception in social psychological experiments. *Psychological Bulletin,* **67** (January): 1–11, 1967.

Kish, L. *Survey Sampling.* New York: Wiley, 1965.

Kitsuse, J. I. "Societal reaction to deviant behavior." *Social Problems,* **9**(3): 247–256, 1962.

Kitsuse, J., & Cicourel, A. V. "A note on the uses of official statistics." *Social Problems,* **II:** 131–139, 1963.

Kluckhohn, C. "Participation in ceremonies in a Navajo community." *American Anthropologist,* **40:** 359–369, 1938.

Kluckhohn, C. "Theoretical basis for an empirical method of studying the acquisition of culture by individuals." *Man,* **39:** 98–103, 1939.

Kluckhohn, C. "The participant observer technique in small communities." *American Journal of Sociology,* **46:** 331–343, 1940.

Kobben, A. J. "New ways of presenting an old idea: The statistical method in social anthropology." *Journal of the Royal Anthropological Institute of Great Britain and Ireland,* **82:** 129–146, 1952.

Kolaja, J. "Contribution to the theory of participant observation." *Social Forces,* **35:** 159–163, 1956.

Komarovsky, M. *The Unemployed Man and His Family.* New York: Holt, Rinehart & Winston, 1940.

Kozol, J. *Death at an Early Age.* Boston: Houghton Mifflin, 1967.

Kriesburg, L. "Occupational controls among steel distributors." *American Journal of Sociology,* **61** (November): 203–212, 1955.

Kriesburg, L. "The retail furrier: Concepts of security and success." *American Journal of Sociology,* **57** (March): 478–485, 1952.

Kroeber, A. L. (Ed.). *Anthropology Today.* Chicago: University of Chicago Press, 1953.

Krueger, C. "Do 'bad girls' become good nurses?" *Trans-Action,* **5** (July-August): 31–36, 1968.

Krueger, E. T. "The value of life history documents for social research." *Journal of Applied Sociology,* **9:** 196–201, 1925.

Krueger, E. T., & Reckless, W. C. *Social Psychology.* New York: Longmans, 1931.

Kuhn, M. "Major trends in symbolic interaction in the past twenty-five years." *Sociological Quarterly,* **5** (Winter): 61–84, 1964.

Labovitz, S., & Hagedorn, R. *Introduction to Social Research.* New York: McGraw-Hill, 1971.

Lang, K., & Lang, G. E. "The unique perspective of television and its effect: A pilot study." *American Sociological Review,* **18:** 3–12, 1953.

Langness, L. L. *Life History in Anthropological Science.* New York: Holt, 1965.

Lasswell, H. D. "The contributions of Freud's insight interview to the social sciences." *American Journal of Sociology,* **45:** 375–390, 1939.

Lazarsfeld, P. F. "The art of asking why." *National Marketing Review,* **1:** 26–38, 1935.

Lazarsfeld, P. F. "Evidence and interference in social research." In D. Lerner (Ed.), *Evidence and Inference.* New York: Free Press, pp. 107–138, 1959.

Lazarsfeld, P. *Qualitative Analysis: Historical and Critical Essays.* Boston: Allyn & Bacon, 1972.

Lazarsfeld, Paul F., & Allen B. "Some functions of qualitative analysis in sociological research." *Sociologica,* **1:** 324–361, 1955.

Lazarsfeld, P. F., & Robinson, W. S. "The quantification of case studies." *Journal of Applied Psychology,* **24:** 817–825, 1940.

Lazarsfeld, P. F., & Rosenberg, M. (Eds.). *The Language of Social Research.* New York: Free Press, 1955.

Leighton, A. *The Governing of Men.* Princeton, N. J.: Princeton University Press, 1946.

Lemert, E. *Social Pathology.* New York: McGraw-Hill, 1951.

Lesser, A. "Research procedure and laws of culture." *Philosophy of Science,* **6:** 345–355, 1939.

Lesy, M. *Wisconsin Death Trip.* New York: Random House, 1973.

Lewis, O. "Introduction." *The Children of Sanchez.* New York: Vintage, 1963.

Lewis, O. "Controls and experiments in field work." In A. L. Kroeber (Ed.), *Anthropology Today.* Chicago: University of Chicago Press, pp. 452–475, 1953.

Lewis, O. *Five Families,* Chapter I. New York: Wiley, 1962.

Lewis, O. *La Vida.* New York: Vintage, 1965.

Lewis, O. *Pedro Martinez.* New York: Random House, 1964.

Leznoff, M. "Interviewing homosexuals." *American Journal of Sociology,* **62:** 202–204, 1956.

Liebow, E. *Tally's Corner.* Boston: Little, Brown, 1967.

Lindeman, E. C. *Social Discovery.* New York: Republic, 1924.

Lindesmith, A. *Addiction and Opiates.* Chicago: Aldine, 1968.

Lindesmith, A., Weinberg, S. K., & Robinson, W. S. "Two comments and rejoinder to 'The logical structure of analytic induction.' " *American Sociological Review,* **17:** 492–494, 1952.

Lipetz, B. "Information, storage and retrieval." *Scientific American,* **215**(3): 224–242, 1966.

Littrell, W. B. "Vagueness, social structure, and social research in law." *Social Problems,* **21** (Summer): 38–52, 1973.

Lofland, J. *Deviance and Identity.* Englewood Cliffs, N. J.: Prentice-Hall, 1969.

Lofland, J. *Analyzing Social Settings.* Belmont, Calif.: Wadsworth, 1973.

Lofland, J. "Editorial introduction—analyzing qualitative data: First person accounts." *Urban Life and Culture,* **3** (October): 307–309, 1974.

Lofland, J. "Replay to Davis—Comment on 'Initial interaction.' " *Social Problems,* **8**(4): 365–367, 1961.

Lofland, J. "Styles of reporting qualitative field research." *The American Sociologist,* **8** (August): 101–111, 1974.

Lofland, J. A., & Lejeune, R. A. "Initial interaction of newcomers in Alcoholics Anonymous: A field experiment in class symbols and socialization." *Social Problems,* **8:** 102–111, 1960.

Lohman, J. D. "The participant observer in community studies." *American Sociological Review,* **2:** 890–897, 1937.

Lombard, G. F. F. "Self-awareness and scientific method." *Science,* **112:** 289–293, 1950.

Lundberg, G. A. "Case work and the statistical method." *Social Forces,* **5**(5): 61–65, 1926.

Mack, R. "Ecological patterns in an industrial shop." *Social Forces,* **32** (May): 351–356, 1954.

Madge, J. *The Tools of Social Science.* London: Longmans, Green, 1953.

Malcolm X. *The Autobiography of Malcolm X.* New York: Grove Press, 1966.

Malinowski, B. *Argonants of the Western Pacific.* London: Routledge, 1932.

Manis, J., & Meltzer, B. (Eds.). *Symbolic Interaction.* Boston: Allyn & Bacon, 1967.

Mann, F. "Human relations skills in social research." *Human Relations,* **4**(4): 341–354, 1951.

Martel, M. U., & McCall, G. J. "Reality-orientation and the pleasure principle: A study of American mass-periodical fiction (1890–1955)." In L. A. Dexter & D. M. White (Eds.), *People, Society and Mass Communications.* New York: Free Press, pp. 283–334, 1964.

Marx, G. T. *Muckraking Sociology: Research as Social Criticism.* New Brunswick, J. J.: Transaction Books, 1972.

Masling, J. "The influence of situational and interpersonal variables in projective testing." *Psychological Bulletin,* **57:** 65–85, 1960.

McCall, G. J. "Symbiosis: The case of hoodoo and the numbers racket." *Social Problems,* **10:** 361–371, 1963.

McCall, G. J., & Simmons, J. L. *Identities and Interactions.* New York: Free Press, 1966.

McCall, G., & Simmons, J. L. (Eds.). *Issues in Participant Observation.* Reading, Pa.: Addison-Wesley, 1969.

McCartney, J. L. "On being scientific: Changing styles of presentation of sociological research." *American Sociologist,* **5** (February): 30–35, 1970.

McEwen, W. J. "Forms and problems of validation in social anthropology." *Current Anthropology,* **4:** 155–169, 1963.

McGinnis, R. "Randomization and inference in sociological research." *American Sociological Review,* **22:** 408–414, 1957.

McHugh, P. *Defining the Situation.* Indianapolis: Bobbs-Merrill, 1968.

Mead, G. H. *Mind, Self and Society.* Chicago: University of Chicago Press, 1934.

Mead, G. H. *The Philosophy of the Act.* Chicago: University of Chicago Press, 1938.

Mead, M. "More comprehensive field methods." *American Anthropologist,* **35:** 1–15, 1933.

Mead, M. & Metrauy, R. *The Study of a Culture at a Distance.* Chicago: University of Chicago Press, 1953.

Melbin, M. "An interaction recording device for participant observers." *Human Organization,* **13**(2): 29–33, 1954.

Mensh, I. N., & Henry, J. "Direct observation and psychological tests in anthropological field work." *American Anthropologist,* **55:** 461–480, 1953.

Merton, R. K. *Social Theory and Social Structure.* Revised edition. New York: Free Press, 1957.

Merton, R., & Kendall, P. "The focused interview." *American Journal of Sociology,* **51** (May): 541–557, 1946.

Metraux, R., & Mead, M. *Themes in French Culture.* Stanford: Stanford University Press, 1954.

Mey, H. *Field-Theory: Study of its Applications in the Social Sciences.* Translated by Douglas Scott. New York: St. Martin's, 1972.

Michels, R. *Political Parties.* New York: Dover, 1957.

Miller S. M. "The participant observer and 'over-rapport.' " *American Sociological Review,* **17:** 97–99, 1952.

Miller, S. *Prescription for Leadership: Training for the Medical Elite.* Chicago: Aldine, 1970.

Miller, S. M., et al. Roby, P., & Steewijk, A. "Creaming the poor." *Trans-Action,* 8 (June): 39–45, 1970.

Mills, C. W. "Situated actions and vocabularies of motive." *American Sociological Review,* **5** (October): 904–913, 1940.

Mills, C. W. *The Sociological Imagination.* London: Oxford University Press, 1959.

Miner, H. "Body ritual among the Nacirema." *American Anthropologist,* **58:** 503–507, 1956.

Moore, J. W. "Social constraints on sociological knowledge: Academics and research concerning minorities." *Social Problems,* **21** (Summer): 65–77, 1973.

Murdock, G. P. "The processing of anthropological materials." In A. L. Kroeher (Ed.), *Anthropology Today.* Chicago: University of Chicago Press, pp. 476–487, 1953.

Nader, L. "Perspectives gained from fieldwork." In Sol Tax (Ed.), *Horizons of Anthropology.* Chicago: Aldine, pp. 148–159, 1964.

Naroll, R. *Data Quality Control.* New York: Free Press, 1962.

Naroll, R., & Naroll, F. "On bias of exotic data." *Man,* **25:** 24–26, 1963.

Nash, D. "The ethnologist as stranger: An essay in the sociology of knowledge." *Southwestern Journal of Anthropology,* **19:** 149–167, 1963.

Nathanson, N. L. "Social science, administrative law, and the information act of 1966." *Social Problems,* **21** (Summer): 21–37, 1973.

Nejelski, P., & Finsterbuch, K. "The prosecutor and the researcher: Present and prospective variations on the Supreme Court's Branzburg decision." *Social Problems,* **21** (Summer): 3–21, 1973.

Nisbet, R. A. *The Sociological Tradition.* New York: Basic Books, 1966.

Oeser, O. A. "Methods and assumptions of field work in social psychology." *British Journal of Psychology,* **27:** 343–363, 1937.

Oleson, V. L., & Whittaker, E. "Role-making in participant observation: Processes in the researcher-actor relationship." *Human Organization,* **26:** 273–281, 1967.

Orlans, H. "Ethical problems in the relations of research sponsors and investigators." In G. Sjoberg (Ed.), *Ethics, Politics and Social Research.* Cambridge, Mass.: Schenkman, pp. 3–24, 1967.

Orne, M. T. "On the social psychology of the psychological experiment." *American Psychologist,* **17:** 776–783, 1962.

Osgood, C. "Informants." In C. Osgood (Ed.), *Ingalik Material Culture.* Yale University Publications in Anthropology, **22:** 50–55, 1940.

Palmer, V. M. *Field Studies in Sociology: A Student's Manual*. Chicago: University of Chicago Press, 1928.

Park, R. "Murder and the case study method." *American Journal of Sociology*, **36:** 447–454, 1930.

Park, R. *Principles of Human Behavior*. Chicago: The Zalaz Corp., 1915.

Passin, H. "Tarahumara prevarication: A problem in field method." *American Anthropologist*, **44:** 235–247, 1942.

Paul, B. "Interview techniques and field relationships." In A. L. Kroeber (Ed.), *Anthropology Today*. Chicago: University of Chicago Press, pp. 430–451, 1953.

Payne, S. L. *The Art of Asking Questions*. Princeton: Princeton University Press, 1951.

Pearsall, M. "Participant observation as role and method in behavioral research." *Nursing Research*, **14:** 37–47, 1965.

Phillips, D. L. *Knowledge from What? Theories and Methods in Social Research*. Chicago: Rand McNally, 1971.

Pitt, D. C. *Using Historical Sources in Anthropology and Sociology*. New York: Holt, Rinehart, and Winston, 1972.

Polansky, N., Freeman, W., Horowitz, M., Irwin, L., Papania, N., Rapaport, D., & Whaley, F. "Problems of interpersonal relation in research on groups." *Human Relations*, **2:** 281–292, 1949.

Polsky, N. *Hustlers, Beats and Others*. Garden City, N. Y.: Doubleday, Anchor Books, 1969.

Polya, G. *Patterns of Plausible Inference*. Princeton: Princeton University Press, 1954.

Ponsansky, N. A. *English Diaries*. London: Methuen, 1923.

Powdermaker, H. *Stranger and Friend: The Way of an Anthropologist*. New York: Norton, 1967.

Psathas, G. *Phenomenological Sociology: Issues and Applications*. New York: Wiley, 1973.

Radin, P. *The Method and Theory of Ethnology*. New York: McGraw-Hill, 1933.

Rainwater, L., & Pittman, D. J. "Ethnical problems in studying a politically sensitive and deviant community." *Social Problems*, **14:** 357–366, 1967.

Reck, A. J. (Ed.). *George Herbert Mead: Selected Writings*. Indianapolis: Bobbs-Merrill, 1964.

Record, J. C. "The research institute and the pressure group." In G. Sjoberg (Ed.), *Ethics, Politics and Social Research*. Cambridge: Schenkman, pp. 25–49, 1967.

Redlich, F., & Brody, E. B. "Emotional problems of interdisciplinary research in psychiatry." *Psychiatry*, **18:** 233–240, 1955.

Reiss, A. "Police brutality—Answers to key questions." *Trans-Action*, **5** (July–August): 10–19, 1968.

Reiss, A. J., Jr. "The sociological study of communities." *Rural Sociology*, **24:** 118–130, 1959.

Reiss, A. J., Jr. "Some logical and methodological problems in community research." *Social Forces*, 33: 52–54, 1954.

Reissman, L. "A study of role conceptions in bureaucracy." *Social Force*, **27** (March): 305–310, 1949.

Rice, S. A. "Contagious bias in the interview: A methodological note." *American Journal of Sociology*, **35:** 420–423, 1929.

Richardson, S. A. "A framework for reporting field relations experiences." In R. N. Adams & J. J. Preiss (Eds.), *Human Organization Research*. Homewood, Ill.: Dorsey Press, pp. 124–139, 1960.

Richardson, S. A. "Training in field relations skills." *Journal of Social Issues,* **8:** 43–50, 1952.

Richardson, S. A., Dohrenwend, B. S., & Klein, D. *Interviewing: Its Forms and Functions.* New York: Basic Books, 1965.

Richter, C. P. "Free research versus design research." *Science,* **118:** 91–93, 1953.

Riecken, H. W. "The unidentified interviewer." *American Journal of Sociology,* **62:** 210–212, 1956.

Riesman, D., & Benney, M. "The sociology of the interview." *Midwest Sociologists,* **18:** 3–15, 1956.

Robinson, W. S. "The logical structure of analytic induction." *American Sociological Review,* **16:** 812–818, 1951.

Roethlisberger, F. J., & Dickson, W. J. *Management and the Worker.* Cambridge, Mass.: Harvard University Press, 1939.

Rogers, C. R. "The non-directive method as a technique for social research." *American Journal of Sociology,* **50:** 279–283, 1945.

Rogers, C. R., & Roethlisberger, F. J. "Barriers and gateways to communication." *Harvard Business Review,* **30**(4): 46–52, 1952.

Rose, A. (Ed.). *Human Behavior and Social Processes.* Boston: Houghton Mifflin, 1962.

Rose, A. "A research note on interviewing." *American Journal of Sociology,* **51:** 143–144, 1945.

Rose, A. "A systematic summary of symbolic interaction theory." A. Rose (Ed.), *Human Behavior and Social Processes.* Boston: Houghton Mifflin, 1962.

Rosenhan, D. L. "On being sane in insane places." *Science,* **179**(4070) (January): 250–258, 1973.

Rosenthal, R. *Experimenter Effects in Behavioral Research.* New York: Appleton-Century-Crofts, 1966.

Roth, J. "Comments on secret observation." *Social Problems,* **9:** 283–284, 1962.

Roth, J. "Hired hand research." *The American Sociologist,* **1** (August): 190–196, 1966.

Roth, J. *Timetables.* Indianapolis: Bobbs-Merrill, 1963.

Roth, J. "Turning adversity to account." *Urban Life and Culture,* **3** (October): 347–361, 1974.

Roy, D. "Banana time: Job satisfaction and informal interaction." *Human Organization,* **18** (Winter): 158–168, 1959–1960.

Roy, D. "Efficiency and 'the fix': Informal intergroup relations in a piecework machine shop." *American Journal of Sociology,* **60** (November), 225–260, 1952.

Roy, D. "Quota restriction and goldbricking in a machine shop." *American Journal of Sociology,* **57** (March): 427–442, 1952.

Roy, D. "The role of the researcher in the study of social conflict: A theory of protective distortion of response." *Human Organization,* **24:** 262–271, 1965.

Roy, D. "Work satisfaction and social reward in quota achievement: An analysis of piecework incentives." *American Sociological Review,* **18:** 507–514, 1953.

Ryave, A. L. & Schenkein, J. N. "Notes on the art of walking." In R. Turner (Ed.), *Ethnomethodology.* Baltimore, Md.: Penguin, 1974.

Sagarin, E. "The research setting and the right not to be researched." *Social Problems,* **21** (Summer): 52–64, 1973.

Sarason, S. *The Culture of the School and the Problem of Change.* Boston: Allyn & Bacon, 1971.

Sarason, S. *The Psychological Sense of Community.* San Francisco: Jossey-Bass, 1974.

Sawyer, E. "Methodological problems in studying so-called 'deviant' communities." In A. J. Ladner (Ed.), *The Death of White Sociology.* New York: Vintage Books, 1973.

Schatzman, L., & Strauss, A. L. *Field Research: Strategies for a Natural Sociology.* Englewood Cliffs, N. J.: Prentice-Hall, 1973.

Scheff, T. J. *Being Mentally Ill: A Sociological Theory.* Chicago: Aldine, 1966.

Schneider, E. V. "Limitations on observation in industrial sociology." *Social Forces,* **28:** 279–284, 1950.

Schuler, E. "Toward a code of ethics for sociologists: A historical note." *American Sociologist,* **3** (November): 316–318, 1969.

Schur, E. M. *Labeling Deviant Behavior: Its Sociological Implications.* New York: Harper & Row, 1971.

Schwab, W. B. "Looking backward: An appraisal of two field trips." *Human Organization,* **24:** 372–380, 1965.

Schwartz, M. S., & Schwartz, C. G. "Problems in participant observation." *American Journal of Sociology,* **60:** 343–354, 1955.

Scott, J. "Black science and nation-building." In J. Ladner (Ed.), *The Death of White Sociology.* New York: Vintage Books, 1973.

Scott, M. *The Racing Game.* Chicago: Aldine, 1968.

Scott, M. B., & Lyman, S. M. "Accounts." *American Sociological Review,* **33:** 46–62, 1968.

Scott, R. W. "Field methods in the study of organizations." In J. G. March (Ed.), *Handbook of Organizations.* Chicago: Rand McNally, 1965.

Scott, R. W. "Field work in a formal organization: Some dilemmas in the role of observer." *Human Organization,* **22**(2): 162–168, 1963.

Seashore, S. E. "Field experiments with formal organizations." *Human Organization,* **23**(2): 164–178, 1964.

Sells, S. B., & Travers, R. M. W. "Observational methods of research." *Review of Educational Research,* **40:** 394–407, 1945.

Selltiz, C., Jahoda, M., Deutsch, M., & Cook, S. W. *Research Methods in Social Relations.* Revised edition. New York: Holt, 1959.

Selvin, H. C. "A critique of tests of significance in survey research." *American Sociological Review,* **22:** 519–527, 1957.

Shaw, C. *Brothers in Crime.* Chicago: University of Chicago Press, 1938.

Shaw, C. R. "Case study method." Publications of *The American Sociological Society,* **21:** 149–157, 1927.

Shaw, C. *The Jack Roller.* (2nd ed.) Chicago: University of Chicago Press, 1966.

Shaw, C. *The Natural History of a Delinquent Career.* Chicago: University of Chicago Press, 1931.

Shibutani, T. *Human Nature and Collective Behavior: Papers in Honor of Herbert Blumer.* Englewood Cliffs, N. J.: Prentice-Hall, 1970.

Shibutani, T. "Reference groups as perspectives." *American Journal of Sociology,* **40** (May): 562–569, 1955.

Shiloh, A. "Sanctuary or prison: Responses to life in a mental hospital." *Trans-Action,* **6** (December): 28–35, 1968.

Siegel, S. *Nonparametric Statistics for the Behavioral Sciences.* New York: McGraw-Hill, 1956.

Simon, J. L. *Basic Research Methods in Social Science.* New York: Random House, 1969.

Silberman, C. *Crisis in the Classroom.* New York: Random House, 1970.

Sills, D. L. *The Volunteers.* New York: Free Press, 1957.

Sjoberg, G. (Ed.). *Ethics, Politics and Social Research.* Cambridge, Mass.: Schenkman, 1967.

Sjoberg, G., & Miller, P. J. "Social research on bureaucracy: Limitations and opportunities." *Social Problems,* **21** (Summer): 129–143, 1973.

Smigel, E. "Interviewing a legal elite: The Wall Street lawyer." *American Journal of Sociology,* **64**(2): 159–164, 1958.

Smith, H. T. "A comparison of interview and observation methods of studying mother behavior." *Journal of Abnormal and Social Psychology,* **57:** 278–282, 1958.

Spencer, G. "Methodological issues in the study of bureaucratic elites: A case study of West Point." *Social Problems,* **21** (Summer): 90–103, 1973.

Spencer, R. F. (Ed.). *Method and Perspective in Anthropology.* Minneapolis: University of Minnesota Press, 1954.

Spindler, G., & Goldschmidt, W. "Experimental design in the study of culture change." *Southwestern Journal of Anthropology,* **8:** 68–83, 1952.

Spradley, J. "The moral career of a bum." *Trans-Action,* **7** (May): 16–29, 1970.

Spradley, J. *You Owe Yourself a Drunk.* Boston: Little, Brown, 1970.

Stanton, A., & Schwartz, M. *The Mental Hospital.* New York: Basic Books, 1954.

Stavrianos, B. K. "Research methods in cultural anthropology in relation to scientific criteria." *Psychological Review,* **57:** 334–344, 1950.

Stone, P. J., Bales, R. F., Namenwirth, J. Z., & Ogilivie, D. M. "The general inquirer: A computer system for content analysis and retrieval based on the sentence as a unit of information." *Behavioral Science,* **7:** 1–15, 1962.

Strauss, A. *The Social Psychology of George Herbert Mead.* Chicago: University of Chicago Press, 1956.

Strauss, A., & Schatzman, L. "Social class and modes of communication." *American Journal of Sociology,* **60**(4): 329–338, 1955.

Strauss, A., Schatzman, L., Bucher, R., Ehrlich, D., & Sabshin, M. *Psychiatric Ideologies and Institutions.* New York: Free Press, 1964.

Strunk, W., Jr. *The Elements of Style.* Revised by E. B. White. New York: Macmillan, 1972.

Stryker, S. "Symbolic interaction as an approach to family research." *Marriage and Family Living,* **21** (May): 111–119, 1959.

Sudnow, D. (Ed.). *Studies in Social Interaction.* New York: Free Press, 1972.

Sullivan, H. S. "A note on implications of psychiatry, the study of interpersonal relations, for investigations in social science." *American Journal of Sociology,* **42:** 848–861, 1937.

Sullivan, M. A., Jr., Queen, S. A., & Patrick, R. C., Jr. "Participant observation as employed in the study of a military training program." *American Sociological Review,* **23:** 660–667, 1958.

Sutherland, E. *The Professional Thief.* Chicago: University of Chicago Press, 1937.

Sykes, G. M. "The corruption of authority and rehabilitation." In A. Etzioni (Ed.), *Complex Organizations.* New York: Holt, Rinehart & Winston, 1962.

Sykes, G. M. "Feeling our way: A report on a conference on ethical issues in the social sciences." *The Journal of Criminal Law, Criminology and Police Science,* **58** (June): 201–213, 1968.

Sykes, G. M. *The Society of Captives.* Princeton: Princeton University Press, 1958.

Szasz, T. *Ideology and Insanity.* Garden City, N. Y.: Doubleday, Anchor Books, 1970.

Tax, S. (Ed.). *Horizons of Anthropology.* Chicago: Aldine, 1964.

Thibaut, J. W., & Kelley, H. H. *The Social Psychology of Groups.* New York: Wiley, 1959.

Thomas, P. *Down these Mean Streets.* New York: Knopf, 1967.

Thomas, W. I. *Social Behavior and Personality.* New York: Social Science Research Council, 1951.

Thomas, W. I. *The Unadjusted Girl.* Boston: Little, Brown, 1931.

Thomas, W. I., & Znaniecki, F. *The Polish Peasant in Europe and America.* New York: Knopf, 1927.

Thompson, J., & McEwen, W. "Organizational goals and environment." *American Sociological Review,* **23**(1): 23–31, 1958.

Thrasher, F. *The Gang.* Chicago: University of Chicago Press, 1927.

Thrasher, F. "How to study the boys' gang in the open." *Journal of Educational Psychology,* **1:** 244–254, 1928.

Tibbitts, H. G. "Research in the development of sociology: A pilot study in methodology." *American Sociological Review,* **27** (December): 892–901, 1962.

Tiryakian, E. "Existential phenomenology and sociology." *American Sociological Review,* **30** (October): 674–688, 1965.

Trice, H. M. "The outsider's role in field study." *Sociology and Social Research,* **41**(1): 27–32, 1956.

Trice, H. M., & Roman, P. "Delabeling and alcoholics anonymous." *Social Problems,* **17**(4): 538–546, 1969–1970.

Trow, M. "Comment on 'Participant observation and interviewing: a comparison.' " *Human Organization,* **16**(3): 33–35, 1957.

Truzzi, M. (Ed.) *Subjective Understanding in the Social Sciences.* Reading, Mass.: Addison-Wesley, 1974.

Turner, R. (Ed.). *Ethnomethodology.* Baltimore: Penguin, 1974.

Turner, R. H. "The quest for universals in sociological research." *American Sociological Review,* **18:** 604–611, 1953.

Vidich, A. J. "Methodological problems in the observation of husband-wife interaction." *Marriage and Family Living,* **28:** 234–239, 1955.

Vidich, A. J. "Participant observation and the collection and interpretation of data." *American Journal of Sociology,* **60:** 354–360, 1955.

Vidich, A. J., & Bensman, J. *Small Town in Mass Society.* Princeton: Princeton University Press, 1958.

Vidich, A. J., & Bensman, J. "The validity of field data." *Human Organization,* **13**(1): 20–27, 1954.

Vidich, A. J., Bensman, J., & Stein, M. R. *Reflections on Community Studies.* New York: Wiley, 1964.

Vidich, A. J., & Shapiro, G. "A comparison of participant observation and survey data." *American Sociological Review,* **20:** 28–33, 1955.

Volkart, E. H. (Ed.). *Social Behavior and Personality: Contributions of W. I. Thomas to Theory and Research.* New York: Social Science Research Council, 1951.

Wald, A. *Sequential Analysis.* New York: Wiley, 1947.

Walker, C., & Guest, R. *The Man on the Assembly Line.* Cambridge, Mass.: Harvard University Press, 1952.

Wallace, S. *Skid Row as a Way of Life.* New York: Harper Torchbooks, 1968.

Ward, D. *Women's Prison: Sex and Social Structure.* Chicago: Aldine, 1965.

Warner, W. L. *The Social System of a Modern Factory.* New Haven: Yale University Press, 1947.

Wax, M., & Shapiro, L. J. "Repeated interviewing." *American Journal of Sociology,* **62:** 215–217, 1956.

Wax, R. H. *Doing Fieldwork: Warnings and Advice.* Chicago: University of Chicago Press, 1971.

Wax, R. H. "Reciprocity as a field technique." *Human Organization,* **11**(3): 34–37, 1952.

Wax, R. H. "Twelve years later: An analysis of field experience." *American Journal of Sociology,* **63:** 133–142, 1957.

Webb, E. J., Campbell, D. T., Schwartz, R. D., & Sechrest, L. *Unobtrusive Measures: Nonreactive Research in Social Sciences.* Chicago: Rand McNally, 1966.

Weber, M. *Economy and Society.* New York: Bedminster Press, 1968.

Weber, M. *From Max Weber: Essays in Sociology.* Translated and edited by Hans Gerth and C. Wright Mills. New York: Oxford University Press, 1958.

Weber, M. *The Methodology of the Social Sciences.* Edited by E. A. Shils & H. A. Finch. New York: Free Press, 1949.

Weis, R. S. "Alternative approaches in the study of complex situations." *Human Organization,* **25:** 108–206, 1966.

Westley, W. "Secrecy and the police." *Social Forces,* **34** (March), 254–257, 1956.

Whyte, W. F. *Human Relations in the Restaurant Industry.* New York: McGraw-Hill, 1948.

Whyte, W. F. "Interviewing for organizational research." *Human Organization,* **12**(2): 15–22, 1953.

Whyte, W. F. "Interviewing in field research." In R. N. Adams, & J. J. Preiss (Eds.), *Human Organizational Research.* Homewood, Ill.: Dorsey Press, pp. 352–374, 1960.

Whyte, W. F. "Observation field methods." In M. Vahoda, M. Deutsch, & S. W. Cook (Eds.), *Research Methods in Social Relations,* Vol. II. First edition. New York: Holt, pp. 493–513, 1951.

Whyte, W. F. "On asking indirect questions." *Human Organization,* **15**(4): 21–23, 1957.

Whyte, W. F. *Street Corner Society.* Chicago: University of Chicago Press, 1955.

Whyte, W. F. "The social structure of the restaurant." *American Journal of Sociology,* **54**(2): 302–310, 1949.

Williams, T. R. *Field Methods in the Study of Culture.* New York: Holt, 1967.

Wilson, J. "Interaction analysis: A supplementary field work technique used in the study of leadership in a 'new style' Australian aboriginal community." *Human Organization,* **21**(4): 290–294, 1962.

Wirth, L. *The Ghetto.* Chicago: University of Chicago Press, 1928.

Wiseman, J. P. "The research web." *Urban Life and Culture,* **3** (October): 317–328, 1974.

Wohl, J. "Traditional and contemporary views of psychological testing." *Journal of Projective Techniques,* **27:** 359–365, 1963.

Wolf, K. K. "A methodological note on the empirical establishment of cultural patterns." *American Sociological Review,* **10:** 176–184, 1945.

Wolfensberger, W. *The Origin and Nature of our Institutional Models.* Syracuse: Human Policy Press, 1974.

Women on Words and Images. *Dick and Jane as Victims.* Princeton, N. J.: Women on Words and Images, 1972.

Young, F. W., & Young, R. C. "Key informant reliability in rural Mexican villages." *Human Organization,* **20**(3): 141–148, 1961.

Zelditch, M., Jr "Some methodological problems of field studies." *American Journal of Sociology,* **67**: 566–675, 1962.

Zetterberg, H. L. *On Theory and Verification in Sociology.* Revised edition. Totowa, N. J.: Bedminster Press, 1963.

Znaniecki, F. *The Method of Sociology.* New York: Farrar & Rinehart, 1934.

Zorbaugh, H. *The Gold Coast and the Slum.* Chicago: University of Chicago Press, 1929.

Author Index

Subject Index